Ishtiaq Jamil
Salahuddin M. Aminuzzaman
Syeda Lasna Kabir • M. Mahfuzul Haque
Editors

Gender Mainstreaming in Politics, Administration and Development in South Asia

Editors
Ishtiaq Jamil
University of Bergen
Bergen, Norway

Syeda Lasna Kabir
Department of Public Administration
University of Dhaka
Dhaka, Bangladesh

Salahuddin M. Aminuzzaman
South Asian Institute of Policy and
Governance (SIPG)
North South University
Dhaka, Bangladesh

M. Mahfuzul Haque
South Asian Institute of Policy and
Governance (SIPG)
North South University
Dhaka, Bangladesh

ISBN 978-3-030-36011-5   ISBN 978-3-030-36012-2   (eBook)
https://doi.org/10.1007/978-3-030-36012-2

This Palgrave Macmillan imprint is published by the registered company Springer Nature
Switzerland AG.
The registered company address is: Gewerbestrasse 11, 6330 Cham, Switzerland

PREFACE

Gender mainstreaming has been on the global agenda as both a mandate and a plan of action since 1995, when it was included in the Beijing Platform for Action. Since then, the commitment to gender mainstreaming has increased globally, along with greater understanding of the concept. However, a number of problems remain. These include conceptual confusion, the lacking representation of women in government, the lacking empowerment of women, and the lack of targeted interventions with close monitoring by respective governments. The road to gender mainstreaming is rocky, to say the least. An instantiation of this is the lacking progress on gender equality, which is the United Nations Sustainable Development Goal no. 5. Women and men are still not earning equal wages for equal work. During the period of 2000–2016, as reported by the UN, women in 90 countries spent roughly three times as many hours doing unpaid domestic and care-related work than did men. Furthermore, women are still being subjected to sexual abuse and violence in different forms in many countries.

The situations mentioned here only give us a cursory glimpse of the problems. Low education, early marriage, domestic violence, acid throwing, sexual harassment, and sexual violence remain unabated in many developing countries. Such practices block the road to gender mainstreaming. This book does not intend to give an account of the patchy progress toward the goal of gender mainstreaming; rather, it discusses an assortment of ideas, concepts, norms, and practices that persist across South Asia and how they relate to gender mainstreaming.

South Asia consists of eight nations—Afghanistan, Bangladesh, Bhutan, India, the Maldives, Nepal, Pakistan, and Sri Lanka. Not all countries are covered in the book. Most of the chapters were first presented as papers at the Conference on Gender Mainstreaming in Politics, Administration, and Development in South Asia in 2017, held at the North South University, Dhaka, Bangladesh. The book includes chapters on Bangladesh, India, the Maldives, Pakistan, and Sri Lanka.

The chapters result from more than a decade of collaboration between four universities: the University of Bergen in Norway, North South University in Bangladesh, Tribhuvan University in Nepal, and the University of Peradeniya in Sri Lanka. This collaboration, which started in 2007 under different collaborative projects financed by the Norwegian government, has resulted in a number of publications, conferences, workshops, seminars, policy briefs, and reports. It has also provided conditions and opportunities for a number of students to pursue master degrees and PhDs at the respective universities. Some projects have developed into South-South and North-South collaborations in teaching, research, and the dissemination of research-based findings. Gender has been an essential ingredient in these joint collaborative projects.

South Asia is vast in terms of population, and it is highly diverse in terms of ethnicity, religion, language, geography, and cultural values. Some countries such as Afghanistan, Nepal, and Bhutan are landlocked, while others such as Sri Lanka and the Maldives are surrounded by oceans. India is enormous, with about 1.35 billion people, and the Maldives archipelago comprises tiny atolls with a total population of 0.5 million. The great diversity also poses serious challenges to gender mainstreaming and raises questions about what gender mainstreaming should incorporate, the areas in which it is most essential, and how it is to be achieved. By signing the Platform for Action of the Beijing Conference in 1995, most South Asian countries committed themselves to achieving gender equality and the empowerment of women in all spheres of administration and development. However, class, caste, social norms, and the rural-urban divide are distinct in South Asia and continue to constrain gender equality and women's empowerment.

This book approaches gender mainstreaming from a policy-and-governance perspective. What have governments done to promote gender mainstreaming? How have they tried try to promote it, and when? And what are the results? These are questions most of the chapters address in one way or another. The focus has been to do within-country analysis rather than cross-country comparisons. Gender mainstreaming policies have implications for the national as well as the local level. The chapters focus on both these levels. Some chapters offer a historical account of a country's efforts toward gender mainstreaming, others focus on specific policies that encounter problems or facilitate opportunities for gender mainstreaming. All the authors are from South Asia, so are able to combine their practical knowledge and experiences with theories, methodology, and data.

The book is relevant for academics, policy formulators and implementers, and students of public administration, political science, policy and governance, sociology, and gender and development studies. Gender in policy formation and governance is an issue that requires more attention, especially in the context of South Asia, where gender roles are segregated and women are increasingly constrained by limited state policies, existing power structures, and restrictive social norms. Overcoming these challenges is essential if gender mainstreaming is ever to be institutionalized. The chapters in this book address some of these challenges.

This book's completion has been made possible by a number of individuals and institutions to whom we owe deep debts of gratitude. Our appreciation and thanks go to the Norwegian Agency for Development Cooperation (NORAD), which has supported collaborative projects that promote gender mainstreaming in education and research in the Global South. We are also grateful for the Norwegian Program for Capacity Development in Higher Education and Research for Development (NORHED), which has supported the publication of this book and played a central role in enhancing South-South and North-South collaborations. We would like to thank our friends and colleagues at the University of Bergen in Norway, Tribhuvan University in Nepal, North South University in Bangladesh, and the University of Peradeniya in Sri Lanka for their continuous support and cooperation in developing the collaborative network. This network has stimulated many students, scholars, and academics in building their capacities and training, not only in education, research, and scientific writings, but also in managing affairs of the state and society.

Special thanks to Arlyne Moi, who has been, as usual, exceptional in copy-editing, and to Sajjad Nayeem for editorial assistance. We would also like to thank the publisher for being patient, as we missed several deadlines in submitting the manuscript. Finally, to our host institutions—the Department of Administration and Organization Theory, University of Bergen, Norway, and the South Asian Institute of Policy and Governance

(SIPG), North South University, Bangladesh—thank you for providing support and a stimulating working environment for scholarly activities and research.

Bergen, Norway   Ishtiaq Jamil
Dhaka, Bangladesh   Salahuddin M. Aminuzzaman
Dhaka, Bangladesh   Syeda Lasna Kabir
Dhaka, Bangladesh   M. Mahfuzul Haque

CONTENTS

1 Introduction: Gender Mainstreaming in Politics, Administration, and Development in South Asia 1
Ishtiaq Jamil, Salahuddin M. Aminuzzaman, Syeda Lasna Kabir, and M. Mahfuzul Haque

2 Gendered Electoral Financing: Two Approaches Toward Funding as an Affirmative Action Measure 19
Ragnhild Louise Muriaas

3 How Policy Folds Back Before Implementation: A Study on Unequal Inheritance Right in Bangladesh 37
Jinat Hossain

4 Gender-Based Harassment and Violence in Higher Educational Institutions: A Case from Sri Lanka 61
Janethri B. Liyanage and Kamala Liyanage

5 'Through the Glass Ceiling, over the Glass Cliff?' Women Leaders in Bangladeshi Public Administration 87
Syeda Lasna Kabir

6   Emerging Leadership Roles of Women in Rural Local
    Government: Experiences from Bangladesh   111
    Mizanur Rahman

7   Gender Budgeting and Governance Challenges: A Case
    Study of Bangladesh   137
    Salahuddin M. Aminuzzaman

8   Empowering Women Through e-Governance in the
    Indian Province of Odisha: Capacity Building as an
    Enabling Measure   157
    Sangita Dhal

9   A Paradigm Shift in Women's Turnout and
    Representation in Indian Elections   181
    Sanjay Kumar

10 Achievements and Challenges for Gender Mainstreaming
    in the Employment Sector of the Maldives   209
    Mohamed Faizal

11 Caught in the Cross-Fire of Religion, Culture, and
    Politics: Women's Sexual and Reproductive Health and
    Rights in Pakistan   231
    Samreen Shahbaz

Index   255

Notes on Contributors

Salahuddin M. Aminuzzaman is Professor of Public Administration and Adviser, South Asian Institute of Policy and Governance (SIPG), North South University, Bangladesh. He has also served as the chair of the Department of Development Studies, University of Dhaka. He is a member of Policy Advisory Group (PAG), Ministry of Local Government, Bangladesh.

Sangita Dhal is Assistant Professor and Post-Doctoral Research Awardee at the Department of Political Science, Kalindi College, University of Delhi, India. She has extensive research experience in areas of e-governance, grassroots democracy, and public policy.

Mohamed Faizal is Secretary General at the National Pay Commission of the Maldives. He has wide-ranging policy interests, with focus on civil service reform, pay reform, performance management, and governance and strategic decision-making in public organizations.

M. Mahfuzul Haque is a former civil servant of the Government of Bangladesh. He is now Assistant Professor, South Asian Institute of Policy and Governance (SIPG) at North South University, Dhaka. He teaches research methodology, development management, organizational behavior and leadership, gender and development, and trust and governance.

Jinat Hossain is a PhD researcher at the Department of Earth and Environmental Sciences at KU Leuven, Belgium. Her PhD is about climate change, gender and social innovation. Her research covers multidisciplinary issues connecting to gender and feminist theories. She works on gendered policy, migration, religion, women's body, sexuality, and masculinity.

Ishtiaq Jamil is Professor at the Department of Administration and Organization Theory, University of Bergen, Norway. His research interests include administrative culture, trust, governance, public policy, institutional theory, representative bureaucracy, and higher education. He is involved in several research projects in South Asia on governance and institutional trust issues.

Sanjay Kumar is Professor and Director of Centre for the Study of Developing Societies (CSDS), India. He has conducted research on electoral politics, state of democracy, and youths in India. He has published widely and is a regular columnist in various English and Hindi nation dallies in India.

Syeda Lasna Kabir is Professor of Public Administration at the Department of Public Administration, University of Dhaka. Her areas of academic and research interests include women's political and administrative participation in South Asia, civil service training, e-governance, administrative culture, migration policies, comparative public administration, organizational behavior, and leadership.

Janethri B. Liyanage has a BSc degree in Chemistry (honors) from the University of Peradeniya, Sri Lanka, and is employed as a probationary lecturer in the Department of Chemistry, University of Peradeniya.

Kamala Liyanage is Professor emeritus at the University of Peradeniya, Sri Lanka. Her research includes gender issues, ethnic studies, good governance, and democracy. She has been the principal investigator of several researches on gender issues and remains active in scientific publications.

Ragnhild Louise Muriaas is Professor of Political Science at the University of Bergen, Norway. Research interest is political financing and gender equality. Selected works include *Gendered Electoral Financing: Money, Power and Representation in Comparative Perspective* (2019) and articles in *Comparative Political Studies, Political Studies* and *Journal of Modern African Studies.*

Mizanur Rahman is Joint Director at Bangladesh Academy for Rural Development (BARD), Comilla, Bangladesh. Since 1996, he has been engaged in conducting social research, projects, and training in his cognate areas, and has published extensively on these issues.

Samreen Shahbaz is working with ARROW as Senior Program Officer, Kuala Lumpur, Malaysia. She has been working for the promotion of sexual and reproductive health and rights. She has been engaged extensively with the national and regional review processes of the Sustainable Development Goals (SDGs) and international human rights accountability mechanisms.

Abbreviations

ADR	Alternate Dispute Resolution
APWA	All Pakistan Women's Association
BCS	Bangladesh's Civil Services
BIMARU	Bihar, Madhya Pradesh, Rajasthan, and Uttar Pradesh
BJP	Bharatiya Janata Party
BNP	Bangladeshi Nationalist Party
BPFA	Beijing Platform for Action
CEDAW	Convention on the Elimination of All Forms of Discrimination Against Women
CII	Council of Islamic Ideology
CSDS	Centre for the Study of Developing Societies
CSO	Civil Society Organization
DEVAW	UN Declaration on the Elimination of Violence Against Women
ECI	Election Commission of India
FATA	Federally Administered Tribal Areas
FPAP	Family Planning Association of Pakistan
FSC	Federal Shariat Court
GEI	Gender Equity Index
GoB	Government of Bangladesh
HDI	Human Development Index
ICESCR	International Covenant on Economic, Social, and Cultural Rights
ICPD	International Conference on Population and Development
KPK	Khyber Pakhtunkhwa
MMA	Mutahida Majlis-i-Amal
MoU	Memorandum of Understanding
NBS	National Bureau of Statistics
NGOs	Non-governmental Organizations

NIMD	Netherlands Institute for Multiparty Democracy
NWDP	National Women's Development Policy
PATA	Provincially Administered Tribal Areas
PEMRA	Pakistan Electronic Media Regulatory Authority
PfA	Plan of Action
PoA	Programme of Action
PTI	Tehreek-i-Insaf
SFYP	7th Five Year Plan
SRHR	Sexual and Reproductive Health and Rights
SVEEP	Systematic Voters' Education and Electoral Participation
TAPP	Technical Assistance Project Proforma
UDHR	Universal Declaration of Human Rights
UNDP	United Nations Development Programme
UPs	Union Parishads
VLE	Village-Level Entrepreneur
WSHGs	Women's Self-Help Groups

LIST OF FIGURES

Fig. 2.1 Increase in women's representation by world regions 20

Fig. 5.1 Increase of women's participation in ministries/the Secretariat (%). (Source: Public Administration Computer Centre (PACC), MOPA. (Updated: March 29, 2014 and March 23, 2018)) 98

Fig. 7.1 Annual allocation of gender budget (as % of total budget) 2011–2016. (Source: Ministry of Finance Database) 146

Fig. 7.2 Gender share as % of the total budget of selected ministries 2015–2016 148

Fig. 8.1 Types of services offered through CSCs. OBC: Other Backward Caste, SC: Scheduled Caste, ST: Scheduled Tribe. (Source: Author) 164

Fig. 9.1 Electoral participation: Men's and women's turnout, 1962–2014 (%) 183

Fig. 9.2 Gender gap in turnout: Lok Sabha elections (1957–2014) (%). (Note: Calculated as the difference between men's turnout (%) and women's turnout (%) for the Lok Sabha election. Source: Authors' analysis of data released by the Election Commission of India) 184

Fig. 9.3 Gender gap in turnout: State assembly elections 1990–2016 (%). (Note: Calculated as the difference between the men's turnout (%) and women's turnout (%) for the state assembly election. Source: Authors' analysis of data released by the Election Commission of India) 185

Fig. 9.4 Gender gap in voting for Congress and BJP (%). (Note: Difference in the percentage vote among women voters and men voters. Source: National Election Studies 2009 and 2014, conducted by the CSDS) 193

Fig. 9.5   Number of female candidates in Lok Sabha elections (1957–2014)   200

Fig. 9.6   Number of male candidates in Lok Sabha elections (1957–2014). (Source: https://i0.wp.com/factly.in/wp-content/uploads/2015/02/Number-of-Male-Contenstants-in-Various-Lok-Sabha-Elections.png?ssl=1)   200

Fig. 9.7   Proportion of increase in male and female candidates   201

Fig. 9.8   Success rate of male vs. female MP candidates (%)   202

Fig. 9.9   Number of women MPs in the Lok Sabha (1952–2014)   202

Fig. 9.10   Proportion of women's representation in the Lok Sabha (1952–2014) (%)   203

LIST OF TABLES

Table 4.1   Distribution of key staff positions among academic staff by gender, 2017   69

Table 4.2   Distribution of academic staff by category, gender, and faculty (permanent staff only), 2017 (as of 31 December 2017)   70

Table 4.3   Distribution of non-academic decision-makers, 2017   71

Table 4.4   Total student enrolment by faculties and gender, 2017   72

Table 4.5   Response on equal treatment from staff and students of the University X (percentage distribution)   73

Table 4.6   Responses of staff and students on gender equality of the University of X (percentage distribution)   75

Table 4.7   Sex-disaggregated data of the key informants of the research   76

Table 4.8   Types of gender-based harassment and violence that took place   76

Table 4.9   Effects of gender-based harassment and violence   80

Table 5.1   Administration of the quota system (until 2018)   96

Table 5.2   Summary of findings: factors affecting the glass cliff in the BCS   104

Table 7.1   Gender gap: South Asian scenario 2018   143

Table 7.2   Gender distribution of economic participation and opportunities   144

Table 8.1   Comparative analysis of women and men CSC operators in Ganjam and Keonjhar districts, 2016–2018   168

Table 9.1   Difference in gender gap in turnout in different states: Assembly elections 1990–2013 (%)   185

Table 9.2   Declining gender gap in turnout in different kinds of states: Assembly elections 1990–2013 (%)   186

Table 9.3   Turnout among men and women voters: Assembly elections since 2010 (%)   187

Table 9.4	Proportion of voters who voted without taking anybody else's opinion into account: Lok Sabha elections 2004–2014 (%)	189
Table 9.5	Whom do voters normally consult while voting? Lok Sabha elections 2009–2014 (%)	190
Table 9.6	State-wise analysis of proportion of voters who voted without taking anybody else's opinion into account (%)	191
Table 9.7	Gender-wise opinions on issues which influenced voting decisions: Lok Sabha elections 2009–2014 (%)	192
Table 9.8	Level of educational attainment of women voters and turnout: Lok Sabha elections 2009–2014 (%)	194
Table 9.9	State-wise pattern of increased literacy rate among women and declining gender gap in literacy (%)	195
Table 9.10	Level of media exposure and turnout among women voters: Lok Sabha elections 2009–2014 (%)	196
Table 9.11	Declining proportion of voters (men and women) not exposed to media: Lok Sabha elections 2004–2014 (%)	196
Table 9.12	State-wise analysis of change in level of media exposure and gender gap on voting: Lok Sabha elections 2009–2014 (%)	197
Table 9.13	Interest in politics and voting	197
Table 9.14	Increasing number of elected women representatives in gram panchayats: 2001–2014 (%)	198
Table 9.15	Women's representation in parliaments of South Asian countries	204
Table 9.16	Electoral participation beyond voting and running for office	205
Table 10.1	Resident Maldivians attending higher education institutions, census 2014	213
Table 10.2	Education level of the employed population (%)	214
Table 10.3	Proportion of employed resident Maldivian population by industries (in percentage), census 2014	215
Table 10.4	Extent of women's representation in political posts (2014)	217
Table 10.5	Mean monthly earnings of women and men, by occupation in Malé, 2010	219
Table 10.6	Average monthly earnings (US$)—main job by education attainment	219

Introduction: Gender Mainstreaming in Politics, Administration, and Development in South Asia

Ishtiaq Jamil, Salahuddin M. Aminuzzaman, Syeda Lasna Kabir, and M. Mahfuzul Haque

INTRODUCTION

Gender mainstreaming is about removing disparities between men and women—about equal access to resources, inclusion and participation in the public sphere, representation in government, and empowerment, all with the aim of achieving equal opportunities for men and women in family life, society, administration, politics, and the economy. Gender mainstreaming does not refer only to women (Monsen, 2010, p. 2). It means that all social and development-related policies must reflect on gender and consider it as an essential element in the policy formulation process.

I. Jamil (✉)
University of Bergen, Bergen, Norway
e-mail: ishtiaq.jamil@uib.no

S. M. Aminuzzaman • M. M. Haque
South Asian Institute of Policy and Governance (SIPG), North South University, Dhaka, Bangladesh

S. Lasna Kabir
Department of Public Administration, University of Dhaka, Dhaka, Bangladesh

© The Author(s) 2020
I. Jamil et al. (eds.), *Gender Mainstreaming in Politics, Administration and Development in South Asia*,
https://doi.org/10.1007/978-3-030-36012-2_1

1

Gender mainstreaming is also about institutionalizing gender equality in development (Mukhopadhyay, 2013), in other words, to provide equitable as well as equal opportunities for people of different genders, classes, castes, and ethnicities, and to validate their sexual diversity. Gender mainstreaming is thus closely linked with gender equality (Walby, 2005). It recognizes that men and women have different needs and priorities and therefore may requires different treatment, but that opportunities should be equal for all, so that men and women can lead equally meaningful lives (Monsen, 2010, p. 8).

The concept of gender mainstreaming was coined by feminist development practitioners in the 1970s and eventually became a prominent concept and strategy to advance the topic of gender in development discourses (Walby, 2005). The UN Fourth World Women's Conference in Beijing (1995) was the occasion that set the agenda for gender mainstreaming through achieving gender equality and the empowerment of women (Moser & Moser, 2005). Since then, it has become a focal point in socioeconomic development programs, not only in the West but also in the developing world. It has now become a "policy frame" through which gender issues, especially those related to women, are incorporated into policies and given due attention. An example is the issue of political and administrative recruitment and the selection process through which a woman can gain a decision-making position in an organization. According to Hafner-Burton and Pollack (2002, p. 2), "The concept of gender mainstreaming promises a revolutionary change in the international and domestic policy process, in which gender issues become a core consideration not simply for specific departments or ministries dealing with women, but rather for all actors across a range of issue-areas and at all stages in the policy process from conception and legislation to implementation and evaluation."

However, along with the concept's advancement and current center-stage position, it has also attracted much debate and controversies on how to incorporate gender issues in development policies and practices, both from theoretical and from practical standpoints (Warren, 2007). According to Walby (2005, p. 321), gender mainstreaming, being a contested concept and practice, "involves the reinvention, restructuring, and rebranding of a key part of feminism in the contemporary era." It therefore requires theory development as a strategy and a practice, in order to promote gender equality.

The dynamic relations between gender and governance have been broadly ignored in mainstream development discourses. In most societies, women's roles are seen as existing mostly in the "private" realm, while men's roles are in the "public" realm (Nussbaum, Basu, Tambiah, & Niraja, 2003). Drawing on global experiences, Brody (2009) observers that women have been treated unequally in all forms of formal and informal processes. He specifically observes that (a) women are unequally treated in the institutions in which they are involved; (b) institutions, in general, fail to acknowledge the "double burden" on women; (c) institutional policies usually fail to recognize gender issues and the nature of the needs of men and women, causing inequalities in decision-making; and (d) the absence of institutional accountability breeds inequality and the violation of women's rights.

GENDER MAINSTREAMING AND ITS ORIGIN

The concept of gender mainstreaming as a strategy and policy process has undergone several stages of development and conceptualization. Understanding these stages requires a discussion on women in development (WID), women and development (WAD), and gender and development (GAD). The different connotations of these three themes illustrate varying assumptions in the stages of conceptualization, policy agendas, and research issues relating to gender mainstreaming.

Women in Development (WID)

WID started gaining prominence in the 1970s and 1980s and was used actively by American liberal feminists. Their concern was women's economic emancipation, which was essential for gender mainstreaming. To end discrimination against women and increase their participation in the economic sector, policies and practices needed to change. In this regard, WID came to be associated with modernization, industrialization, and urbanization—the major post-colonial policy agenda in developing countries in the 1950s. It was expected that modernization, with emphasis on education, would create a modern workforce that would benefit men and women equally. However, modernization and its promise of women's emancipation were highly criticized in the 1970s, as modernization had not led to women's advancement. To the contrary: women's position was downgraded. Agriculture is a case in point: processes of mechanization ended up favoring men more than women, whereas in traditional forms of agriculture, women play a larger role. In addition to criticism associated with modernization, other critics of WID pointed to the problems of "quick" or "single fix" approaches to women's empowerment. Examples here are to give women access to appropriate technology, offer income-generating activities, or give women access to skills and education. The problem is that such measures, in isolation, do not take into account the contexts in which women live—their class, religion, caste, race, and culture. If these contexts do not support women's increased empowerment, then technological innovations, work, educational opportunities, and so forth are easily appropriated by other social and family actors such as male family members. Women usually have no defense against such social action (Rathgeber, 1990, pp. 491–492).

Women and Development (WAD)

Against the backdrop of criticism of WID, the concept of WAD evolved in the mid-1970s. Because it combined Marxist and feminist perspectives, it was termed as a neo-Marxist feminist approach (Rathgeber, 1990, p. 493). WAD's major argument is that women have always been an essential part of the economy; they are not newcomers, as WID claims, and their work inside and outside the house has sustained society. This maintenance of society, however, has also led to the maintenance of an international order of inequality. In this regard, the dependence of both women and men on an international system creates dependence and subordination. The international system promotes class differences and makes both men and women in the Third World, especially in Africa, dependent on the same system that oppresses them. Without addressing class structure, differences, and domination, gender mainstreaming interventions, and strategies may remain an illusion. WAD argues that women's position will improve when the international system becomes more egalitarian. WAD, however, fails to critically analyze the relationships between gender, class, varying modes of production, and social structures such as patriarchy.

Gender and Development (GAD)

This concept emerged in the 1980s and has its theoretical roots in socialist feminism. It takes a more holistic approach to analyzing the gender situation; it does not restrict its scope to women's problems but also asks critical questions about gender roles. According to Rathgeber (1990, p. 494), "GAD is not concerned with women per se but with the social construction of gender and the assignment of specific roles, responsibilities, and expectations to women and to men." GAD focuses on the male and female genders and emphasizes equity and social justice. It recognizes women's contribution both inside and outside the household, rejects the private-public dichotomy, and asks questions about why inside-the-house activities are not counted as being *as* valuable as outside-the-house activities.

GAD views the concept of "sex," that is to say, the distinction between male and female, as biological, while it views "gender" as a social construction in which the relations between women and men are socially formed and therefore mutable. This relationship is not fixed (Cornwall, 2007). The social construction of gender roles promotes discrimination and subordination, so GAD proponents would like to see an end to it.

But GAD takes a more proactive approach to women's roles, seeing them as agents of change. It is concerned with ensuring women's legal status, their right to own land and to receive an inheritance. It emphasizes the reexamination of social structures and institutions and commits to "structural change and power shifts" (Rathgeber, 1990, p. 495).

As the above discussion suggests, gender mainstreaming encompasses a broad range of activities, thoughts, planning, and questions about how to make both sexes act and behave in a manner that respects the premises and preferences of everyone, no matter their gender. Gender mainstreaming would be impossible without both sexes thinking and acting freely in social space. This means families and other social actors such as religious leaders must also accommodate and create space for individuals, either male or female, to act according to their preferences without fear of reprisal and harassment. State policies, economic progress, and advocacy by civil society may facilitate gender mainstreaming and empowerment, but as long as the social context within which the sexes operate does not facilitate such freedom, the empowerment of women and gender equality remain a farfetched dream.

Gender Planning

Associated with gender mainstreaming is gender planning, which aims to ensure equal status between men and women (Moser, 1989, 1993). This requires renewed thinking and planning regarding the policy instruments that are available, and what new instruments are required to lift women out of subordination and to empower them. Gender planning is therefore essential for ensuring that women acquire equality, equity, and social justice.

In the context of developing countries, it is recognized that women and men have different roles and thus also different needs (Moser, 1989, p. 1799). Recognizing this fact is one thing, but incorporating it appropriately into gender planning is quite another. It requires theoretical conceptualizations and methodological tools. Women are becoming increasingly active in the public sphere, for instance, through migration and seeking employment at home or abroad. An important issue is thus how policies and policy-makers should respond to the different needs of women.

Women's roles—for instance, their reproductive role (child rearing and family care giver), productive role (income-generating employment), and community engagement roles (forming social organizations to manage the needs of neighborhoods, such as water, firewood, etc.)—are often unrecognized and subordinated to men's seemingly more productive role (main breadwinner). That means women's reproductive and community-managing roles remain invisible and unacknowledged in the community and by the state. Even women's economic role in society often remains undervalued, invisible, and counted as "free work," just as is their reproductive role. For instance, women in South Asia do a large portion of work in agriculture but are seldom given the title of "farmer." This invisibility causes them to be deprived of economic benefits and professional identity.

In the past decades, different policies and programs have been adopted, especially in the developing world, and directed toward women with low income. These can be classified as (a) welfare, (b) equity, (c) anti-poverty, (d) efficiency, and (e) empowerment (Moser, 1989, p. 1808). These policies, although non-linear, initially started with helping poor women gain inclusion in some development programs by providing free goods and services, and thereafter giving them the same status as men in development projects. It was deemed important to reduce poverty, to recognize women's contributions in the private sphere, and to train them in skills that could enhance their delivery capacity and engagement in the formal economy thorough paid employment, all of which would hopefully result in self-reliance and increased self-confidence. This entailed the empowerment of women in decision-making, enabling them to assume leadership roles and to meaningfully participate in governance. But even though welfare, anti-poverty measures, and recent efficiency policies have been the dominant policy approaches in the developing countries, their implications often contain gender-biased norms and measures.

The current focus is on promoting equity and empowerment, but these policies also often pose challenges. The equity-based approach has brought about a few successes in women's representation in politics, employment, leadership, and administration, but the representation of ethnic, transgender, queer, disabled, and other minority groups often remains unaddressed. Incorporating all these groups into polices would entail a social transformation with far-reaching consequences for social power-structure configurations. Such empowerment further entails increasing the power of women to become self-reliant and able to make decisions for themselves. That said, the concept of empowerment is still geared largely toward the more limited scope of ensuring women's participation in policy formulation and implementation.

Revisiting Gender Mainstreaming

The landscape of gender mainstreaming is beset with contested concepts, strategies, and practices. Is it all-inclusive? What about its present status in the age of globalization and technological revolution? Technological innovations, democratization, and participatory governance are promoting freedom, choice, and increased capability (Sen, 1999). As Sen notes, choice itself is a valuable feature in a person's life as regards attaining capabilities, as "[t]he 'capability set' would consist of the alternative functioning vectors that she can choose from" (Sen, 1999, p. 75). But this also triggers several questions: Do gender mainstreaming policies open up many alternative functioning vectors for women? What kinds of options are available and accessible to different classes, castes, ethnicities, and queer groups? We must also consider whether the mainstreaming debates are incorporating new issues such as the digital divide, equal access to the use of technology, the rights of minorities, the inclusion of disabled, LGBT, and queer groups in policy processes, all in order to provide them with the same opportunities everyone else in society should have. These issues require renewed thinking and inclusion in gender mainstreaming debates, discourse, and policies.

Another issue is that while globalization has definitely made nations wealthier, we simultaneously observe greater income disparities and wider gaps between the rich and the poor within rather than across countries. At the same time, globalization has introduced competition and market-based principles and interests in society. Some groups, such as the poor and families whose head of household is a woman, are pushed back and marginalized, sometimes driven away from their lands, which are then appropriated by powerful economic and unscrupulous actors. What kind of choices and justice do these poor men and women have when they are marginalized? In the age of globalization, new challenges are surfacing, so to what extent are government policies taking account of these new challenges?

With the revolution in information and communication technology (ICT) and social media, there is easier access to information and other online services that facilitate gender mainstreaming, but we also observe that ICT and social media give people with bad intentions more room for maneuver. Take, for instance, the increasing technology-facilitated stalking, abuse, and harassment of women and minorities. In this sense, technology is quickly outpacing society and the state's ability to monitor, control, and restrict the technology if necessary, especially mobile versions. Without proper control and supervision, we observe the increasing use of vulgar sites, even by adolescents, and the use of social media to harass, stalk, humiliate, and abuse girls and women (Woodlock, 2017, p. 586). Unless young people critically evaluate this technological development and easy access, their worldview and mindset regarding sexuality will be distorted. Some cyber laws have been formulated, but without the active engagement of the wider community and societal institutions such as schools and families, the abuse of technology poses a serious threat, not least in portraying women as a commodity. In the case of India, according to Arnold et al. (2002, p. 759), "While discrimination against young girls that results in excess female mortality has been widely documented through the years [...] the recent sharp increases in the gap of female-male sex ratios are commonly assumed to be the result of the rapid spread of the use of ultrasound and amniocentesis for sex determination, followed by sex-selective induced abortions." The use of ultra-sonogram technology to ascertain whether babies are healthy is thus leading to the abortion of girl fetuses simply because Indian society has a preference for boys.

Micro-level issues relating to family, community, and society are also important for gender mainstreaming. Therefore, policies aimed at such mainstreaming should include men, parents, in-laws, priests/clergies, and other related key persons, to ensure a more fair, just, and equitable gender practice in private, public, and community life. For instance, women's double or triple roles might bring more problems than solutions. Does gender mainstreaming take this into consideration? Do the policies offer alternative solutions for working mothers, to create a balance between their productive and reproductive roles?

On the other hand, among certain classes, women's economic involvement and empowerment has created new challenges for men. Men's traditional breadwinning role is changing. Societal transformation and changing gender roles that have come about through women's economic empowerment need further attention and more discussion. Who will play the household role? Who will pay the bills? How can women and men create a balance between private and public life? How can the state offer the best alternatives for the working couple/parents, so they can perform both productive and reproductive roles? How do men perceive and treat women when they (the women) become breadwinners and decision-makers? Is the society ready for women's empowerment, in particular, women's equal participation in the economy and in decision-making process? Although gender mainstreaming policies encourage women to engage in productive and income-generating activities, these issues need to be considered in the wider and long-term policy agenda.

GENDER MAINSTREAMING IN SOUTH ASIA

The challenges of gender mainstreaming in South Asia have been daunting, especially in the contexts of patriarchal, religious, and caste-based social norms and values. Despite huge differences in the South Asian nations in terms of geography, language, ethnicity, socio-demographic characteristics, and politics, these countries share one common feature: men's dominance in politics, administration, and economic activities. Gender segregation is distinct in the division of labor and in who occupies the private and public spheres. Women have been subservient to the policy preferences of their male counterparts. However, in recent years, more and more women are participating in politics at the local and national levels, in administrative and top-level positions, and in formal economic activities.

The processes and strategies for gender mainstreaming in South Asia may be an outcome of three factors that have pushed for women's empowerment, inclusion, participation in the public sphere, and engagement in the formal economy. The first is the formulation and implementation of a number of gender-related affirmative policies by the state, which allow women to be recruited to the civil service and local government, and which have set up education schemes for girls. The second is policy-transfer advocacy by international and multilateral organizations and national and international NGOs. Third, globalization of the economy has allowed South Asian nations to join the global village. This has resulted in rapid economic growth and opened avenues for women to join the formal economy, for instance, the garment sector. Along with this is micro-finance and other social intervention programs spearheaded by NGOs. These give women small loans and help them manage their economic activities.

Despite such policy interventions and strategies, social contexts embedded with thick cultural and religious values and patriarchal norms are impeding gender mainstreaming. For example, women must seek male (father or husband) permission in major decisions such as choosing paid jobs or traveling outside the private sphere. As a result, men have far greater mobility than do women, and women are left with the role of caring for children, the elderly, and managing household chores. Women are also paid less, and their jobs usually have a lower social ranking than men's jobs. As Mehta (2007, p. 4) puts it, there is a power differential between men and women, with greater value being awarded to "the characteristics, work, and behavior of males over those of females."

Moreover, because of marginalization and a lack of access to information, women are less empowered and, as such, more vulnerable to disasters. The 1991 cyclone in Bangladesh exemplifies that the "mortality levels amongst females over the age of ten were three times higher than those of males" (Twigg, 2004, cited in Mehta, 2007, p. 9). Also, "in the Asian tsunamis, five times as many women as men are believed to have died" (Chew & Ramdass, 2005, cited in Mehta, 2007, p. 9).

In South Asia, patriarchal norms are dominant and influence public policies and the actions of public institutions and social actors. So we can rightly ask: Have social values and norms developed to the point where they can expedite gender mainstreaming, or is some social mobilization needed to trigger and bring about social transformation? It is possible to observe a slow process of change in women's increased participation in education, local and national governance, and in their exercise of leadership roles. But such forms of empowerment can only be enjoyed by the happy few. Given the enormous population size, the level of poverty, and inadequate redistributive policies, the South Asian nations may require many more years to achieve substantial gender mainstreaming in accordance with gender development theorists' expectations—unless some radical social reform processes happen. This would require a holistic broad-based partnership strategy between the state, civil society, international actors, and the business community, to incorporate gender mainstreaming in all policies and programs (Kabeer, 2003; Panday, 2013).

The issue of institutionalizing gender in policies and practices remains elusive. In terms of statistics on women's access to health and education, participation in local governance, and engagement in economic activities, some South Asian nations may show an impressive record, but in real terms, has gender mainstreaming been institutionalized to the point where women have gained meaningful participation, representation, and become involved in decision-making (Jahan & Mumtaz, 1996)? Have gender equality and equity been ensured? To what extent have gender equality and equity been given serious attention in policies, or do government actors use the terms merely to lend more legitimacy to their policies (Mukhopadhyay, 2013)?

Over the past few decades the South Asian countries have emphasized policies to enhance welfare, efficiency, and poverty reduction. In recent years, however, there has been a noticeable thematic shift toward empowerment, rights, and capability approaches. Interestingly, in South Asia, the theoretical discourses on gender and development have been relatively advanced compared to the actual practice and implementation of gender policies (Baruyah, 2005). The South Asian countries also suffer from a paradox: Most of them have experienced the rule of a female head of the state, in some cases even for many years, but women's empowerment and political engagement are still insufficient. The poor participation of women in politics and governance therefore seems deeply embedded in South Asian culture (Omyedt, 2005).

In the South Asian context, legal equality becomes useless if actual inequalities are due to institutional flaws (Banskota, 2012). Drawing examples from Pakistan, Ahmad and Sohaib Murad (2010) note that the gender gap cannot necessarily be addressed by creating a new scope, but that socio-demographic and cultural factors play a role in letting the gender gap continue. An Indian study (Dijkstra et al., 2007), meanwhile, shows a more promising picture. The researchers observe that at the local government level, women are respected and rated as competent, fair, and flexible. Yet for structural and cultural reasons, the contributions of women tend to remain invisible. This invisibility poses a serious threat to democratic governance.

There is hardly any comparative research on governance from a gender perspective in South Asia. Nor are there many research-based empirical studies on broader gender issues such as access to resources, equality between the genders, women's participation in governance and the workforce, their voice in the public sphere, and the implications of all such matters on governance institutions and processes. As Caroline Moser (2005, pp. 577–578) points out, more than two decades have passed since the *Beijing Plan for Action* (1995) was formulated. What then is the status of gender mainstreaming? Its success depends on four issues: (a) recognizing gender equality and gender mainstreaming as policy issues that need serious attention, (b) setting policy agendas for gender mainstreaming and thereafter formulating gender policies, (c) translating policies into reality by implementing them, and (d) properly accounting for and evaluating the policies, to measure their success in terms of policy outcomes and impact.

Taking stock and renewing our thinking have become essential. The above-mentioned stages (WID, WAD, GAD) are important points of departure and require serious attention if gender mainstreaming is a goal; otherwise it will simply be window dressing, in the developing world as well as elsewhere. In the context of South Asia, we do observe a number of policies undertaken in the recent past on anti-poverty, social welfare, and efficiency, but there have been few on equity and empowerment. Some policies favoring micro-credit and other social intervention programs are argued to be enhancing equity and empowerment, but we need to understand empowerment within a wider socio-economic and political context. These policies may have a minimal effect as far as reducing poverty and increasing social welfare, but unless there is some form of social transformation, they will fail to bring about change in the power structure. Class, caste, culture, and religious values are strong in South Asia and define the power structure and distinction between male and female roles. These social constructions are difficult to overcome. As such, the poor—both men and women—are likely to be marginalized, dominated, and influenced by the existing power structure and socio-cultural values.

Despite opposition and protest, positive discrimination in the form of affirmative policies is necessary to trigger changes in South Asia. But there is also a need to further investigate what impact these policies have in terms of more varied and increased representation and participation in politics, administration, and development. Putting a policy into effect is not enough. Equally important is a mechanism to evaluate it, assess its impact, and adjust it accordingly. This is because most policy-related challenges are visible only after the policy is implemented. Policies that can overcome or cope with the challenges would gain more legitimacy and societal support, and the gender mainstreaming process would become a fact.

The above discussions signify the importance of gender mainstreaming and conducting research on its various aspects. Keeping this in mind, the book presents studies from Bangladesh, India, the Maldives, Pakistan, and Sri Lanka. Our point of departure is policy cycle, with major focus on policy formulation, and its subsequent implementation and evaluation. How, for example, the issue of gender is incorporated in a nation's policies such as budget and ensures administrative, and political representation, how policy contents have been altered and revised, how policies have evolved over the years to respond to the issue of gender mainstreaming, how policies fold back before being implemented, and what major consequences and impacts these have had for uplifting women both in the rural and in the urban settings. We also focus on issues such as gender violence and inadequate policies in this regard. The chapters are results of years of empirical research and field-level experiences of authors with authentic examples to establish linkages between state and local institutions with social and gender needs. It is, therefore, useful text and resource to practitioners and students in disciplinary areas such as politics, public policy, public administration, development studies, sociology, and international relations both to conduct and choose a topic for research and to generate debates about gender mainstreaming.

THE BOOK

The chapters in this book, most of which were presented as papers at a conference in 2017, cover diverse topics and address a broad range of issues. Common to them all, however, is the theme of gender mainstreaming. The chapters look at how gender-related issues are incorporated into policy formulation and governance, how they have fared, what challenges they have encountered when these policies were put into practice, and their implications and fate. In short, the focus is on gender mainstreaming and the challenges it encounters. The authors have used varied frameworks to analyze gender mainstreaming at the micro and macro levels, and mostly within the scope of a single country.

In Chap. 2, Ragnhild Louise Muriaas discusses examples of how public financial incentives have recently been used to motivate women to seek political leadership and to stimulate key gatekeepers to demand women leaders. The chapter concludes that such initiatives can work, both in tandem with and as a substitute to gender quotas, but that their efficiency depends on the institutional context and the design of the measure.

Jinat Hossain, in Chap. 3, examines how a policy folds back even before implementation, due to resistance from certain societal segments. Drawing on the fate of Bangladesh's National Women's Development Policy (2011), Hossain observes that the successful implementation of a gender policy depends on the amount of change it aims to achieve and the nature of the opposition it may encounter from various quarters with contrary interests. She also notes that ruling regimes tend to compromise with religious leaders, to comply with the public's religious sentiments, and to opt for a safe political settlement.

In Chap. 4, Janethri B. Liyanage and Kamala Liyanage analyze gender-based violence in institutions of higher learning in Sri Lanka. They find that both students and staff at these institutions face various types of gender-based harassment and violence, and that the horrendous experiences have an immensely negative impact on their academic lives. The root causes of such violence are gendered socialization, unequal power relations, gender identities, gender performance, and the patriarchal structure of the institutions.

In Chap. 5, Syeda Lasna Kabir observes that female members of bureaucracy in Bangladesh tend to face a host of institutional and behavioral challenges. Eventually, they are pushed to the edge of a phenomenon termed the "glass cliff"—an invisible barrier partly analogous to the well-known "glass ceiling" which keeps women from reaching senior-level positions. While both the glass ceiling and the glass cliff result in limited engagement in policy-making roles, a lack of room for maneuver, reduced empowerment, and invisible inequality in the peer group environment, a glass cliff typically emerges when a woman assumes a position of leadership when the chance of failure is heightened. Extrinsic factors such as work/life balance and subjective discrimination also figure into the scenarios.

Mizanur Rahman, in Chap. 6, studies the role of women member of grassroots-level local government (*Union Parishad*) in Bangladesh, observing that even with the existing legal framework, women can make a difference to transform rural society. Amid their ceaseless struggle and constrained participation in government, woman leaders were able to make differences in providing "culturally suitable judgment" for rural women in the village court. The trained women leaders were found to be relatively more sensitive and responsive to women's causes and gender issues. They also initiated a form of transformative politics that increased community welfare and social justice in local government.

In Chap. 7, Salahuddin M. Aminuzzaman observes that with the given political dynamics of Bangladesh, gender budgeting is stalled and handicapped by a combination of factors such as a lack of political direction and follow-up, inadequate conceptual clarity, a lack of professional competence and skills, weak monitoring of the results, and, most importantly, poor supervision and a weak or non-existent demand for it. Civil society, women activists, and the media have not yet been able to generate an adequate demand for gender budgeting. Furthermore, there is noticeable institutional weakness, which means it is impossible to do the in-depth gender analysis that is required to prepare gender budgets and to monitor them.

Sangita Dhal, in Chap. 8, presents a case study from the Indian province of Odisha, examining e-governance and its implications for the empowerment of women. Capacity building through the application of technology is considered one of the enabling mechanisms for accomplishing the larger goal of women's empowerment in the state, but as Dhal observes, the journey toward women's liberation and social emancipation is hampered by the challenges of social, economic, and political disempowerment.

In Chap. 9, Sanjay Kumar finds that political representation and participation are the most effective ways to put Indian women's interests on the political agenda and to let their voices to be heard. This is why women's involvement in the electoral process is particularly important. However, the pronounced gender gap in electoral participation in India remains an untenable dilemma for Indian democracy. Women constitute close to half of the total electorate, yet remain under-represented at the polling booth. This is an undeniably discouraging aspect of Indian elections.

Chapter 10, by Faizal Mohamed, looks into the changing economic landscape of the Maldives. The shift to service and manufacturing, combined with migration to urban centers, has inadvertently diminished women's participation in economic activities and confined a significant proportion of them to household duties. Policies for gender mainstreaming have been an integral part of successive governments. But despite positive strides, deep-rooted cultural beliefs, coupled with inconsistent and inappropriate institutional policies, continue to contribute to work and wage inequalities. Thus, a more focused, strategic, and holistic realignment of gender policies is needed in order to build on the recent achievements, enabling women to further break into leadership positions and narrow the pay gap.

Chapter 11, by Samreen Shahbaz, examines gender equality and women's and girls' sexual and reproductive health and rights (SRHR) in the context of Pakistan. It critically reviews the extent to which the Pakistani state has met its international commitments on SRHR and the critical factors for the lack of adequate laws to ensure such rights. Shahbaz finds that identity politics continue to intersect with religious idioms, local sociocultural norms, and traditions. This has led to serious gaps in SRHR-related laws and policies and limited progress on Pakistan's international SRHR commitments.

References

Ahmad, R. H., & Sohaib Murad, H. (2010). Gender gap in Pakistan: A socio-demographic analysis. *International Journal of Social Economics, 37*(7), 541–557.

Arnold, F., Kishor, S., & Roy, T. K. (2002). Sex-selective abortions in India. *Population and Development Review, 28*(4), 759–785.

Banskota, S. S. (2012). Gender and democracy: An overview for Nepal. In *Linking environment, democracy and gender* (pp. 33–47). Emerald Group Publishing Limited.

Baruyah, B. (2005). Gender and development in South Asia: Can practice keep up with theory? *Canadian Journal of Development Studies, 26*(special issue), 677–688.

Brody, A. (2009). *Gender and governance: Overview report.* Brighton, UK: Bridge Publications, IDS.

Cornwall, A. (2007). Revisiting the 'gender agenda'. *IDS Bulletin, 38*(2), 69–78.

Dijkstra, J. K., Lindenberg, S., & Veenstra, R. (2007). Same-gender and cross-gender peer acceptance and peer rejection and their relation to bullying and helping among preadolescents: Comparing predictions from gender-homophily and goal-framing approaches. *Developmental Psychology, 43*(6), 1377.

Government of Peoples' Republic of Bangladesh. (2011, March). National Women Development Policy. Ministry of Women and Children Affairs. Retrieved from https://www.unescogym.org/wp-content/uploads/2017/05/Bangladesh-National-Women-Policy-2011English.pdf. Last consulted on May 22, 2019.

Hafner-Burton, E., & Pollack, M. A. (2002). Mainstreaming gender in global governance. *European Journal of International Relations, 8*(3), 339–373.

Jahan, R., & Mumtaz, S. (1996). The elusive agenda: Mainstreaming women in development [with comments]. *The Pakistan Development Review, 35*(4), 825–834.

Kabeer, N. (2003). *Gender mainstreaming in poverty eradication and the millennium development goals: A handbook for policy-makers and other stakeholders.* Commonwealth Secretariat International Development Research Centre, Canadian International Development Agency (CIDA).

Mehta, M. (2007). *Gender matters: Lessons for disaster risk reduction in South Asia.* Kathmandu: The International Centre for Integrated Mountain Development (ICIMOD). ISBN 978 92 9115 024 3.

Monsen, J. (2010). *Gender and development* (2nd ed.). London: Routledge.

Moser, C. O. N. (1989). Gender planning in the third world: Meeting practical and strategic gender needs. *World Development, 17*(11), 179–185.

Moser, C. O. N. (1993). *Gender planning and development theory, practice and training.* London: Routledge.

Moser, C. O. N. (2005). Has gender mainstreaming failed? A comment on international development agency experiences in the South. *International Feminist Journal of Politics, 7*(4). https://doi.org/10.1080/14616740500284573

Mukhopadhyay, M. (2013). Mainstreaming gender or reconstituting the mainstream? Gender Knowledge in Development. *Journal of International Development, 26*(3), 356–367. https://doi.org/10.1002/jid.2946

Nussbaum, M., Basu, A., Tambiah, Y., & Niraja, G. J. (2003). *Essays on gender and governance.* New Delhi: Human Development Resource Centre, UNDP.

Omyedt, G. (2005). Women in governance in South Asia. *Economic and Political Weekly, 40*(44–45), 4746–4752.

Panday, P. K. (2013). *Women's political participation in Bangladesh: Institutional reforms, actors and outcomes.* New York: Springer.

Rathgeber, E. M. (1990). WID, WAD, GAD: Trends in research and practice. *The Journal of Developing Areas, 24*(4), 489–502.

Sen, A. (1999). *Development as freedom.* Oxford: Oxford University Press.

Walby, S. (2005). Gender mainstreaming: Productive tensions in theory and practice. *Studies in Gender, State & Society, 12*(3), 321–343. https://doi.org/10.1093/sp/jxi018

Warren, H. (2007). Using gender-analysis frameworks: Theoretical and practical reflections. *Gender & Development, 15*(2), 187–198. https://doi.org/10.1080/13552070701391847

Woodlock, D. (2017). The abuse of technology in domestic violence and stalking. *Violence Against Women, 23*(5), 584–602.

CHAPTER 2

Gendered Electoral Financing: Two Approaches Toward Funding as an Affirmative Action Measure

Ragnhild Louise Muriaas

INTRODUCTION

All over the world, there has been a steady increase in the number of women who have been elected into political office during the last two decades. Yet while Asia started out as one of the best achievers in 1997, with 14 percent of elected offices held by women, the changes in this part of the world are growing at a slower speed than in most other world regions. Currently, Europe, the Americas, and Sub-Saharan Africa have

This chapter is based on a keynote address given at the International Conference on Gender Mainstreaming in Politics, Administration and Development in South Asia and Beyond, North South University, Dhaka, Bangladesh, November 18–19, 2017. The talk is based on findings from the project *Money Talks: Gendered electoral financing in democratic and democratizing states*, funded by the Research Council of Norway (grant number 250669/F10).

R. L. Muriaas (✉)
Department of Comparative Politics, University of Bergen, Bergen, Norway
e-mail: Ragnhild.Muriaas@uib.no

higher rates of women in elected offices, and the Arab states (which were far behind Asia in 1997) are currently just two percentage points behind Asia (see Fig. 2.1). In the rest of the world, gender quotas have taken off and been a contributing factor to the increase in women holding elected office, but gender quotas are much rarer in Asia. There are reserved seats for women in Pakistan and Bangladesh, as well as legislated gender quotas in Nepal, but these quotas never challenge the over-representation of men. Instead of discussing why quotas are not creating the same momentum in Asia as in other parts of the world, I will discuss a less common, but evolving, type of intervention to increase gender balance in political recruitment—that of gendered electoral financing. Knowing that there is a vast economic participation and opportunity gender gap (Gender Gap Report, 2018), how has funding currently been used as a means to increase the number of women in elected office?

We can start with some examples. In 2006 and 2011, female electoral candidates in Zambia received training and cash to become better equipped to win seats in first-past-the-post elections for the national legislature. Similar initiatives have also been taken elsewhere, for example, in the 2009 and 2014 Malawi elections. Ahead of the 2014 parliamentarian elections in Malawi, an initiative known as the '50–50 Campaign' provided campaign materials and cash to female candidates amounting to US$413 for parliamentary candidates and about US$138 for local government

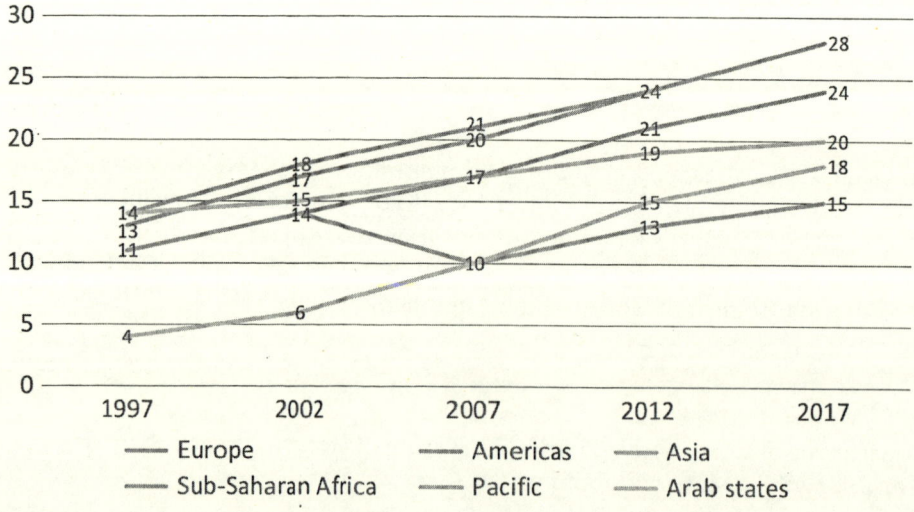

Fig. 2.1 Increase in women's representation by world regions

candidates. This was an extension of the initiative taken five years earlier, when female aspirants who sought political party nomination as candidates received about US$127 in cash, in addition to free airtime and campaign materials (such as T-shirts and posters). Western donors and Malawi's national government sponsored both initiatives.

Other examples are the efforts of EMILY's List in the United States. EMILY's List is a US political action committee that seeks to train women who want to run for political office in the United States and helps them build electoral campaigns. This unique initiative has a political agenda and supports only those members of the Democratic Party who share the views of EMILY's List on abortion rights, healthcare, and education. The initiative is funded by individual donors, with the idea being that even ordinary people can get involved in politics and help fund women's campaigns by paying a membership fee, donating money, participating on the majority council, or even buying a T-shirt.[1] In the context of Asia, the WIN WIN scheme in Japan was inspired by EMILY's List. WIN WIN provided donations to candidates who exhibited strong commitment to gender issues (Gaunder, 2011). This is similar to the non-partisan 50:50 parliament initiatives in the UK and Ireland, where income from membership fees and the sale of merchandise goes to training and motivating women to run for elections.[2]

These initiatives stand as only a few examples of how funding can be used as an incentive for women to seek election to political office. Other initiatives target political parties rather than female candidates themselves: A party may be financially sanctioned or rewarded, based on whether or not it reaches a certain threshold of gender balance on its candidate ticket for elections. In South Korea, the Political Fund Act of 2010 provides additional funding to the parties that nominate more women candidates. It stipulates that 10 percent of the total financial assistance must be spent on women's political representation, and that failure to do so would result in funding being withdrawn (Eunyoung, 2013; Yoon & Shin, 2015). Similar provisions are found in France, Portugal, and Chile. Money is typically seen as a barrier to women's inclusion in elected public office worldwide, but these new initiatives also see money as the solution to women's

---

[1] Additional information about the organization is available on its website at https://emilyslist.org (last visited March 26, 2018).

[2] For information on these initiatives, see https://5050parliament.co.uk (UK) or http://5050-group.com/blog/ (Ireland) (last visited March 26, 2018).

underrepresentation (Muriaas, Wang, & Murray, 2020). The purpose of this chapter is: First, to provide a theoretical background for why the underrepresentation of women in politics has emerged as a salient issue and how it has recently been tied to factors related to electoral funding. Second, to show how different actors across the globe have started to use funding as an affirmative action measure, but with distinctively different approaches, focusing on either the demand or the supply side of politics.

Increased Focus on the Number of Women in Elected Office

The question of why different kinds of gendered electoral financing schemes have emerged across the world is tied to the what we may term the utility turn in issues related to women's representation. Questions that used to be addressed as a women's rights issue are increasingly framed as a matter of effectiveness and used in the utility discourse (Skjeie & Teigen, 2005). Women's increased involvement in politics is favored not just as a matter of fairness toward sub-groups that have been excluded from politics in the past due to historical discrimination, but important because power-sharing between the sexes brings an added value (Sénac, 2008). As Mansbridge observes, the utility turn represents a move away from the argument that "descriptive representation by gender will be good for women to the argument that such representation will be good for the polity" (2005, pp. 631–632). For instance, the current focus on Sustainable Development Goals (SDGs) is also affected by the idea that gender equality bodies will enrich the public sphere.

"Achieve gender equality and empower all women and girls" is goal number five of the Sustainable Development Goals promoted by the UN (UN, 2015, p. 18). One of the specific targets of this goal is women in leadership, that is, to "[e]nsure women's full and effective participation and equal opportunities for leadership at all levels of decision-making in political, economic and public life" (p. 18). This international aim of promoting equal rights for women is driven by a normative commitment to women's empowerment and the belief that gender equality supports economic development. Scholars argue that gender gaps in political participation, education, access to health, land rights, and employment opportunities cause economic inefficiency and hinder women from reaching their full potential as caregivers, workers, and citizens (Duflo,

2012). The reasoning is that since women compose half of the population, structural discrimination that makes it difficult for them to participate fully in the economy of a country has repercussions for the general level of education and employment.

The link between gender equality and economic development can be exemplified through the international campaign on ending child marriage. This international campaign has a goal of promoting (i) legal reforms that establish a minimum age for marriage at 18 and (ii) policies to ensure that these new laws are implemented. The argument used to convince decision-makers to carry out such policies is that child marriage is not only a serious ill and a human rights issue in and of itself, but is also a practice that negatively impacts economic development. The following causal mechanism explains how age of marriage have consequences for a country's gross national product: Girls—and boys—who wed young drop out of school. Consequently, a high prevalence of child marriage in a country has a negative impact on the general level of education in a society. Literacy and math skills are likely to remain at a low level if the practice of early marriage is not curbed. Furthermore, women who become pregnant at a young age are more likely to suffer certain health problems due to birth complications. In turn, women's health problems make them less effective as mothers and workers, and this has further negative consequences for the production of goods and services in a country. Gender equality is good economics.

For this reason, international development organizations frequently link gender equality to market-led growth goals. The question that remains is how this again is related to women's political representation. Panday (2008) argues that in Bangladesh, it is recognized that the goals of equality, development, and peace cannot be achieved without the active representation of women, not just at the local level, but also at the national level. Still, her research finds that in Bangladesh, like elsewhere, women are often criticized when they attempt to negotiate in the public domain. Kabeer (1999) argues that access to resources is a pre-condition for political participation because it provides the agency needed to make choices freely. Hence, women's access to land, girl's education, participation in credit programs, and new wage opportunities in Bangladesh are linked to the inclusion of women in decision-making structures. Again, this is linked to assumptions about what is known as "substantive representation" (Pitkin, 1967): Female representatives are more likely to act in the interest of other women. They are supposedly more responsible for other women's needs, since they share their experiences. For example, women understand why girls who study at schools with no bathroom facilities stay home one week each month. This has emerged as a prime example of why it sometimes takes a woman to understand low school attendance. Hence, women should be in political offices to clarify these gender issues.

Some scholars have criticized this assumed relationship between the gender of a political representative and the understanding of key issues—or at least they have suggested that the theory needs to be nuanced. Childs and Krook (2009), for instance, assert that women will not be able to form strategic coalitions with each other to promote legislation related to women's issues, even if they grow more numerous in legislative chambers, because similar to men, they are partisans focusing on getting the politics of the party implemented. Instead, Childs and Krook argue that what we need to study is how substantive representation occurs and to look for critical actors (whether female or male) who will make sure that women-friendly policies emerge.

Nevertheless, even if only some women elected to political office will act in line with recommendations from the international agenda on gender equality, it is more likely that such critical actors will emerge if a substantial number of women make it into political offices. Hence, emphasizing the need to focus on critical actors and actions has not curbed the enthusiasm of those who fight for more women in elected offices. The argument was perfectly phrased by the former British Prime Minister David Cameron in 2005 (quoted in Childs & Webb, 2012, p. 5):

> The recruitment of women has got nothing to do with crude political calculation, or crazed political correctness. [...] If you put eight Conservative men round a table and ask them to discuss what should be done about pensions, you'd get some good answers [...] but what you are less likely to get is a powerful insight into the massive unfairness relating to women's pensions. We need people from diverse backgrounds to inform everything we do.

According to this perspective, women offer different perspectives on all kinds of policies—small and large—including those that are less visible on the international agenda. Gender perspectives need to be mainstreamed into all kinds of policies and reforms.

Consequently, and according to Edgell (2017), the idea that gender equality is all about political efficiency and economic development has made gender quota policies a mainstay within the global development discourse. Very few argue openly against the importance of having more women in politics, and there has been constant growth in the representation of women in politics in the last decades. Furthermore, gender quotas have proven quite effective in many countries. Data from the UN show that the proportion of women in national parliaments has increased globally from 13.2 percent in 2000 to 23.4 percent in 2017. At the same time, 39 percent of countries worldwide have used some form of quota system to increase women's representation in politics. This is quite a change, but the flipside of these numbers is that 76.6 percent of all seats in national parliaments are held by men, and 61 percent of countries worldwide have not adopted gender quotas.

Hence, despite the upswing in the use of gender quotas worldwide, men are overrepresented in politics worldwide. With the emerging reliance that economic and political opportunities are linked, new approaches using funding as an affirmative action measure is increasing. What is interesting with these new approaches is distinctively different decisions regarding how change must occur. All affirmative action measures using funding to increase gender balance in political recruitment classifies as an instance of gendered electoral financing. 'Gendered electoral financing' can be defined as *interventions using finances as a remedy to promote gender balance in political office* (Muriaas et al., 2020). Different funding interventions target different groups of actors, however. First, I will discuss why high election costs are seen as a barrier for women in politics and, second, how different types of gendered electoral financing use different approaches to change.

Gender Balance and High Election Costs

It is widely assumed that money influences elections and thus shapes how interests gain representation in democratic systems. In a study of the status of women employees in the government sectors of India, Pakistan, and Bangladesh, Kabir (2013, p. 101) shows that women are nowhere near to being full and equal participants in public policy choices. Financial resources are a prerequisite for competing in elections and are frequently held to constitute a barrier for women's entry into politics everywhere (Murray, 2012). This is thought to be especially so in developing countries, where women's socio-economic status is disproportionately low relative to that of men. First, women are less resourced than men and often lack control over their family's money, property, and other assets. It is ironic that a woman has the political right to run for the presidency in, for instance, Sudan, but she must ask her husband (or father, or brother) whether she is allowed to run for office and to get access to the resources the family possesses.

Second, women have less access to resource networks. Higher education and working in a career provide people with networks. Women typically have less education and are less active in the labor market. This reduces their opportunities to build contacts and friendship within networks that could help further their election campaigns and promote their political careers. One example was offered by a female member of parliament from Tunisia, who spoke at an international conference on women's political rights organized by International Institute for Democracy and Electoral Assistance (IDEA) and the Netherlands Institute for Multiparty Democracy (NIMD). She said that she was pushed through as a candidate by the pharmaceutical organization she belonged to. The organization's leadership asked all its members to donate a little something for her campaign. She got elected, but to get that necessary financial support, she had to be a pharmacist.

Furthermore, as found by Bauer and Darkwah (2020), there are also problems of gender stereotypes. Usually it is men who are in a position to finance a political campaign. However, it can be problematic in many cultures for a woman to take money from a man, since she would be expected to give the man something in return. Although some men would provide a political contribution, others would never do so without at least hinting at getting a return of some sort. Such cultural practices create gender stereotypes that negatively impact women's opportunities to become elected, since it is difficult for them to do fundraising.

Up until recently, the academic literature on political campaign spending was mainly based on studies of elections in the United States. The seminal studies of women's access to campaign funds in the United States, conducted in the 1980s and 1990s, find that women are no less able than men to raise adequate funds for competitive campaigns (Burrell, 1985; Werner, 1997, p. 81). Importantly, however, these studies have been conducted in a context where parties are more institutionalized and have a stronger label than in most democratizing states. Furthermore, even in this context, Fox (1997) finds that women perceive fundraising to be more difficult than their male counterparts. More recent studies of public-funding programs in the United States reveal that public-funding schemes increase the pool of women candidates willing and able to run for state legislative offices (Mayer, Werner, & Williams, 2006, p. 247). Even in a mature democracy, public funding is key to women.

Furthermore, this research from the United States does not take into consideration the effects of weak economies and weak party organizations. Consequently, it is unclear to what extent findings from US elections are relevant for 'the Global South.' In their qualitative comparative analysis of differences and similarities between six different cases using gendered electoral financing, Muriaas et al. (2020) finds that funding is a barrier across regional divides. Yet, it seems like party organizations in established democracies are expected to cover campaign expenses, but in many new democracies, party affiliation is not based on ideological affinities. Rather, an aspiring candidate does not necessarily have a long-term commitment to a political party, and nominated candidates are to a great extent expected to cover campaign expenses themselves (Muriaas, 2009). In short, the raising of funds by parties and candidates is a matter of unregulated self-help (UNDP, 2007, p. 116). For example, in a study of the cost of electoral campaigning in Brazil, Samuels (2001, p. 21) finds that "candidates cannot rely on strong party organizations to drum up votes, and cannot cheaply provide voters with clear partisan cues." Instead, candidates standing for elections may have to rely on personal 'machines' that thrive on access to, and distribution of, clientelistic goods (Ames, 1995; Mainwaring, 1999).

That parties are not institutionalized has some repercussions for the recruitment of women into politics. Matland (1998) identifies access to resources as the most essential condition for explaining variation in women's descriptive representation in developing countries. According to him, it is only when the number of women with the necessary resources becomes substantial that the opportunity for effective interest articulation exists in such contexts (p. 120). Still, according to Muriaas et al. (2020), while there is a great variation in party organizations' ability to fund candidates election campaigns, the process of candidate selection was a particularly expensive hurdle for female candidates.

In studies of primaries, researchers such as Rainbow Murray (2012), Wang and Muriaas (2019), and Gretchen Bauer and Akusua Darkwah (2020) have found that funds spent on election campaigns in the UK, Ghana, and Zambia are enormous. Their studies show that an aspirant who seeks to win a party's nomination in a first-past-the-post electoral system may need to mobilize the support of a core group of party members by providing food, transport, and gifts. Even after their nomination, aspirants often must give some kind of gift or token of appreciation to the delegates who were involved in the actual process of selecting candidates.

Furthermore, as mentioned in a talk by Rainbow Murray (2019), on the basis of her fieldwork in the UK study, a candidate must personally pay for many expenses while on the campaign trail, examples being food, telephone bills, time off work, and (in some cases) a residency in the constituency where he or she plans to run. All these expenses must be paid upfront, without any security about the outcome of the process. Only one person per constituency will ultimately win a nomination from a political party, and even if an aspirant wins that nomination, he or she will still need to beat candidates from other parties' tickets before gaining a seat in the national legislature. In cases where there is a well-working party-funding system or the aspirant seeks nomination from the ruling party, the costs of actually running in the election may even be less than the costs of gaining nomination, since more expenses would be covered by the party at the election stage. Nonetheless, the election campaign also presents important personal costs, such as taking time off a job or paying for child care.

TURNING FUNDING TO WOMEN'S FAVOR: INCENTIVES TO CHANGE

Gendered electoral financing rests upon the assumption that if money is a barrier for women, it could also be seen as a solution. As early as 1995, the Beijing Platform for Action identified the high cost of contesting elections as one of the main barriers to women in politics. Since then, the importance of funding measures to overcome this barrier has gradually gained ground among international actors, including bilateral and multilateral donor organizations and international nongovernmental organizations. Despite the fact that alternative measures for increasing women's political integration (such as financial strategies) have been adopted in a number of countries, there is little knowledge about their impact and relative effectiveness. The most comprehensive research projects so far are two initial overviews of non-quota strategies used globally (Krook & Norris, 2014) and of political finance measures to promote women's participation (Ballington & Kahane, 2014). Currently, the issues of (i) public party funding, in general, and (ii) targeted public funding as a tool to increase gender equality in politics, in particular, have gained attention from International IDEA and NIMD. Nonetheless, scholarly work on these issues is needed, although some research is beginning to address laws imposing financial sanctions or benefits on parties based on the gender balance they achieve on their candidate slates (Muriaas et al., 2020).

As already discussed, gendered electoral financing includes interventions that use finance as a remedy to promote gender balance in political office. Muriaas et al. (2020) differentiate two types of intervention schemes that use funding as an incentive to get more women elected to political office: (1) schemes aimed at changing parties' likelihood of nominating women (incentivizing parties) and (2) schemes aimed at changing women's ambitions (campaign cost relief for women). What is interesting with these two different approaches is that they take different approaches to who needs to change, partiers or women. What is interesting with this is that they supposedly address different mechanisms: Incentivizing parties is most likely to address the demand for women while the incentivizing women mechanism targets the supply side of candidates. But which one of them is more likely to produce change?

Incentivizing Parties

One current trend we have seen (in countries ranging from France and Ireland to South Korea and Ukraine) to incentivize political parties to adopt more gender-balanced party lists is the distribution of public funding to parties based on whether they meet certain thresholds of gender balance. Such incentives can be presented as a 'stick' (punishment) or a 'carrot' (reward), as follows: Legislation can dictate that a political party will be *financially punished* if it does not comply with a gender quota law that requires a certain number or percentage of candidate lists to be allocated to candidates of a stipulated gender. Of course, such legislation is only effective if the country's system of public-funding works and the party's funding is actually reduced if it does not comply with the quota. In addition, there is a great deal of difference with regard to where a country's legislation may set the bar. Some countries aim for gender parity and require parties to have close to a 50:50 gender ratio. They may set harsh penalties for parties that do not comply, for example, a loss of *all* public funding or a loss of 60 percent of funding they would otherwise be entitled to. Other countries set a lower bar (e.g. that 20 percent of candidates should be women), and they also may set a milder punishment (e.g. a 20 percent cut in campaign financing).

Financial reward is another way of incentivizing parties. In certain countries, for instance, Croatia and Ukraine, parties get an extra financial reward if they nominate a certain number of women as candidates. There are several ways of using this 'top-up' system. First, the threshold a party must reach could be anything from 5 percent to parity. Similarly, the reward may differ in size and in kind. For example, in the Ukraine, a public-funding 'pot' is earmarked for parties that reach the threshold. The pot is divided between the parties like a cake: If only one party meets the threshold, it may eat the whole cake by itself, but if several parties comply with the gender quota, the cake is sliced into pieces. In other countries, the parties receive a fixed amount of funding calculated according to the seats won or the number of candidates on the party's list.

The key challenge to making such policies work is that public funding needs to work (Ohman, 2018). This does not always happen in new democracies, where there is no public party funding, or where such funding is deeply affected by rampant corruption. Furthermore, sanctions must hit where decisions are made. If decisions on who gets on the party lists are taken locally, but the central party organization experiences the penalty, the incentive may not work very well. It could also be that those at the party's center are so well-resourced that public funding is not something they have to take into account, while the grassroots political party organizations (or even the smaller parties) taste the repercussions of financial sanctions. Hence, small and new parties with less sponsors and party-owned resources (like land or houses) are more likely to take actions based on these incentives. Finally, we cannot forget that political parties are machines designed to win political seats. Although it is sad, many parties will not recruit women if they are afraid this might cost them a seat. A seat in parliament is more important than less or more public funding.

Incentivizing Women: Campaign Cost Relief for Women

Funding women's election campaigns is perceived as particularly suitable in candidate-centered systems, such as single-district member systems. In such systems, the personal financial costs of electioneering tend to be high (Norris, 1993, p. 328). Within candidate-centered systems, candidates compete twice, first in the primaries and then (if they are successful) in state or national elections. As discussed earlier, to be viable competitors, candidates must raise money, build coalitions of support, create campaign organizations, and develop campaign strategies—and all of these may pose greater challenges for women than for men in societies that are historically patriarchal (Lawless & Pearson, 2008, p. 68).

In the absence of gender quotas, targeted funding of women's campaigns has been used to increase gender balance in political recruitment. Such targeted funding is different from a gender quota, which demands that parties go out and find women to recruit into politics. The assumption is that targeted funding will trigger a new supply of female candidates by motivating women to run for election, since they know they can receive extra funding. Extra funds or a reduction in fees could be critical for candidates, particularly women, since studies have found that the lack of access to networks with resources is a key barrier to women entering politics (Kayuni & Muriaas, 2014; Muriaas, 2009).

According to Sidhu and Meena (2007), targeted electoral financing of women may work as a tool for leveling the playing field between the genders, reducing election costs, cutting down on corruption, and increasing oversight. The National Democratic Institute, for instance, worked to promote women's electoral campaigns in Kenya in 2013 and in Sierra Leone in 2002, through intensive leadership and campaign training, as well as by buying air time (Svåsand, 2014). In a study of a funding campaign targeting women aspirants in the 2009 Malawian elections, Kayuni and Muriaas (2014) find that the campaign proved efficient in *motivating* women to compete in the elections (i.e. to seek nomination in primaries or as independent candidates), but it did not effectively address the *obstacles* women faced in the party primaries. A recent study of gender and elections in Ghana by Gretchen Bauer and Akosua Darkwah (2020) examines how reducing filing fees for women who seek a nomination from a political party or for the general elections might be a gendered campaign-financing tool for women. Of course, such an intervention would be most effective in cases where filing fees are high and candidates are paying them from their own pockets.

The challenge to such campaign-cost relief as an intervention strategy to motivate women to run for election is that it might not be sufficient to make a difference. As Bauer and Darkwah's (2020) study of Ghana reveals, parliamentarians see this as just a drop in the bucket. However, some feedback mechanisms may operate in these circumstances. For example, perhaps seeing that at least some costs are covered would encourage women to participate in political life. Nonetheless, several questions remain about the appropriate mechanisms to motivate women to engage in politics: Who should receive funds? Should there be funds available for all female aspirants, or only for women who are registered as candidates? Will pouring more cash into the system simply reinforce the problem of too much money in politics? We definitely need more research to look into these dynamics before we can provide recommendations about how and when campaign cost relief can make a difference to female aspirants.

DEMAND FOR WOMEN OR SUPPLY OF WOMEN?

The two strategies that I have discussed above handle the issue of women's agency in different ways.

Along with gender quotas, strategies that incentivize parties affect what has been called 'demand-side' factors in politics.[3] Demand-side explanations suggest that the onus for change lies not on women but on political elites: gender quotas and funding incentives work most effectively when they are addressed to the leadership of a political party (Krook, 2010, p. 709). The message is "Go and get those women or you will not get funds," or "so that you can get a reward." Such explanations hold that social bias in legislatures reflects the prejudices of selectors—the party insiders who choose candidates in many political systems—against women (Norris & Lovenduski, 1993, p. 378).

On the other hand, 'supply-side' explanations emphasize a lack of resources, knowledge, and motivation as factors that negatively affect women's access to political office. Cuts in filing fees or fresh cash directed toward women is meant to inspire them to run for office, even though competition is stiff. Supply-side solutions focus on equipping women with resources and thereby triggering their ambitions to run and present themselves as available to political parties. The beauty of supply-side solutions that directly fund women is that they help women become less dependent on men for political participation. Rather than relying on an 'altruistic' male, whether it be their husbands (or fathers or brothers) or a political

[3] An influential line of theory uses the economic model of supply and demand to identify factors that may influence recruitment in different political systems (Norris, 1993, p. 310). In a perfect political market, the forces of supply and demand should eventually produce equilibrium, as pointed out by Krook (2010, p. 710), and the proportion of representatives who are women should mirror the proportion of women in the population. Of course, this is seldom the case, as women are underrepresented in almost every national legislature around the world.

party leader, these funding measures equip women to get elected on their own steam. They have access to funds of their own and do not have to rely on laws that require men (often the gatekeepers in political parties) to go out and find them. In addition, such funding measures may even avoid some of the negative aspects of gender quota policies. In short, supply-side measures aimed at equipping female aspirants to run for political office are game changers that can make women more independent in the political arena.

Concluding Remarks

The question of how is it possible to address the inequalities that hold women back and deprive them of opportunities and rights has gained attention over the last few decades. Just one example is that gender equality is number five on the list of the Sustainable Development Goals (SDG), and the platform aims to empower women through addressing structural issues that hinder their economic and political opportunities. A lack of resources is widely seen as one factor that affects women's opportunities to get elected to political offices. Although the role of money in elections varies across different countries and world regions, money is likely to shape political recruitment almost everywhere. Many now claim that a problem with gender quotas is that they do not address the inequalities that keep women from being favored choices in politics. Gender quotas regulate the number of women in politics without identifying the structural mechanisms that hinder women from participating in politics more, such as less access to financial resources.

Along with gender quotas, gendered electoral financing is introduced as an alternative or enforcing mechanism that tries to alter how money is typically channeled into a political system. Although current efforts to introduce gendered electoral-financing schemes have proven vulnerable and difficult to implement, they force scholars, activists, and politicians to focus on the relevance of money for political advancement. When women are underrepresented in politics, this new agenda claims, it is not just because women are different from men in how they appear; it is because structural factors keep them from having what is necessary for a successful political career, namely, financial resources. Hence, even if gendered electoral-financing schemes have limited results to show for in actually being effective in ensuring that women get elected to political office on a larger scale, they have been powerful for putting the financial costs of running an election on the agenda.

REFERENCES

Ames, B. (1995). Electoral strategy under open-list proportional representation. *American Journal of Political Science, 39*(2), 406–433.

Ballington, J., & Kahane, M. (2014). Women in politics: Financing for gender equality. In E. Falguera, S. Jones, & M. Ohman (Eds.), *Funding of political parties and election campaigns: A handbook on political finance* (pp. 301–342). Stockholm: International IDEA.

Bauer, G., & Darkwah, A. (2020). Some money has to be going. Discounted filing fees to bring more women into parliament in Ghana. In R. Muriaas, V. Wang, & R. Murray (Eds.), *Gendered electoral financing: Money, power and representation in comparative perspective*. London and New York: Routledge.

Burrell, B. C. (1985). Women's and men's campaigns for the U.S. House of Representatives, 1972–1982: A finance gap? *American Political Research, 13*(3), 251–272.

Childs, S., & Krook, M. L. (2009). Analysing women's substantive representation: From critical mass to critical actors. *Government and Opposition, 44*(2), 125–145.

Childs, S., & Webb, P. (2012). *Sex, gender and the conservative party: From iron lady to kitten heels*. Basingstoke and New York: Palgrave Macmillan.

Duflo, E. (2012). Women, empowerment and economic development. *Journal of Economic Literature, 50*(4), 1051–1079.

Edgell, A. B. (2017). Foreign aid, democracy, and gender quota laws. *Democratization, 24*(6), 1103–1141.

Eunyoung, S. (2013). Ten years' experience of gender quota system in Korean politics. *GEMC Journal, 4*, 98–104.

Fox, R. L. (1997). *Gender dynamics in congressional elections*. Thousand Oaks, CA: Sage.

Gaunder, A. (2011). WIN WIN's struggles with the institutional transfer of the EMILY's List model to Japan: The role of accountability and policy. *Japanese Journal of Political Science, 12*(1), 75–94.

Kabeer, N. (1999). Resources, agency, achievements: Reflections on the measurement of Women's Empowerment. *Development and Change, 30*(3), 435–464.

Kabir, S. L. (2013). *Women's participation in South Asian civil services: A comparative analysis of India, Pakistan and Bangladesh*. Dhaka: A. H. Development Publishing House.

Kayuni, H., & Muriaas, R. L. (2014). Alternatives to gender quotas: Electoral financing of women candidates in Malawi. *Representation, 50*(3), 393–404.

Krook, M. L. (2010). Beyond supply and demand: A feminist-institutionalist theory of candidate selection. *Political Research Quarterly, 63*(4), 707–720.

Krook, M. L., & Norris, P. (2014). Beyond quotas: Strategies to promote gender equality in elected office. *Political Studies, 62*(1), 2–20.

Lawless, J., & Pearson, K. (2008). The primary reason for women's underrepresentation? Reevaluating the conventional wisdom. *Journal of Politics, 70*(1), 67–82.

Mainwaring, S. (1999). *Rethinking party systems in the third wave of democratization: The case of Brazil.* Stanford: Stanford University Press.

Mansbridge, J. (2005). Quota problems: Combating the dangers of essentialism. *Politics & Gender, 1*(4), 622–638.

Matland, R. (1998). Women's representation in national legislatures: Developed and developing countries. *Legislative Studies Quarterly, 23*(1), 109–125.

Mayer, K. R., Werner, T., & Williams, A. (2006). Do public funding programs enhance electoral competition? In M. McDonald & J. Samples (Eds.), *The marketplace of democracy: Electoral competition and American politics* (pp. 245–267). Washington: Brookings Institution & Cato Institute.

Muriaas, R. L. (2009). Reintroducing a local-level multiparty system in Uganda: Why be in opposition? *Government and Opposition, 44*(1), 91–112.

Muriaas, R. L., Wang, V., & Murray, R. (2020). Introducing the concept of gendered electoral financing. In R. Muriaas, V. Wang, & R. Murray (Eds.), *Gendered electoral financing: Money, power and representation in comparative perspective.* London and New York: Routledge.

Murray, R. (2012). Parity in France: A dual-tack solution to women's underrepresentation. *West European Politics, 35*(2), 343–361.

Murray, R. (2019). *"It's a rich man's world": The (gendered) costs of running for office in the UK.* Paper presented at the EXPG conference, Amsterdam, 4–6 July 2019.

Norris, P. (1993). Conclusions: Comparing legislative recruitment. In J. Loveduski & P. Norris (Eds.), *Gender and party politics* (pp. 309–330). London: Sage.

Norris, P., & Lovenduski, J. (1993). "If only more candidates came forward": Supply-side explanations of candidate selection in Britain. *British Journal of Political Science, 23*(3), 373–408.

Ohman, M. (2018). *Gender-targeted public funding for political parties: A comparative analysis.* Report, International Institute for Democracy and Electoral Assistance (IDEA), Stockholm, Sweden.

Panday, P. K. (2008). Representation without participation: Quotas for women in Bangladesh. *International Political Science Review, 29*(4), 489–512.

Pitkin, H. F. (1967). *The concept of representation.* Berkeley: University of California Press.

Samuels, D. (2001). Money, elections, and democracy in Brazil. *Latin American Politics and Society, 43*(2), 27–48.

Sénac, R. (2008). Justifying parity in France after the passage of the so-called parity laws and the electoral application of them: The 'ideological tinkering' of political party officials (UMP and PS) and women's NGOs. *French Politics,* *6*(3), 234–256.

Sidhu, G. L., & Meena, R. (2007). *Electoral financing to advance women's political participation: A guide to UNDP support.* New York: UNDP.

Skjeie, H., & Teigen, M. (2005). Political constructions of gender equality: Travelling towards … a gender balanced society? *NORA—Nordic Journal of Feminist and Gender Research, 13*(3), 187–197.

Svåsand, L. (2014). *Promoting pragmatic political parties: Exploring international party assistance and its impact on party manifestos in new democracies.* Paper for annual meeting of the Midwest Political Science Association, Chicago, IL, 3–6 April.

UN. (2015, October 21). Transforming our world: The 2030 agenda for sustainable development, GA res. A/RES/70/1. Retrieved from https://undocs.org/A/RES/70/1.

UNDP. (2007). *Electoral financing to advance women's political participation: A guide to UNDP support.* New York: UNDP.

Wang, V., & Muriaas, R. L. (2019). Candidate selection and informal soft quotas for women: Gender imbalance in political recruitment in Zambia. *Politics, Groups, and Identities, 7*(2), 401–411.

Werner, B. L. (1997). Financing the campaigns of women candidates and their opponents. *Women & Politics, 18*(1), 81–97.

World Economic Forum. (2018). *The Global Gender Gap report, 2018.* Geneva, Switzerland. Retrieved December 11, 2019 at 2018, from http://www3.weforum.org/docs/WEF_GGGR_2018.pdf

Yoon, J., & Shin, K.-Y. (2015). Mixed effects of legislative quotas in South Korea. *Politics & Gender, 11*(1), 186–195.

CHAPTER 3

How Policy Folds Back Before Implementation: A Study on Unequal Inheritance Right in Bangladesh

Jinat Hossain

INTRODUCTION

All public policies face oppositions during implementation either from society or from the administrative apparatus that implements it. As a result, some policies are implemented but a host of others remain partially implemented or remain unimplemented. Routine policies face little opposition but new or novel policies are always at the risk of encountering oppositions from different quarters. The worst is the case for those policies which are new and implemented in a top-down manner without involving the stakeholders in the stages of both policy formulation and policy implementation. This indicates that even with good intentions a policy may be opposed seriously if the policy cannot incorporate the mood and sentiments of a society.

This chapter presents such a worst-case scenario in the case of Bangladesh and analyses how a policy folds back before its implementation.

J. Hossain (✉)
Division of Geography and Tourism, Department of Earth and Environmental Sciences, Katholieke Universiteit Leuven (KU Leuven), Leuven, Belgium
e-mail: jinat.hossain@kuleuven.be

I. Jamil et al. (eds.), *Gender Mainstreaming in Politics, Administration and Development in South Asia*,
https://doi.org/10.1007/978-3-030-36012-2_3

Considering unequal inheritance right issue in Bangladesh as a case, this study explores how National Women's Development Policy (NWDP), which contained regulations on ensuring women's equal inheritance right, was discontinued long before its implementation.

Gender discrimination in the case of land ownership as well as control over property is one of the most important constraints in ensuring gender balance in economic well-being, social status and empowerment (Agarwal, 1994a). Women's equal inheritance right has long been ignored in policies and analysis, particularly in South Asia (Agarwal, 1994b). Bangladesh is not an exception to this trend, though the country has taken significant positive stands in favour of women's rights and privileges. In the last few decades, women in Bangladesh have made significant progress in terms of mobility, migration, education, maternal health and their involvement in different income generating activities, both in urban and in rural areas (Kabeer, 1991; Khan, 2013). There are significant changes noticed in terms of girls' education, legal action against gender violence and implementation of affirmative policies or ensuring quotas for women's employment in the public sector (Kabeer, 2011). Furthermore, non-governmental organizations (NGOs), such as Grameen Bank and Bangladesh Rural & Advancement Committee (BRAC), have targeted the poorer section of women in the country and have been working for improving their lives through a micro-credit programme (Kabeer, 2011). Women's involvement in the ready-made garments industry speeded up women's participation in the public domain (Bhattacharya, Rahman, & Raihan, 2002). Thus, Bangladesh has a achieved a remarkable track record in overall women's empowerment that contributed to a significant number of social changes (Khan, 2005). However, despite some positive changes, women in Bangladesh, compared to male counterparts, remain much behind in many areas (Kabeer, 2001; Chowdhury, 2009; Hossain & Tisdell, 2005; Mahmud et al., 2014; Kabeer, 2001; Hashemi, Schuler, & Riley, 1996).

The government is also putting significant efforts in introducing and implementing new policies, acts and laws in favour of women (Khan & Ara, 2006). Even the Constitution of Bangladesh guarantees equal rights for both men and women in every sphere of life (Andaleeb & Vanneman Wolford, 2004). The Constitution clearly states that the state shall not discriminate any citizens on the grounds of religion, race, cast, sex or place of birth (Bangladesh Const. art. 18; 1 & 3). Furthermore, Bangladesh has also been a signatory to different international conventions supporting gender equality and women's empowerment, for example, CEDAW

(Convention on the Elimination of All Forms of Discrimination Against Women) or the Beijing platform (Huda, 1997; Karim, 2004; Khan, 2005). All these commitments and obligations have significantly contributed to the formulation of new policies and programmes in favour of women's progress. Yet, some laws and policies are still contradictory and, to some extent, seem to be discriminatory for women. For instance, inheritance laws in Bangladesh (as the case is similar in other countries in South Asia) provide lower shares of landed property to women than to men (Agarwal, 1994a; Sourav, 2015). Especially personal and family matters including, marriage and inheritance-related issues which are practised based on religion, and these laws vary from one religion to the other (ibid.). For example, according to the *Sharia* law, followed by the Muslim community, a female is entitled to only half of what a male receives from the paternal property (Quran: 4:7, 11). According to Hindu laws, Hindu women do not inherit any paternal property (Agarwal, 2003). Consequently, these laws help male to inherit more than a female (Zaman, 1999).

The importance of getting equal access to property for better socioeconomic status of the women is evidenced in literature (Agarwal, 1994a, 2003). However, the Government of Bangladesh (GoB) has tried to adopt policies to protect women's equal rights of property since the last two decades (Sourav, 2015). National Women's Development Policy has been seen as a milestone in ensuring gender equality in Bangladesh by offering women access to property. But this policy, declared in 2011, failed to be successfully implemented due to the violent protests from certain groups of people. Even though the policy was formulated with the right intention to provide women, irrespective of religious belonging with equal share in paternal property, but the policy failed because it failed to read and cope with religious sentiment in the Bangladeshi society.

From this background, this study explains how policies fold back before it is implemented, even though it contained elements of neutrality and fair distribution of property, ensuring equality and justice in a society. From a policy design perspective, this policy adopted a rational model whereby it was supposed to ensure equal rights as enshrined in the Constitution for both men and women in terms of inheritance of property. However, in between the formulation to implementation stage, it was stopped because of severe opposition to it from different social groups, especially the religious groups.

To understand why and how this inheritance law folded back, terminated or stepped back, we need to understand how policy generates and mobilizes social and organizational oppositions. All policies encounter oppositions depending on the nature of the policy. Some policies generate severe opposition in society, leading to civil disobedience, and may threaten the survival of the regime. These oppositions are difficult to handle sometimes, and the only way left to the regime is to discontinue this policy if no compromise or negotiation is possible to contain the opposition and to avoid serious threat to the survival of the regime.

Objective

With this backdrop, this study aims to explore how and why policy folds back before implementation? It has four objectives:

- How the National Women Development Policy was formulated? Who were the major actors in its formulation?
- Why the policy was discontinued? What was the nature of the opposition and why the government failed to contain the opposition?
- What the government could have done during the policy formulation and implementation stages to address the opposition and implement the policy?
- What possible consequences the non-implementation of the policy have contributed to?

Theoretical Underpinning

Different scholars stressed different variables for the study of policy implementation. The discussions in this study expanded on different issues like identifying the limitations of policy formulation and implementation process and ended through developing different measures, theories and models for making policy successful. Van Meter and Van Horn (1975) explained conceptual understanding of policy implementation. According to them, the possibility of effective policy implementation mostly depends on the type of policy, the degree of change it suggests and the degree of consensus it draws. The probability of successful outcome of policy implementation gets higher if the policy entails marginal change with high goal consensus. They proposed a model to outline the description and analysis of the policy implementation process.

Matland (1995) noticed that the implementation literature lacks a proper theoretical structure. Reviewing organizational theory literature, he identified how ambiguity and conflict affect policy implementation.

However, he combined different factors behind these ambiguities/conflicts and provides a more theoretically grounded approach for implementation. He referred to traditional top-down and bottom-up models based on the public administration tradition to identify the reasons behind unsuccessful policy implementation. He argued that micro-level actors and factors normally control the process, while in most of the cases, the policy stages are highly political in nature and commonly emphasized by top-down models. Matland's model explains where the most important conflicts are likely to lie in policy implementation and proposes probable measures to overcome those.

Thomas and Grindle (1990) have discussed policy formulation and implementation through two different models. They discussed linear model, which is more about policy formulation. As discussed by them, policy formulation helps the government to take action to implement it, though implementation is very much crucial. In most of the cases, the outcome of implementation is often uncertain, ranging from unsuccessful to successful, sometimes even with limited expected outcome. This kind of policy is more common in a hierarchic system where policies are formulated at the top and implemented in a top-down manner.

Instead, they suggested an alternative model—the interactive model, which builds on a political economy approach. In this model, Thomas and Grindle (1990) assumed that a state of equilibrium surrounds the pre-established policy set; revising or altering the policy set might impact on this equilibrium, either positively or negatively. This might cause some response/reaction among those who have the possibility to be affected by the change of new policy. However, this model opens for revisions at any stage depending on the reaction or opposition coming from different sources. The interactive model considers policy reform as a long-term undertaking where the revision might be taken at different steps. Thomas and Grindle (1990) argue about the risk and probable challenges of a new policy while implementing.

From the above discussion, it can be ascertained that when a policy is new or novel and aims at a big change in society in terms of modifying the existing socio-cultural norms, it must be carefully designed and implemented by bringing in different stakeholders at different stages of policy-making. Usually the implementation of such a policy requires a longer time frame and has to be combined with both top-down and bottom-up approaches. This means involvement of a mixture of government institutions and other social organizations that have a stake in the policy to be included in different stages of policy-making. If only a top-down model of policy formulation and implementation is followed, then the policy is very likely and surely to be met by societal oppositions and the fate of the policy may be sealed. The interactive model by Thomas and Grindle (1990) suggest how to cope with different oppositions both societal and institutional and which resources to mobilize to overcome such oppositions. The first lesson is to combine both top-down and bottom-up models in policy implementation so that different stakeholders may have an opportunity to be a part of it and suggest options for change, alteration and modification.

In the case of Bangladesh, given the hierarchic nature of policy-making, most policy decision are top down, usually decided by the party in power. Though Bangladesh introduced parliamentary democracy in 1991 (except for a period of two years from 2007 to 2008), its democratic practices have remained weak. Usually the party leadership enjoys absolute power and the opposition is either ignored in major policy-making process or harassed if it opposes a policy. The parliament as a forum of democratic discourse and deliberation has remained non-functional. What is most characteristic of governance in Bangladesh is excessive centralization of the authority, personalized leadership and patriarchy, which govern its policy-making process (Jamil, Askvik, & Dhakal, 2013). Such a system of governance is based on party loyalty rather than on legitimacy from below. Hence all policy decisions face a problem of legitimacy, as these are top down and lack societal foundation, that is, support from below. This becomes more critical when a policy is considered to be a threat to existing socio-cultural and religious values. Moreover, strong polarization along the two major political parties has almost fragmented all segments of society, from professional groups (lawyers, engineers, doctors, teachers, etc.), to labour unions, to civil society, to religious groups. Therefore, any policy taken during one regime faces strong opposition and is eventually suspended or terminated with the change of government. The National Women Development Policy ensuring women's equal inheritance right was such a policy which was likely to receive strong opposition from different groups often politically motivated.

Political Settlement in Policy Issues

The other theory that can be used to explain why this policy folded back is Mushtaq Khan's (2010) political settlement framework. This framework is based on political settlement among powerful groups. Applied to public policy context, it means that certain policies may generate opposition from different quarters, and depending on the intensity and relative strength of this opposition, conflicts may vary from being less to very severe. If this opposition cannot be contained, it may threaten the survival of the regime. In such a situation, political settlement is an option to maintain the status quo and balance of power and allows the regime to continue without being threatened or serious opposition. Combining political settlement theory with Thomas and Grindle's interactive model to policy implementation, we argue that oppositions to any policy is quite common but if opposition is difficult to contain, then political settlement is a way out and often adopted by governments to quell opposition in order to maintain the status quo. However, as regards the policy, political settlement may fold back the policy and it remains latent until a new window of opportunity opens up.

Methods

The study follows a qualitative research method and uses both primary and secondary sources of data collection. In-depth interviews were carried out with the following respondents:

1. Policy-makers and officials (5 in total) who worked on the policy formulation and implementation stages, officials who had worked/ currently working in the Ministry of Women's and Children Affairs and Department of Women Affairs during the time of policy formulation and implementation.
2. Lawyers (5 in total)—dealing with family laws, in particular those with expertise on inheritance issues as mentioned in the *Sharia* law and in other religions.
3. Academics and researchers working on women's rights and gender equality (5 in total) who have been a prominent voice on the debate regarding equal inheritance issues and significant personalities during policy formulation.
4. Women activists (4 in total) who have been working significantly from the grassroots to the national level to mobilize people and lobbying to policy-makers for ensuring gender equality in every sphere of life and to incorporate it in policies and programmes.
5. Islamic religious scholars (3 in total) and Hindu priests (3 in total) to find out the reasons and facts of the failure of the policy to be implemented. A total of 25 respondents were selected purposively from different categories and professions who are aware and have knowledge on this issue.

The secondary sources of data were obtained from reviewing different religious books, particularly interpreting different verses on the issue of land distribution and women's right. This study also analysed different versions and draft of the National Women Development Policy that came out in 1997, 2004, 2008 and 2011. It also analysed different newspaper articles (both in the local and English languages) and news that were published at that time of policy formulation, implementation and public reaction that was generated afterwards.

RESULT AND DISCUSSION

In the following we present findings on what was the inspiration behind this policy and why and how it was formulated, what roles did the government play, and what implications it had for the non-implementation of the policy?

Formulation of National Women's Development Policy

The Background

The Government of Bangladesh (GoB), inspired by international laws and initiatives of the local and international NGOs, became very concerned about ensuring gender equality by signing different conventions in favour of women and formulating different state laws and policies. It ratified CEDAW[1] with reservations on two articles. The government is much criticized for its reservations: (1) Article 2 and (2) Article 16(1c). In addition, the country is also proud to be a signatory to the Beijing Platform for Action (BPFA) that was signed in 1995.

According to the officials of the Ministry of Women's and Children Affairs, women activists and key informants, signing in BPFA is the biggest push for GoB to formulate the National Women's Development Policy. According to one academic (Key Informant A),

> After singing BPFA, Bangladesh was committed to introduce new policies to ensure gender equality in every sphere of life. The National Women Development Policy that was formulated in 1997 was perhaps the outcome of this conference.

---

[1] The Convention on the Elimination of All Forms of Discrimination against Women.

However, after reviewing the convention, experts have identified 12 critical areas where the signatory countries need to take sufficient measures to work on. Among these identified areas, one was to integrate gender perspectives in legislation, public policies, programmes and projects. The policy strongly suggests that the member states initiate national machinery for the advancement of women. Within two years of signing in BPFA, GoB formulated the National Women's Development Policy in 1997. One key informant (Key Informant B) argued,

> *Government seems to be strongly committed to formulate new laws and policies, even to amend the existing laws that are discriminatory for women. With the continuation of being a signatory to BPFA, National Women's Development Policy came out in 1997. It actually met the long-cherished demand of the women activists in order to get equal rights, particularly in regard to equal inheritance right.*

In 1997, the NWDP, for the first time, came out with different measures for women's advancement in Bangladesh. The important step that came out in this policy is to meet the commitment of ensuring equality in inheritance right for both men and women. However, in Section 7.2 of the 1997 policy, it was stated that 'Women would be given full and equal rights, and control over earnings, inheritance, wealth, loan, land and wealth earned through technology and market management, and new laws would be enacted to achieve this goal' (GoB, 1997). Women activists expressed their satisfaction after the declaration of NWDP by the government. The same Key Informant B stated,

> *NWDP, 1997 was satisfactory with its content and formulation process, yet this is unfortunate that it did not see the light of implementation properly. The present Awami League Government made unreasonable delays in the whole process of its implementation and they actually delayed the implementation till the next election. After then they made another commitment that they would implement this policy if they come to the power in the next term.*

However, the policy went up in smoke with the change of government. In 2004, the Bangladeshi Nationalist Party (BNP)-led government reformulated the policy again, changing some important clauses, including equal inheritance right. In the 9.13 clause of this draft policy, right to equal property through inheritance and the right to land were dropped. A new phrase was espoused that would perhaps give women equal access and control over wealth earned through the management of market. This actually diminishes the possibility of ensuring equal rights for women in property and inheritance (Gayen, 2011). At that time the BNP-led government was also criticized for the role that it played and the way of formulating this policy (ibid.). From the point of view of women's activists, the government did not sufficiently discuss and take opinions of experts, activists, NGO workers and civil society before the policy formulation. This policy also did not see the light of implementation. Furthermore, in 2008 the Caretaker government again initiated the NWDP, where it kept the issue of having equal access to property alive. However, this is for the first time that different Islamic groups went against the policy, particularly the clause that mentioned about women's equal inheritance right. This resulted in the failure of the policy to be implemented.

In the 2008 electoral manifesto, the Bangladesh Awami League (AL; at present the party in power) promised to reformulate the Women's Development Policy based on the policy initiated in 1997. However, in 2011 the government reinitiated to declare the Women's Development Policy by revising the 1997 policy. Thus, the National Women Development Policy 2011 was initiated from the Ministry of Women and Children Affairs. The declaration of this policy came out on 8th March, on International Women's Day, and it was planned to be implemented from 2013. Yet, the policy brought some confusions with the content of the new policy, particularly in regard to inheritance rights. Key Informant B recalled different reactions after the declaration,

> In the following day of the policy declaration, there was a very misleading headline published in many of the national dailies. The newspapers reported that the National Women Policy 2011 has been declared with the provision of equal property inheritance rights for both men and women. The reports and headlines were very much convincing. The common people even women activists of the country thought that the policy (NWDP) ensured equality in property. But, from the very day of the declaration, religion-based political parties boycotted the policy. In addition, they also declared resistance against it, claiming that it had given men and women equal inheritance rights which is anti-Quran, i.e. against the Sharia Law. It took a while for the women activists and scholars to understand that the policy did not in fact provide equal property rights.

However, after the declaration, a question raised, what actually was stated in this new policy? In clause 25.2, the policy stated, 'to give women the rights to wealth and resources earned through income, succession, loan/credit, land and market management' (GoB, 2011, p. 42). That means, according to the newly proposed policy, women would get control over or access to property that they already earned or owned. Whereas, in the 1997 policy, it stated to give full and equal rights and control over earning, inheritance, wealth, loan and wealth, and it also proposed to enact news laws to achieve this goal. Therefore, the Women Development Policy 2011 is certainly one step backwards from the policy of 1997, particularly in relation to the right to inheritance of property.

Pre-formulation Work of NWDP
According to the key informants, women activists and development workers, in 1997, the government had done sufficient groundwork before formulating the policy. After BPFA, it seemed to be much willing/interested to formulate a policy for women advancement. It has chosen representatives from different sectors, that is, women activists, civil society, local government, NGOs and development workers, political representatives, stakeholders, teachers, religious leaders, Imams, Madrasa teachers, legal-aid groups, entrepreneur from unions, sub-districts and districts, and so on and called for discussion. Women activists and organizations expressed their satisfaction with the government's initiatives and procedures of formulating the policy, though they were disappointed with the slow implementation of the policy. However, in 2004, according to the key informants, the BNP-led government announced the policy all of a sudden, without necessary pre-formulation work. In 2008, there were many discussions, meetings and seminars before the policy was formulated. Yet, the policy did not meet the expectations of women activists, particularly in relation to inheritance right. In 2011, the AL-led government apparently seemed to be interested to declare the policy at the beginning. A representative of the government, Mr. D explained the steps of this policy formulation in the following manner,

> *In the beginning, we asked Bangladesh National Lawyers Association to give us a draft proposal of the policy. At the same time, we also arranged several meetings and panel discussions in the capital and also in different parts of the country. We took opinions from academics, political leaders, and lawyers, members of local government, women leaders, activists, religious leaders, and development workers before formulating the policy. Our intention was to make it sure that the policy formulation takes place in a democratic way where representatives from every group participate and share their opinions.*

Despite taking these measures, religion-based political groups strongly protested the policy from the day it was declared. Though the policy did not state anything clearly about equal inheritance rights for men and women, these groups assumed that the policy proposed the equal provision and which, according to them, is completely anti-Islamic. On the other hand, at the beginning of the declaration of the policy, women activists and leaders congratulated the government for taking such revolutionary steps in ensuring gender equality. Later, after reviewing and understanding the clause of the policy more clearly, women activist groups and leaders also opposed the policy, stating that that policy did not meet the long-cherished demand of women activists while it did not clarify anything that ensured women's equal share in inheritance as men.

Discontinuation of Policy: Opposition, Reaction and Failure

Inheritance System in Different Religions

Though Bangladesh has a secular legal system, in matters relating to family, inheritance and marriage, it follows the laws prescribed by different religions. The Muslims, who constitute most of the population (88.8%), follow the *Sharia* law in their family, marriage, property distribution and other personal matters (BBS, 2013). One of the Islamic scholars explained the share of inheritance issue as per the *Sharia* law and clarified reasons behind it:

> *According to Sharia Law, a daughter normally inherits half as much as her brother. People might think that this law discriminates women. But, if we consider other privileges that women get, this idea would turn to be wrong. Islam does not give women equal share with property, because, firstly, women get dower[2] from the husband in marriage. Dower is women's right and a husband must have to pay it during the time of marriage or after marriage depending on wife's preferences. In addition, in Islam, women are not supposed to be responsible for their own maintenance, rather it is the responsibility of the*

[2] Dower or *mahar* is a sum of money or other property to be paid or delivered to the wife. It is either specified or unspecified, but in either case, the law confers a mandatory right of *mahar* or dower on wife. The mahar belongs to the wife and she can deal with it in the manner she likes it—neither her husband, husband's relations nor even her relations can dictate her in the matter of using the *mahar* money or property (http://www.preservearticles. com/2012030124287/what-is-a-mahar-or-dower-in-muslim-law.html, accessed September 21, 2016).

father, brother or husband to provide all kinds of maintenance cost for women within his ability. Again, women also inherit her husband's property after his death.

However, many women activists do not completely agree with this opinion and denied the 'privileges' that *Islam* offers to women. According to them, providing maintenance or dower by the husbands makes women more dependent and submissive rather than being privileged.

The other religious groups in Bangladesh are Hindu, Buddhists and Christians. The second major religious group in Bangladesh is Hindu, with around 10% of the population (BBS, 2013). Both Hindu and Buddhist women do not get any property from their father or mother. One of the Hindu priests argued,

Women don't own any parental property. This is because the father gives everything within his ability when the daughter gets married. It can include money, jewellery, property, domestic appliances, furniture or anything that the father feels to give as gifts to his daughter. Moreover, unlike males, females do not take their own responsibility. All her maintenance and responsibility belong to the father before marriage, to husband in marital life and to son if the husband dies. Thus, even though women don't get inheritance, they get many other benefits from the males in different stages of their life.

However, there always remain different debates and interpretations of religious laws. According to the religious leaders, religion does not discriminate women; rather it gives better privileges. On the other hand, women activists, scholars and academics claim that religion leaves women in a secondary position and makes them more dependent on men. On this aspect, one of the key informants, B, said,

There is no doubt that all the religions of the world are male based. Women's equal share in the inheritance does not articulate in any of the religions that are mostly practiced in Bangladesh, except Christianity. I am not sure if the Christians in Bangladesh practice it or not. Religious leaders are against equal share of inheritance and to me their stand seems to be very irrational. However, providing maintenance to women and giving dower comes just as rule in paper that does not even strongly practiced among all the Muslims. There are many families where female maintains the family. Female headed households are common in both urban and rural areas. Then, how they can protest against equality in inheritance while these so-called religious norms are not commonly practiced?

On the other hand, as mentioned earlier, Bangladesh is signatory to CEDAW and other international conventions. On top of that there have always been demands from women activists as well as international communities to change such laws that discriminate women from equal access to property and inheritance. Furthermore, approximately 10% of the population of Bangladesh belongs to religious groups other than Islam, whose life is not governed by the *Sharia* law. Therefore, the key informants and women activists questioned, why the *Sharia* law would constraint the policy formulation as well as implementation while it discriminates the *Muslim* women and also women from other religions.

Immediate Reaction After the Declaration of Policy
The policy declared in 2011 apparently appeared to propose women's equal right to access and control over all earned and inherited property and resources. Several oppositions from Islamic groups came out as a reaction when the policy was just drafted. They claimed this policy as anti-*Islamic*, because the *Sharia* law does not permit women to get an equal share in property. Immediately after the policy draft was declared, the Islamic Law Implementation Committee, a combination of some religion-based political organizations called *Hartal*,[3] came out on the streets and violently opposed the policies. Several reports noted their strong reactions against the policy, such as the pickets attacked motor vehicles of common people, including members of parliament, vandalized vehicles, set fire to petrol pumps and police vans. Many madrasa students and religious activists came out on the streets in funeral garb that indicated their readiness to sacrifice their lives to resist this policy. The protests continued in Dhaka did spread in the whole country and conflicts and clashes between the Islamic groups and law enforcers were reported at several districts too. These incidents caused injury to both policemen and common people. Though the government tried to negotiate with the Islamic groups, stating that there is nothing mentioned in the policy that goes against Islam, still the movements continued.

Then the government took a serious step in order to remove the confusion of *Islamic* groups by calling approximately 150 leaders of the Bangladesh Jamiatul Modarasin, a pro-Awami League platform of Madrasa teachers. However, on April 20, 2011, after a dialogue with them, the current Prime Minister of Bangladesh reassured that her government has

---

[3] Blockade.

already removed all contradictions with respect to the *Sharia* law from the National Women Development Policy. However, despite reiterated assurances from the Prime Minister that nothing would be done against the scriptures, the Islamic Law Implementation Committee announced country-wide protests for several days against the implementation of the policy.

Women activists, on the other hand, kept protesting against government's role in formulating and implementing this policy. According to them, 2011 National Women's Development Policy does not say anything clearly about ensuring women's equal rights in inheritance and property. Rather it even stepped back from the 1997 Women's Development Policy that guaranteed women's equal right in inheritance. As the policy declared that women will have equal access to inherited property, it does not actually mean that women have the right to get equal access in inheritance and property. Again, the government's claim about this policy, articulating that the new policy does not go against Islam or the *Sharia* law but is an attempt to ensure gender equality, actually showed the dual role of government. On the one hand, this policy does not fulfil the commitment of CEDAW by ensuring gender equality with its unclear statements about equal share in inheritance. On top of that, women activist groups were even more disappointed with the government's passive role in finalizing the draft and proceeding further with the policy. However, because of strong opposition and vandalism from Islamic Law Implementation Committee and resilient criticisms from women's activists, the government actually pulled back the process and the policy had an abrupt end without being implemented.

As discussed above, in a nutshell, we finally got three different opinions about the policy. *First*, according to the GoB, the policy is a progressive move to ensure women's rights without conflicting with the *Sharia* law. *Second*, the religious groups and parties believe that the policy is completely anti-*Islamic* and should be sparred. Finally, the *third* force comprising of women activists and the female wings of some leftist parties rejected this policy. As per their view, the current version of NWDP has not contained any indication of equality in sharing inheritance.

Government's Role in the Implementation Process

The NWDP was a path-breaking policy in ensuring equal rights for women in terms of inheriting property. Given the novelty and the degree of change the policy promised to bring in terms of sharing of property, it was very likely that it would invite oppositions. One group of women activists and gender experts argue, the government instead of entering into dialogues with different stakeholders, made the policy in a top-down manner without any room for discussions. Even the major opposition political parties were side-lined. But the government officials denied that claim, stating that they had invited the stakeholders from each and every related group of people from society and took their opinion during policy formulation process. In answer to their claim, another group of women activists agreed that the government nominated and invited representatives from different sectors, yet the selection did not reflect the voice of the women activists who had worked long for gender equality and women empowerment in this country. In the same vein, the Islamic religious group also believed the discussion with the government during the time of policy formulation does not represent the verse of Quran. Despite having different lines of demand, both groups agreed that the nomination of stakeholders from the government to share opinion was politically chosen and contained biasness. Therefore, the impression of the policy at an initial stage of policy formulation was that the opinion from the stakeholders neither meets the demand of the women activists, nor of the Islamic priests. On top of that, after analysing the process involved in policy formulation, the analysis discloses a half-hearted effort on the part of the government without doing serious homework and an unbiased selection process of the stakeholders during the formulation of the policy and its subsequent implementation. Again, the officials of GoB denied this objection and claimed that the policy was formulated based on sufficient groundwork with the involvement of relevant stakeholders before it was adopted. Even they referred to the meeting held on April 20, 2011, when the Honourable Prime Minister called the Islamic leaders for a dialogue after declaring the policy. Despite these efforts, the government failed to create a consensus among different stakeholders. As such the government was taken aback and could not anticipate the intensity of the protest. Thus, it had to give in to societal pressure and abandoned the policy's implementation.

Therefore, the government resorted to political settlement with powerful religious groups in society in order to avoid serious violence and clashes all over the country. Religion has a deep root in Bangladeshi society and most people display high respect for religious values. In such a situation amidst protests by various religious groups and which may hurt religious sentiments and incite mass agitation, the government thought it wise not to pursue the policy anymore and add more 'oil to the fire'. As a result, the government opted for a settlement. This type of political settlement is in fact a compromise to maintain the status quo and not threaten social harmony despite being aware of the fact that implementing the policy which would have ensured radical inheritance rights for women. To avoid unsettling the government or at least absorb the shock, political settlement became an option for the government.

On the other hand, women activists were expecting that the government would implement the previous policy formulated in 1997. Women activists and lawyers even referred different examples from the past that many religious doctrines have been changed over the course of time. Legal expert Barrister F argued in this regard,

> *We found that the Islamic family law has been changed at different times. In 1939 and in 1961, Muslim Family Law has different clauses that do not really follow the exact Sharia Law. Law regarding Halala marriage (NikahHalala)[4] has been changed going beyond the Sharia's interpretation. Marriage and divorce registration has been made obligatory, which was not mandatory in Sharia. All these amendments were made previously. But now, with the issue of inheritance, strong oppositions are taking place as if we never had any amendment before.*

Thus, referring to these previous examples, lawyers, women activists and academics argue that there is nothing wrong in changing or revising the *Sharia* law. Furthermore, there are examples that different *Muslim* countries amended the *Sharia* law and implemented a gender-equal policy in their country. Many *Muslim* countries have taken off their reservation from CEDAW and are trying to fully implement it. Women activists think that the government is actually capitalizing its political interest by not ensuring gender equality in the country. A women activist, C, said,

> *There a big political interest working against the policy being implemented. First of all, the majority of the people of the country are Muslims and the government does not want to disappoint them. The government believes that by implementing the policy that contradicts with Islam might negatively impact*

[4] A couple who underwent a divorce cannot remarry unless the woman marries another man truly, and then her second husband dies or divorces her. In this case the marriage (*nikah*) of the woman with her second husband is called *nikah halala* (https://en.wikipedia.org/wiki/Nikah_Halala, accessed September 21, 2016).

*on their popularity during the election. Therefore, the Awami League govern-
ment did not proceed further with the policy formulated in 1997 even after its
declaration. Again, in 2011, we see that an important clause related to inheritance right was changed under the pressure of religious group which really
surprised us.*

Why the GoB Backed Out?

In Bangladesh, policy culture suffers from a lack of consistency and devia-
tions. The nature of policy and what policy is more likely to be adopted
and implemented depend on the type of regime. The two major political
parties that have shared state power since 1991 hardly agree on major
policies and are constantly at loggerheads. This has resulted in frequent
policy shifts and policy instability.

Bangladesh is predominantly a Muslim country, but it also has a reputa-
tion that it is secular and tolerant to other religious values. However, the
party in power (the Awami League) portrays itself as a secular party compared to the main opposition party, the Bangladesh Nationalist Party
(BNP), which has allied with Islamic fundamentalist parties and always
criticizes the Awami League as anti-Islamic and blames it as a close ally of
India, a relationship which is not considered as very popular in Bangladesh.
Given the dominant religious values and sentiments of the majority of the
people, the Awami League is cautious to implement any policy that might
go against the dominant religious sentiments in the country. At the same
time, it tries to appease other liberal groups, especially women activists,
that it is also working for them.

This is a big dilemma for the Awami League government to combine
its secular stand and at the same time be cautious in going against the
dominant religious sentiments, which might threaten its survival. Despite
having good intentions with this policy formulation, the policy was formulated without discussing and consulting with the opposition political
party—the BNP. In fact the relationships between these two parties are
antagonistic, which has had serious consequences for the national consensus on many issues and has halted or slowed down many critical national
policies (such as the implementation of the Chittagong Hill Tracts Peace
Treaty of 1997) crucial for the development process and nation building.

What Could the Government Do?

The efficiency of a government is measured by the level of good governance. In other words, to what extent it is capable of making sound policies and implementing it accordingly. In this regard, the capacity of the

government comes into question. In some cases, the capacity depends on how the government foresees the probable societal consequences of a policy. If the possibility of opposition to a particular policy is assumed to be high, then the government has to delegate the decision-making authority to different veto players in order to incorporate or co-opt their preferences. In a country where one-party rule dominates, oppositions from stakeholders are likely to be instigated by the political opposition because these are the avenues to harass the sitting government and make their voices heard. It, however, could not be ascertained in this study whether the opposition from the religious groups was instigated by the main opposition political party. The government claims that it had extensive dialogues with different Islamic groups, but when the policy was about to be implemented, it faced serious challenges from the religious groups. This could be due to the fact that there are religious groups or different constellation of religious groups which could be mobilized and show strong opposition to government policy. In this case, the government failed to locate and anticipate these groups and the strength and intensity of opposition these groups could unleash.

In addition, wider deliberation and mobilization of different groups could have been a strategy before adopting and subsequently implementing the NWDP. A consensus is required between conflicting interests and less governmental intervention from above is necessary to lower societal and political resistance.

Third, the purpose of the policy and expectations from it could have been widely circulated in society to make people more aware of it.

Consequences of Non-implementation of the Policy

Non-implementation of this policy has left a serious dent in ensuring gender equality in Bangladesh. In order to ensure gender equality and to mitigate discrimination against women, it is obligatory for the state to withdraw the remaining reservations from CEDAW, argued women activists of the country. Article 2, for instance, mandates that the state signing the convention has to ensure gender equality in all its domestic legislation, by abolishing discriminatory laws and endorsing new provisions (The United Nations, 1988). Article 16 (1c) states that the state has to initiate appropriate measures to eliminate discrimination against women in every sphere, including marriage and family relations (The United Nations, 1988). Moreover, the Constitution of Bangladesh also assures equal rights for women and men. Thus, keeping the reservation in Article 2 contradicts with Articles 10, 19, 27, 28 and 29 of the Constitution of Bangladesh. The GoB, after having a review by the Ministry of Law, Justice and Parliamentary Affairs, has committed to take out these reservations in the periodic report in 2004. Thus, Bangladesh is obligated to ensure gender equality in every sphere of life and National Women's Development Policy actually comes as a result of constant international and national commitments by the country.

Key informants of this study think that Bangladesh can learn by looking at the examples of other Islamic countries that ratified CEDAW without any reservation and are seriously working on it. It is also notable that 29 out of 57 member countries of the Organisation of Islamic Cooperation (OIC) have ratified the Convention fully without any reservations. Many countries have withdrawn initial reservations during the review process. It has been a challenge for Bangladesh to meet the Millennium Development Goals, Beijing Platform for Action and Commission on the Status of Women if the country keeps the reservations. The non-implementation of the National Women's Development Policy has actually made Bangladesh pull back from meeting international commitments and constitutional obligations. Moreover, implementing this policy is actually on the election manifesto of the party in power but it has failed to meet it until now. What is a more serious blow is that the present and subsequent governments may find it difficult to implement a policy of this stature because of the nature and volume of oppositions. These oppositions may gain more strength and mobilize even more on a larger scale to thwart any attempt to implement such policy in a patriarchal and man dominated society such as Bangladesh.

Another opinion from the key informants is that the Government of Bangladesh has shifted its priority from an anti-poverty approach to empowerment. Key informant A argues,

> It has been around 20 years that the government has been considering NWDP with several revisions. Undoubtedly the government has changed their approach in terms of gender equality and women empowerment. They are more focusing of women's participation in employment, education and economic involvement. However, that might be one reason for why the government does not seem to be serious about this policy.

Yet, the officials working for the government do not really think that the policy is not implemented. According to them the policy is still on its way of implementation. Regarding the reactions of the religious group, they argue that the government actually negotiated with the Islamic groups and there is no more confusion with the policy. But they agree that it has disappointed the women activists who had a long-lived demand of women's equal right in inheritance. Yet, the government took a serious consideration of the contextual confusion that rose after policy formulation, and to it, the context at present is not favourable for women's equal share in inheritance at all. Therefore, the officials working for the government with this policy clarify their stand, arguing that the policy is a progressive step to ensure women's rights, but not actually conflicting with the *Quran*. They assured that no policy or amendment would be taken that goes against *Islam*. So, the policy contained a footnote stating that, 'Notwithstanding anything contained in this policy, during enactment of the law, anything contrary to the Holy *Quran* and *Sunnah* shall be void' (GoB, 2011, p. 68).

The government's attempts to withdraw the provision of equal inheritance from NWDP reflects 'political settlement'. This long-expected provision was withdrawn at the policy formulation stage in the wake of massive opposition from the religious fundamentalist groups. The Islamic fundamentalist groups staged strong protests, including violent demonstrations and vandalism. The government realized that formulating such a policy of providing equal inheritance right may agitate Islamic fundamentalists as well as upset the sentiments of Muslim communities. It was also wary of losing popularity among Muslims, especially during elections, who comprise 90% of the total population of the country. As a response to the opposition and in order to acquiesce to the other demands by the Islamic fundamentalist groups, the government incorporated some demands, especially those put forward by Hefazat e Islam. The demands included the removal of some secular contents from primary and secondary education textbooks, allocating more budget for the development of Islamic education and recognizing the Dawra-e Hadith Certificate in Qawmi madrasas as equivalent to postgraduate degrees in Islamic Studies and Arabic, and so on, which the government has accepted. Put to the acid test by religious fanaticism, the AL-led government bowed down and struck political negotiation with the Islamic fundamentalist groups. This, however, caused dissatisfaction among women activists, NGOs, international NGOs and members of civil society. Although such political settlement based on negotiation and bargaining may resolve the problem of instability, conflict and violence, it may also cause policy delays for an indefinite period and compromise issues of women's empowerment and equal rights in inheritance.

CONCLUSION

Policy formulation and its implementation might be a big challenge when a government faces opposition from certain groups of people. However, in the case of Bangladesh, the National Women's Development Policy could not see the light even after the formulation of four different drafts in the last 20 years. The opposition and reactions were so strong that the policy failed to be implemented, even though the country has committed internationally to ensure gender equality in every sphere of life. Also, in a country where national consensus on major policies is a serious concern, opposition is likely to emerge from many holds—religious, political and social. Moreover, one-sided policy by the party in power has been a major problem in Bangladesh, leading to policy instability. Similarly, serious opposition to any policy, irrespective of how it was formulated, is also seriously impeding policy implementation and good governance in Bangladesh. In order to pacify serious opposition and obviate the threat to its survivability, the present government chose political settlement or compromise to bail itself out of the threatened political order.

Cultural values are deep rooted and influence how people behave and relate to each other. In the case of gender relations, different cultures have different prescriptions and these are hard to alter or modify overnight. Therefore, policies of this stature, which intend to alter or modify certain cultural values, require a longer time frame, strong commitment and mobilization on the part of the government, high political consensus and inclusion of different stakeholders. A radical or revolutionary change effort carried out hurriedly in a top-down manner is not the right recipe and is very likely to face opposition, as was witnessed in the implementation of the National Women's Development Policy in Bangladesh. The way this policy has been opposed in society has only demonstrated that rational policy-making based on altruistic intentions may not fare well if it lacks wider societal acceptance and goes against mainstream socio-cultural and religious values. The final outcome of this would likely to be falling short of its goal, that is, non-implementation of policy.

Acknowledgements I want to express my heartiest gratitude to Ishtiaq Jamil, PhD, Professor, Department of Administration and Organization Theory, University of Bergen, Norway, for his constant support and supervision to bring this chapter to this stage. The work would not have been possible without his initiative and guidance. I am also thankful to the Higher Education Quality

Enhancement Project (HEQEP), University Grants Commission (UGC) for funding this small-scale research project.

REFERENCES

Agarwal, B. (1994a). Gender and control over property: A critical gap in economic analysis and policy in south Asia. *World Development, 22*(10), 1455–1478.

Agarwal, B. (1994b). *A field of one's own: Gender and land rights in South Asia* (Vol. 58). Cambridge University Press.

Agarwal, B. (2003). Gender and land rights revisited: Exploring new prospects via the state, family and market. *Journal of Agrarian Change, 3*(1–2), 184–224.

Andaleeb, S. S., & Vanneman Wolford, G. (2004). Participation in the workplace: Gender perspectives from Bangladesh. *Women in Management Review, 19*(1), 52–64.

Bangladesh Const. art 28 (1), & 18 (3). Retrieved August 28, 2017, from http://bdlaws.minlaw.gov.bd/sections_detail.php?id=367&sections_id=24576

BBS. (2013). *Statistical pocket book*. Government of Peoples Republic of Bangladesh.

Bhattacharya, D., Rahman, M., & Raihan, A. (2002). Contribution of the RMG sector to the Bangladesh economy. *CPD Occasional Paper Series, 50*, 6.

Chowdhury, F. D. (2009). Theorising patriarchy: The Bangladesh context. *Asian Journal of Social Science, 37*(4), 599–622.

Gayen, K. (2011, May). 'Equal property rights': Much Ado about nothing'. *Forum- A Monthly Publication of Daily Star, 5*(5). Retrieved January 24, 2017, from http://archive.thedailystar.net/forum/2011/May/right.htm

Government of Peoples' Republic of Bangladesh (1997). *National Women Development Policy*. Ministry of Women and Children Affairs.

Government of Peoples' Republic of Bangladesh (2011, March). *National Women Development Policy*. Ministry of Women and Children Affairs. Retrieved August 22, 2017, from https://www.unescogym.org/wp-content/uploads/2017/05/Bangladesh-National-Women-Policy-2011English.pdf

Hashemi, S. M., Schuler, S. R., & Riley, A. P. (1996). Rural credit programs and women's empowerment in Bangladesh. *World Development, 24*(4), 635–653.

Hossain, M. A., & Tisdell, C. A. (2005). Closing the gender gap in Bangladesh: Inequality in education, employment and earnings. *International Journal of Social Economics, 32*(5), 439–453.

Huda, S. (1997). Women's movement in Bangladesh. *Asian Women, 5*, 133–143.

Jamil, I., Askvik, S., & Dhakal, T. (2013). Understanding governance in South Asia. In I. Jamil, S. Askvik, & T. Dhakal (Eds.), *In search of better governance in South Asia and beyond*. New York: Springer.

Kabeer, N. (1991). The quest for national identity: Women, Islam and the state in Bangladesh. In *Women, Islam and the state* (pp. 115–143). London: Palgrave Macmillan.

Kabeer, N. (2001). Conflicts over credit: Re-evaluating the empowerment potential of loans to women in rural Bangladesh. *World Development, 29*(1), 63–84.

Kabeer, N. (2011). Between affiliation and autonomy: Navigating pathways of women's empowerment and gender justice in rural Bangladesh. *Development and Change, 42*(2), 499–528.

Karim, L. (2004). Democratizing Bangladesh: State, NGOs, and Militant Islam. *Cultural Dynamics, 16*(2–3), 291–231.

Khan, F. C. (2005). Gender violence and development discourse in Bangladesh. *International Social Science Journal, 57*(184), 219–230.

Khan, M. (2010). Political settlements and the governance of growth-enhancing institutions. Retrieved December 17, 2019, from https://eprints.soas.ac.uk/9968/1/Political_Settlements_internet.pdf

Khan, M. I. (2013). Social changes in contemporary Bangladesh. *Journal of the Asiatic Society of Bangladesh, 58*(2), 263–276.

Khan, M. R., & Ara, F. (2006). Women, participation and empowerment in local government: Bangladesh union Parishad perspective. *Asian Affairs, 29*(1), 73–92.

Mahmud, K. T., Parvez, A., Hilton, D., Kabir, G. M. S., & Wahid, I. S. (2014). The role of training in reducing poverty: The case of agricultural workers receiving microcredit in Bangladesh. *International Journal of Training and Development, 18*(4), 282–290. https://doi.org/10.1111/ijtd.12039

Matland, R. E. (1995). Synthesizing the implementation literature: The ambiguity-conflict model of policy implementation. *Journal of Public Administration Research and Theory, 5*(2), 145–174.

Sourav, M. R. I. (2015). Unjust land right of women in Bangladesh. *International Research Journal of Interdisciplinary Multidisciplinary Studies, 1*(3), 5–13.

Thomas, J. W., & Grindle, M. S. (1990). After the decision: Implementing policy reforms in developing countries. *World Development, 18*(8), 1163–1181.

Van Meter, D. S., & Van Horn, C. E. (1975). The policy implementation process: A conceptual framework. *Administration & Society, 6*(4), 445–488.

The United Nations. (1988). Convention on the elimination of all forms of discrimination against women. Retrieved August 22, 2017, from http://www.un.org/womenwatch/daw/cedaw/text/econvention.htm

Zaman, H. (1999). Violence against women in Bangladesh: Issues and responses. *Women's Studies International Forum, 22*(1), 37–48. https://doi.org/10.1016/S0277-5395(98)00093-4

CHAPTER 4

Gender-Based Harassment and Violence in Higher Educational Institutions: A Case from Sri Lanka

Janethri B. Liyanage and Kamala Liyanage

Introduction

Gender-based harassment and violence are not new phenomena in tertiary-level educational institutions in Sri Lanka. In the recent past, several university teachers were accused of sexual harassment and violence. A few such cases even went up to the courts. A female vice-chancellor revealed at a public event that several male teachers were barred from teaching due to their involvement in incidents in which female students were sexually harassed (*Mawbima*, March 24, 2016, p. 1). At one university in Sri Lanka, four such incidents were reported to the vice-chancellor recently, and these are now under investigation.

Gender-based discrimination, harassment, and violence against women have become a matter of concern for some gender-sensitive individuals in

J. B. Liyanage
Department of Chemistry, Faulty of Science, University of Peradeniya, Peradeniya, Sri Lanka

K. Liyanage (✉)
Department of Political Science, University of Peradeniya, Peradeniya, Sri Lanka

the universities of Sri Lanka. With the leadership of the University Grants Commission, Sri Lanka, the document *Strategies for Universities: Preventing Sexual and Gender-Based Violence*[1] has been prepared and issued by a gender-sensitive group of university teachers. The Senate of the University of Peradeniya appointed a special committee to draft a code of ethics, a policy, and guidelines for the prevention of gender-based discrimination, harassment, and violence,[2] which was approved by the university authorities in 2017. The Council of the University of Peradeniya has appointed a Committee against Gender-Based Violence and Sexual Harassment in 2018, to monitor and investigate such incidents within the university.

Such incidents have also received attention from the state, the non-governmental sector, and civil society organizations. Numerous policies and strategies have been formulated in Sri Lanka to implement preventive measures and provide redress for victims. Some of the national policies that have incorporated strategies on gender-based violence are the *National Health Policy*, the *National Policy on Youth*, the *National Family Policy*, the *Plan of Action Supporting the Prevention of Domestic Violence Act*, the *Guidelines for a Code on Sexual Harassment*, and so forth. Despite having such a policy framework and comprehensive national plan of action, gender-based harassment and violence continue to take place in the private and public sphere in Sri Lanka. This, it is argued, is due to the insufficiency of the application of the measures (Jayasundere, 2009, p. 1).

THE RESEARCH SETTING AND OBJECTIVE

Although the issues related to direct sexual violence and gender-based discrimination have been increasing rapidly in higher educational institutions in Sri Lanka, only a few systematic studies have been done on the problems (Gunarathne, 2014; Gunawardena, Weerasinghe, Rajapakse, Wijesekara, & Chathuranga, 2011; Liyanage, 1996, 2000; Liyanage, Vandort, & Paramaguru, 2012; Perera, Abeynayake, & Galabada, 2006). Documentary evidence suggests that all this research has mainly paid attention to dating and ragging (bulling new university students during the first few months, hazing, initiation ceremonies, etc.) among students.

---

[1] Preventing Sexual and Gender-Based Violence: Strategies for Universities, 2015, Colombo: Care International Sri Lanka.

[2] The second author served as a co-chairperson of this committee.

However, it is fundamentally necessary to examine, through scholarly research, the nature of gender-based harassment and violence, the root causes of the phenomena, and how gendered socialization, patriarchal culture, and gender performance may relate to such violence.

To this end, data were collected from different types of respondents of a state university of Sri Lanka. The name of the university has deliberately been kept anonymous and instead 'University of X' has been used. Other facts and data pertaining to the University of X are also avoided to preserve its anonymity. The University of X guarantees equal access to "all persons of either sex" and prohibits discrimination based on differences such as the sex, race, creed, class, and religion of staff members and students.

In the above-explained context, the main objective of the research is to examine the nature of the gender-based harassment and violence faced by staff members and students in the University of X. What are the causes of gender-based harassment and violence, and how does such behavior relate to gendered socialization and gendered performance? In this research we also tried to examine whether violent activities or behavior reproduces gender roles, identity, and relations, and whether gender-equality policies mandated for Sri Lankan universities are practiced in the University of X.

Conceptual Framework and Definitions

Feminist theorists have defined the term 'gender' according to different perspectives. Some describe gender as status given to men (masculinity) and women (femininity) by the society and culture, while Adkins (1995) views it as a dynamic process. Yet other theorists define gender as performance (Butler, 1990, 1993), or as something one does, as in the phrase 'doing gender' (West & Fenstermarker, 1995; West & Zimmerman, 1987).

In general, therefore, gender is defined as a set of characteristics, roles, and behavior patterns that are socially and culturally constructed to distinguish men and women from each other. It refers to a web of cultural symbols, normative concepts, institutional structures, and internalized self-images. This points to a process through which social constructions define masculine and feminine roles and articulate these roles within power relationships. The term gender, therefore, refers neither to women nor to men, but to the relationships between them, to the roles given by the community to each, and to the ways in which societies are divided according to ideas regarding the status, capabilities, and the aspirations of men and women (Commonwealth Secretariat, 2000). These are learned from generation to generation through gendered socialization processes and vary widely within and between cultures (United Nations, 1995). Some examples of socially constructed gender differences include different duties given to men and women, different perceptions of preferences and capabilities of the sexes, different recognition, and varying pay rates for similar occupations. These gender statuses, identities, and relationships also depend on a particular socio-economic, cultural, and political context, and they are affected by other factors such as race, ethnicity, class, religion, caste, age, and so on (Connell, 1987).

Socially constructed gender differences often lead to gender-based discrimination that denies equal treatment, equal opportunities, and equal outcomes for both men and women. The kind of socialization we have been exposed to through generations has shaped us into believers of various gender stereotypes and prejudices. These have been internalized and naturalized to the point where gender inequalities and gender-based discrimination arising from them are hardly visible or a matter of concern to most people in society.

According to Judith Butler, gender is constructed through a person's performance of gender. Individuals learn gender performance both consciously and unconsciously and are unaware that they are performing a gender role. They accept the gender identity assigned to them by their own behavior or performance and which is again interpreted and repeated within the discourse of gender relations in a cultural and social context. Thus, gender performativity is a repetitive act that serves to reproduce itself perpetually (Butler, 1990, p. 2). Butler's concept of gender performativity extends the idea by suggesting that it is through performance that gendered subjectivities are constructed. She argued that "gender proves to be performative, that is, constituting the identity it is purported to be" (Butler, 1990, p. 25). For Butler, gender performance demonstrates the instability of masculine subjectivity; a 'masculine identity' exists only as the actions of individuals who stylize their bodies and actions in accordance with a normative binary framework of gender. In addition, the performance of gender makes male power and privileges appear natural and normal rather than socially produced. The ideology and practice of gender or masculinity and femininity is produced within institutions or society and through everyday interactions between people; it is diverse, unequal, dynamic, and negotiable (Kimmel, 2000). West and Fenstermarker (1995, p. 37) contend that cultural beliefs about underlying and essential differences between men and women and social structures that constitute and are constituted by these beliefs are reproduced by the accomplishment of gender.

Gender-based violence in its simplest form is violence against women based on women's subordinate status in society. It includes any act or threat by men or male-dominated institutions that impose physical, sexual, or psychological harm on a woman or girl because of her gender. It involves men and women, in which the female is usually the target, and emanates from unequal power relationships and status between them (MacKinnon, 1979). Gender-based violence includes a host of harmful behaviors that are directed at women and girls because of their sex, including abuse, sexual assault, dowry-related murder, marital rape, selective malnourishment of female children, forced prostitution, female genital mutilation, and the sexual abuse of female children. It is often known as 'gender-based' violence because it evolves in part from women's subordinate status in society. Many cultures have beliefs, norms, and social institutions that legitimize and therefore perpetuate violence against women. The same acts that would be punished if directed at an employer, a neighbor, or an acquaintance often go unchallenged when men direct them at women, especially within the family. It encompasses threats of violence and coercion. It can be physical, emotional, psychological, or sexual in nature, and can take the form of a denial of resources or access to services.

Specifically, violence against women includes any act of verbal or physical force, coercion, or life-threatening deprivation directed at an individual woman or girl that causes physical or psychological harm, humiliation, or arbitrary deprivation of liberty, and which perpetuates female subordination (Heise, Ellsberg, & Gottemoeller, 1999). Gender violence occurs in both the 'public' and 'private' spheres. Such violence not only occurs in the family and in the general community, but is sometimes also perpetuated by the state through policies or the actions of agents of the state such as the police, military, or immigration authorities. Gender-based violence happens in all societies, across all social classes, with women particularly at risk from men they know.

Gender-based violence and harassment are based solely on a person's gender, and those who have the power to control the behavior of others can use their power and privileges to that end. Gender-based violence and harassment encompass the opposite sex as well as same-sex interactions that keep victims in their place. Such actions range from verbal comments and jokes to threats, sexual assault, and rape. The *UN Declaration on the*

Elimination of Violence Against Women (DEVAW) defines gender-based violence as "any act of gender-based violence that results in, or is likely to result in, physical, sexual or psychological harm or suffering to women, including threats of such acts, coercion or arbitrary deprivation of liberty, whether occurring in public or in private life" (UN DEVAW, 1993, Article 1). According to MacKinnon (1979, p. 1), gender-based harassment refers to the unwanted imposition of a sexual requirement in the context of a relationship of unequal power. Central to the concept is the use of power derived from one social sphere to lever benefits or impose deprivations in another social sphere. The one is sexual, the other is material, and the cumulative outcome is particularly potent. Gender-based harassment includes verbal abuse, pressure for sexual activity, unwanted patting and pinching, demanding sexual favors, making threats, and so forth.

Till (1980, p. 7) has used the term 'academic gender-based harassment' and defined it as the use of authority to emphasize the gender or gender identity of the student or junior staff in a manner which prevents or impairs that person's full enjoyment of educational benefits or opportunities.

Dziech and Weiner (1990) opine that gender-based harassment and violence occur at higher educational institutions because university culture mostly operates on male-based norms, and women have to abide by these norms or else incur trouble. Leach (2013) argues that gender-based harassment in university-level education is higher in countries with weak educational systems, low levels of accountability, high levels of poverty, and gender inequality. It is more prevalent in institutions where educators are poorly trained, underpaid, and severely under-sourced (Beninger, 2013). According to Sharma (2013), gender-based harassment in education includes: (1) inappropriate sexualized comments or gestures; (2) unwanted physical contact such as touching, pinching, or groping, and the threat of failing on exams; and (3) sexual assault and rape. Sexual harassment could also include sexual favors in exchange for good grades or preferential treatment in class. The perpetrators can be students, lecturers, teachers, or administrative staff.

RESEARCH METHODOLOGY

The study employed both quantitative and qualitative methodologies to highlight the research issue. With regard to qualitative methodology, we collected narratives and experiences from 47 people (21 staff members, among which 19 were females and 2 were males, and 26 students, among which 21 were females and 5 were males). In addition, we conducted face-to-face interviews with 31 randomly selected staff members (22 females, 9 males) and 47 students (26 females, 21 males). These were considered key informants (hostel wardens, sub-wardens, student counselors, deputy proctors, security personnel, health center staff, key decision-makers, and student leaders such as members of the student union, women's activists, etc.)

As regards collecting quantitative data, we conducted a questionnaire survey among 73 staff members (both academic and non-academic) and 198 students, representing all nine faculties of the university. To conduct the survey, we used a pre-defined and pre-tested questionnaire that contained both quantitative and qualitative questions.

Data were collected during 2015 and 2016. For the purpose of this study, we did not analyze data sets separately according to categories such as ethnicity, academic staff, non-academic staff, and students. Rather, we treated all men as one group and all women as another, even though there are ethnic, regional, class, and rural-urban divisions among them.

Equality Policies in the State University

The University of X is committed to creating a place for study and work, free from all types of harassment, intimidation, and exploitation for its students and staff, in line with applicable national and international laws, charters, and conventions.[3]

Efforts to ensure gender equality at the university have included an analysis of the university acts, by-laws, rules, and regulations, with the aim of determining whether policies related to gender equality exist, and whether they ensure equal status and equal value to both men and women in the university. Equality, including gender equality, is accommodated for by Section 30 of the *Universities Act No. 16* (1978). It reads as follows:

---

[3] Articles 10, 12(1) and (2), and 14(1) of the Constitution of Sri Lanka (1978); Women's Charter of Sri Lanka (1993); the Prevention of Domestic Violence Act of 2005 of Sri Lanka; Prohibition of Ragging and Other Forms of Violence in Educational Institutions Act (1998); United Nations International Covenant on Civil and Political Rights (1966); Convention on the Elimination of Discrimination Against Women (CEDAW) (1981), and its Optional Protocol (1983); Vienna Declaration on the Elimination of Violence Against Women (1993); and the ILO Conventions, Sections 19 and 345 of the Sri Lankan Penal Code (Amendment) Act, No. 22 (1995).

Subject to the provisions of sections 29(c) and 31, a University shall be open to all persons of either sex and whatever race, creed or class, who are citizens of Sri Lanka, and other persons who are lawfully in Sri Lanka, and no test of religious belief or profession shall be adopted or imposed in order to entitle any such person to be admitted as a teacher or student of the University, or to hold any appointment therein or to graduate thereat or to hold, enjoy or exercise any advantage or privilege thereof.

A close investigation of the university's acts and by-laws reveals that men and women are not given equal status and value as prescribed by those same acts and by-laws. The *Universities Act No. 16* (1978) often uses 'he' as the generic term when referring to key decision-makers in the university system, such as the chairman of the University Grants Commission, the auditor general, the vice-chancellor, the rector, registrar, bursar, deans of faculties, heads of departments, and members of the senate and the faculty board. In *By-Law No. 1* (1996), relating to students' discipline, and in the *University Student Union By-Law No. 1* (2003), we find the generic term 'he' used to refer to both male and female students of the university, especially when referring to the office bearers and members of the Student Union. However, the *Prohibition of Ragging and Other Forms of Violence in Educational Institutions Act, No. 20* (1998) uses the gender-neutral term 'person,' while the *Examination Procedure, Offenses and Punishment Regulation No. 1* (2008) uses the gender-inclusive term 'he/she' to refer to men and women in the university.

The failure to acknowledge both men and women by conscious or unconscious use of 'he' as the generic term to refer to both sexes leaves out the participation and representation of females in the university system altogether and reinstates the historical marginalization of women in the public sphere. The use of the term 'he' to denote key officers also confirms the historical identification of men as active, prominent, and dominant figures holding important and privileged positions in society.

The examination of *Hostel Rules* at the university revealed that the female students are given the time limit of 7:30 pm to return to their hostel compound, while male students do not need to be in their hostel until 10:00 pm. Both male and female students who participated in interviews stated that the time limit given to males and females was discriminatory to both sexes and in different ways. The students opined that the restriction was strictly monitored only for females, and that they had to go through the ordeal of obtaining 'late passes' from their hostel wardens if they needed to return to hostel later than 7:30 pm. This would be the case, for example, if they wanted to attend university events, participate in field trips, *kuppi*,[4] and so on. Data revealed that these regulations were not strictly observed for the male students, and both male and female respondents confirmed that the time restriction for male students is not monitored or enforced strictly by the university authority.

There is no special provision at the university that ensures equal treatment of both female and male students or to prevent gender-based discrimination and guarantee that staff members and students will not be treated less favorably due to their sex. Furthermore, there is no structured mechanism to ensure that rules and regulations in the university are equally applied to both genders and to monitor that equality is maintained.

MALE AND FEMALE REPRESENTATION IN THE UNIVERSITY

This section includes gender-segregated data on the number/percentage of male and female key decision-makers, staff, and students in the university. Men occupy around 75 percent of the key positions available at the university. The percentage of male representation in important decision-making committees is also significantly higher than that of the females (Table 4.1).

Table 4.1 Distribution of key staff positions among academic staff by gender, 2017

Position	Male	Female
Chancellor	1	
Vice-chancellor	1	
Deputy vice-chancellor	1	
Deans	9	
University council	29	4
Heads of departments	70	10
Directors of post-graduate institutes	3	
Directors of centers and units	28	3
Academic development and planning com.	5	3
Finance committee	11	2
Senate higher degrees committee	13	4
Senate research committee	15	5
Librarian	1	
N (percentage)	187 (86%)	31 (14%)

[4] *Kuppi* is a term used in the university context to refer to group tutoring which senior students offer to juniors.

As the Table 4.2 demonstrates many male academics of the University X are representing the higher academic levels as professors and Senior lectures while many female academics are in the lower levels such as lecturer and probationary lecturer (Table 4.2).

In the General Administration Division and Services Division, the percentage of male staff members is approximately 71 percent. The Library

Table 4.2 Distribution of academic staff by category, gender, and faculty (permanent staff only), 2017 (as of 31 December 2017)

Faculty	Professor/senior professor			Associate professor			Senior lecturer-1			Senior lecturer-11		
	M	F	T	M	F	T	M	F	T	M	F	T
Agriculture	23	7	30	1	2	3	14	6	20	16	9	25
Allied health science	1	0	1	0	0	0	1	2	3	7	6	13
Arts	16	5	21	1	0	1	31	18	49	41	20	61
Dental sciences	11	10	21	0	0	0	4	3	7	6	7	13
Engineering	16	1	17	0	0	0	19	3	22	48	17	65
Management	1	0	1	0	0	0	2	1	3	4	3	7
Medicine	17	8	25	1	1	2	8	11	19	20	21	41
Science	20	11	31	1	0	1	6	10	16	22	13	35
Veterinary medicine	4	1	5	1	0	1	4	4	8	12	8	20
Other academic Staff[a]	0	0	0	0	0	0	1	7	8	1	3	4
Total	109	43	152	5	3	8	90	65	155	177	107	284

Faculty	Lecturer			Lecturer (probationary)			Total		
	M	F	T	M	F	T	M	F	T
Agriculture	3	2	5	11	11	22	68	37	105
Allied health science	1	11	12	4	24	28	14	43	57
Arts	9	11	20	10	6	16	108	60	168
Dental sciences	1	3	4	4	5	9	26	28	54
Engineering	1	0	1	8	10	18	92	31	123
Management	3	3	6	4	17	21	14	24	38
Medicine	5	6	11	9	8	17	60	55	115
Science	0	7	7	12	11	23	61	52	113
Veterinary medicine	1	0	1	2	6	8	23	19	42
Other academic Staff[a]	1	2	3	3	3	6	6	16	22
Total	25	45	70	67	101	168	472	365	837

Source: *Statistical Handbook*, University of X, 2017

[a]'Other academic staff' refers to the academic staff of the library and English-language teaching unit

Table 4.3 Distribution of non-academic decision-makers, 2017

Designation	Male	Female
Registrar	1	–
Deputy registrar	3	1
Senior assistant registrar	5	8
Assistant registrar	6	8
Bursar	1	–
Deputy bursar	2	1
Senior assistant bursar	6	2
Assistant bursar	5	4
Senior assistant internal auditor	–	2
Senior medical officer	1	
Curator	2	–
Director physical education	1	
Statistical officer	–	1
Workshop engineer	1	–
Chief marshal	1	–
Public relations officer	1	–
Chief security officer	1	
N (percentage)	37 (58%)	27 (42%)

Network is the only division dominated by a large percentage of females (among 12 senior assistant librarians, only 2 are men). Among decision-makers of the non-academic staff, more than 57 percent of the positions are occupied by men, and the representation of women (43 percent) among them is higher than among the decision-makers of the academic staff (Table 4.3).

In this university, a relatively large number of females are involved in providing services that are supposedly 'feminine,' such as medical and nursing services requiring 'feminine traits' of patience, understanding, nurturing, and caring. In contrast, a striking number of males provide services that are supposedly 'masculine,' such as higher-level decision-making, marshaling, proctoring, and security services that call for 'masculine traits' like courage, physical prowess, and the ability to 'protect' the vulnerable. After making demands for years, one female marshal and a few security guards were recently recruited by the university authority. The authors attempted to find out if the reason for such gender-segregated occupations is the gender stereotyping on the part of recruitment bodies in the university, or if the applicants' own gender stereotyping was involved, by analyzing gender-segregated records of the applicants for the above staff positions. However, the absence of such records in the university made it impossible for the authors to come to any concrete conclusion.

The female student population at the University of X is higher than its male student population (Table 4.4). Statistics show that the number of male students is strikingly higher at the Faculty of Engineering, while the number of females is higher at the Faculty of Arts (Table 4.4).

The significant gap between the number of male and female students in the faculties for arts, medicine, and dentistry reveals yet another instance of gendered socialization; these are considered 'feminine' disciplines, while mathematics and engineering are 'masculine' disciplines that call for 'rational' thinking.

Through our questionnaire, we collected data from 73 staff members (45 females and 28 males) and 198 students (143 females and 55 males from all nine faculties), who answered questions regarding whether the University of X practices gender-equal treatment, has a gender-inclusive culture, and adopts mechanisms for resolving any reported gender-related discriminatory practices. Data collected during our research on these issues are presented in Tables 4.5 and 4.6, and show that discriminatory practices based on people's gender identity do exist at the university. More than 41 percent of staff respondents believe that women are treated less favorably than men in the recruitment and selection processes for university positions. It is also evident from Table 4.5 that for more than 50 percent of the respondents, women are less favorably treated in research and academic activities. The majority of the respondents believe that women are less favorably treated in relation to recognition (55 percent), opportunities to get involved in institutional development (74 percent),

Table 4.4 Total student enrolment by faculties and gender, 2017

Faculty	Male	Female	Total	Percentage of female students
Agriculture	315	625	940	66.5
Allied health science	257	527	784	67.2
Arts	842	3554	4396	80.8
Dental science	137	258	395	65.3
Engineering	1271	390	1661	23.5
Management	238	377	615	61.3
Medicine	539	749	1288	58.2
Science	997	1160	2157	53.8
Veterinary science	144	243	387	62.8
Total	4740	7883	12,623	62.5

Source: *Statistical Handbook*, University of X, 2017

membership in inquiry boards and other important boards (60 percent), and training and staff development (53 percent), and that they experience instances of gender-based harassment (90 percent). More than 50 percent of respondents say that women are less favorably treated with respect to the provision of facilities such as rest rooms, recreation, and sports. Around 45 percent mention that women are not treated equally when nominations and appointments are made for decision-making positions. However, 69 percent believe that men and women are treated equally when it comes

Table 4.5 Response on equal treatment from staff and students of the University X (percentage distribution)

	Respondents	Percentage		
		Less favorable treatment toward women	Less favorable treatment toward men	Equal treatment for both men and women
Recruitment and selection	Staff	41	11	48
Research and academic work		52	11	37
Recognition in the university community		55	3	42
Institutional development opportunities		75	4	21
Membership in inquiry boards		61	5	34
Rest room/toilet facilities		53	13	35
Recreation/sports facilities		54	9	37
Training and staff development		53	24	23
Remuneration		0	0	100
Promotions		27	3	70
Representation in decision-making positions		46	3	51
Instances of harassment		91	2	7
Obtaining leave		17	–	83

(*continued*)

Table 4.5 (continued)

	Respondents	Less favorable treatment toward women	Less favorable treatment toward men	Equal treatment for both men and women
		Percentage		
Admission	Students	5	6	89
Accommodation		12	6	82
Interacting with academic staff		35	19	46
Subject selections		21	13	66
Assessment/results		11	15	74
Orientation programs		47	17	35
Leadership in student unions		85	6	9
Extra-curricular activities		68	6	26
Representation in student bodies		83	5	12
Sports		52	5	43
Hostel rules/late passes		66	9	25
Punishment/inquiry board decisions		10	57	33
Cultural and religious activities		63	3	34
University 'subculture'		75	7	18
Functions at the university		72	5	23
Library facilities		29	3	68
Canteen facilities		55	7	38
Safety/security	Staff	74	–	26
	Students	88	5	7
Dress codes/code of behavior	Staff	79	–	21
	Students	94	2	4

to granting promotions, and 100 percent of this group of informants have recognized the equal remuneration policies in the university.

The majority of the students perceive that female students are treated less favorably in relation to representation in student unions (83 percent), leadership in student union activities (85 percent), hostel rules (66 percent), sports (51 percent), and cultural and religious activities (63 per-

Table 4.6 Responses of staff and students on gender equality of the University of X (percentage distribution)

	Respondents	Percentage			
		Yes	No	No response	Heard from others
Discrimination based on gender	Staff	37	24	16	23
	Students	77	23	–	–
Gender-inclusive culture	Staff	19	70	11	–
	Students	29	71	–	–
Bullying/harassment based on gender	Staff	34	22	14	31
Family friendly policies	Staff	21	79	–	–
Need for a mechanism to resolve gender issues	Staff	64	29	7	–
Gender equality in student politics	Students	3	94	3	–
Examination matters involved in gender	Students	27	73	–	–

cent). Both female staff (74 percent) and students (87 percent) mention that females are less favorably treated in relation to security, dress code (78 percent and 93 percent), and incidents of sexual harassment. However, 56 percent of respondents say that male students are treated less favorably in disciplinary matters and punishment imposed by the university authority.

GENDER-BASED VIOLENCE AT THE UNIVERSITY OF X: ANALYSIS OF THE CASE STUDIES

Evidence suggests that until recently, most cases of gender-based harassment and violence in the university context in Sri Lanka were ignored by lawmakers and others in authority. The situation at the University of X is no exception. Most cases of gender-based harassment and violence have not been recorded here. Keeping this issue in mind, we adopted a mixed-method approach for data collection in order to gain a better understanding of the major issue of this research. Initially we collected data from our respondents through a questionnaire survey. After the survey, we conducted 47 case studies (21 staff members, of which 19 are female and 2 are male; 26 students, of which 21 are female and 5 are male). This helped us to triangulate data.

In identifying the cases, we used sources such as student counselors, the university health center, wardens and sub-wardens, marshals, staff, and students. We listened to 32 individuals' narratives related to the violent incidents they faced. However, the 47 respondents were the key informants of this research, and we collected data from them through observation and face-to-face interviews. Sex-disaggregated data of the key informants are presented in Table 4.7, while types of gender-based harassment and violence that we learned of during the data collection process are presented in Table 4.8.

Five male students were key informants for the research, and they all reported having experienced severe ragging that included forced sexual acts and sexual cruelty. Of the two male staff members, one had been forced by a female colleague to go on a date, and the other faced some incidents related to character assassination, which tarnished his academic career. Data revealed that three female staff and one student had 'consensual' sexual

Table 4.7 Sex-disaggregated data of the key informants of the research

Category	Distribution of age group				Academic qualification				Marital status	
	20–26	27–39	40–49	50–61	PhD	MA/MSc	First degree	Student	Married	Single
Number	26	13	6	2	5	9	7	26	11	36

Table 4.8 Types of gender-based harassment and violence that took place

Type/category of incidents	Number of incidents
Sexual attacks	6
Rape	3
Stabbed to death	1
Unwanted abortion	2
Sexual cruelty	2
Wife battering	3
Character assassination and intervening in recruitment and promotion	5
Forced dating	4
Verbal abuse due to rejection of sexual favors	3
Touching and patting	5
Demand for sexual favor	4
Threat of rape due to rejection of student leader's decisions	2
Ragging of a sexual nature	7

relations with four male staff members. Although some view these relations as 'misusing the power of senior male colleagues to exploit powerless female juniors,' the authors observed and heard from various sources, including these women on different occasions, who spoke of how they use male power to their own advantages, and how they feel 'privileged' to have such intimate relations with powerful males (such as the head of the department and director of an institute, etc.). However, for most of the female informants, it was a matter of suffering due to harassment and violence. No female academic staff member used violence against men, but some senior female students have used violence against junior women. In terms of frequency, only 39 percent of the cases of violence ended with just one episode; 30 percent of the cases were victimized 4–10 times, while around 31 percent of the victims were exposed to violence 2–3 times.

Data reveal that most of the incidents happened in public places such as lecture rooms, student common rooms, individual staff rooms, the university park, behind the gymnasium and student center, on a public bus or train, or on a street. However, wife beating happened in both public and private locations such as the home or university staff quarters. Evidence suggests that most of the violent events took place during the evening or night.

Gender-Based Violence at the University of X: The Consequence

Fourteen victims whom we learned about in this study went to a hospital or the university health center. One died at a hospital, three had abortions after getting treatment from local Ayurvedic physicians but later were admitted to a hospital, one was treated for a broken arm, the rest obtained medications. Seven went to see psychiatrists. One case was reported to the police station, another five were reported to the university authority, and seven asked for help from teachers, friends, or family members. One case was resolved by the court and another by the university authority. A recent case has been investigated by a senate-appointed special committee. This female victim met the department head and the dean, both male, five times. At first, the department head did not take her complaint seriously, and she was chased out of his office by the dean. As a result, she submitted a written complaint to the vice-chancellor. In two other cases, the authority took no action. The rest of the victims did not ask for any help from anybody, fearing that the incident could become known to others, or out of fear of further harassment/violence and adverse consequences, or out of fear of unnecessary intervention in matters related to their medical examination, permanent recruitment, and promotion. Most of the victims requested assistance only when the violence resulted in serious physical injury, pregnancy, or a threat to their academic career/examination results. Data reveal that 7 staff members and 12 students shared their experiences with teachers, friends, or family, and only 3 of them obtained assistance. Eight victims reported that they were discouraged by teachers or friends and were asked to keep quiet.

According to the narratives given by two young female graduates, they were not given the opportunity to join the department even though they passed the final-year examination with a first class (honors). Both women consider that they were denied the opportunity because they rejected a senior lecturer's request for sexual favors. One female staff member, when referring to her negative experiences, expressed fear that she might be denied promotion due to having rejected her department head's sexual advances. One married victim blamed her husband for having extra-marital affairs with some young students and for neglecting her family. However, she stated that "I don't mind if my husband sleeps with a thousand women, it is not an issue for me, if he maintains the family by taking care of the children, because the family is more important."

One female respondent mentions that her husband is always suspicious about her to the extent that when she gets home at the end of the day, he smells her clothes to check whether she has had any physical contact with anybody at her workplace. According to her, "wife beating is a normal practice at my home, especially on those days that I get home late. My only worry is our son, who is planning to take revenge on the father one day." One battered woman believes that she faces violence because of her property, received from her late husband: "Immediately after my husband's sudden death, his brother came to live with my family. Since I am young and have three little children, I accepted him as a protector to us. However, later he tried to kill me when I refused to give him a piece of land owned by my late husband."

Three female staff members who had 'consensual' sexual relations with senior male staff members are married and pretend or demonstrate that their relationship is similar to "a relation of an academic child and a father." They speak openly about their lovers in the university community and appreciate the assistance they receive in doing their post-graduate studies, research, and so forth. They and their lovers treat each other in a very decent manner, they claim. Husbands and family members of these women know all three men, and they too treat these males as "very senior, helpful teachers." However, all three wives of the male staff members have several conflicts with their husbands' on-staff lovers, and have even come to the university premises to address the issues. This was mainly after they received scandalous information about their husbands' "secret trips, exchanging gifts, and attending events together." One wife committed suicide, but there were even rumors that she was killed by the male professor. Meanwhile, all three female academics who were involved in these affairs completed their post-graduate studies, published research reports, articles, and books with the support of the male seniors, and have been able to climb the academic ladder. Similarly, a female student has received a first class (honors) due to 'generous support' given by her supervisor, and she expected to join the university staff. However, due to information received by the university authority regarding the sexual affair between her and the male teacher (her supervisor), she was not selected for the position.

Three first-year female students have been severely ragged by male as well as female senior students, and one of them states that "during the rag season, my femininity was thoroughly abused. I had to describe my body and explain the specific purpose of the female organ in front of them. They forced me to elaborate on what menstruation is, and on what it meant to be a lesbian. I became quite distraught and weak." A female fresher expresses that "during ragging, some of us faced utterly helpless and very painful situations. The psychological shock and unpleasantness we suffered during ragging in the first few weeks at university will definitely affect us for the rest of our life." Two boys were sexually assaulted and forced to do illicit activities with seniors. One left the university and, after psychiatric treatment for nearly one year, re-enrolled with the next batch of students. The other boy left the hostel and, thanks to support and counseling from his family and some staff members, had been able to continue his studies after the two-month ragging period.

Another girl highlights the despicable behavior of certain *Bhikkhu*[5] students while watching a drama: "As soon as the lights went off, a *Bhikkhu* seated behind us stretched his legs and started stroking my back. I turned around and started glaring at him but he seemed quite unconcerned. I wanted to shout and scold him but, fearing the reaction of the society, I kept quiet." A young female graduate told about why she was unable to obtain a permanent position:

---

[5] A *Bhikkhu* is an ordained male monastic ('monk') in Buddhism.

My supervisor helped me a great deal when I was doing my final year of research. However, after I joined the staff as a temporary lecturer, I realized that he was trying to make advances. He told me "You can share my office since you don't have one. I will drop you at your boarding house. I like thin, smart girls like you." However, since I avoided him, he started spreading nasty rumors. Finally, as the head of the department, he influenced the university authority and interfered in the selection. As a result, I was not selected for the permanent position.

Another female staff member notes her experience: "One day while I was reading some reports in the library, I realized that the library assistant who helped me find reading materials was hanging around me. All of a sudden, he started squeezing his private part. I got my books and ran out of the library."

Two male staff members say that they too faced gender-based harassment and one tells how "a final-year girl in his class repeatedly requested, tried to motivate, and even pushed him to date her." Another mentions that "I treat students as our children, and when they come to their final year, we establish very close relations, mainly in supervising their research. However, a male colleague misinterpreted this relationship and spread various rumors about me which not only had a negative impact on my career but also adversely affected my personal and family life." Data presented in Table 4.9 reveal that a vast majority of the respondents consider that the harassment/violence has had negative effects on their life.

Table 4.9   Effects of gender-based harassment and violence

Type of effect	Number of incidents
Major physical injury	5
University drop-out	2
Academic year loss	1
Psychological sufferings	8
Became socially inactive	4
Severe situation at the workplace	4
Denied employment opportunity at the university	2
Fear in relation to marriage	2
Fear of not getting future promotion	3
Negative impact on academic life	7
Chronic headache	1
Other	8

Root Causes of Gender-Based Harassment and Violence

It is extremely difficult to recognize the factors responsible for many forms of harassment and violence in the university because the majority of incidents remain unreported. However, interviews with victims, identified staff, and students, and observations of the related incidents have revealed some contributing causes. The study suggests that several complex and interconnected factors occurring in various social, cultural, and structural contexts have left women and some junior men vulnerable to such violence. Around 70 percent of interviewees and victims report that harassment and violence occur because women and junior men (first year) are in weaker and helpless positions, or that they fail to resist in active ways. According to them, generally harassment and violence directed at women or junior men are a manifestation of historically unequal power relations between men and women or senior men and junior men. Factors such as patriarchal structures, socio-economic forces, belief in the superiority of males and the inferiority of females, gender-stereotype attitudes, traditions, and practices have all contributed to creating such imbalances of power relations.

Many respondents say (and we observe) that men are generally motivated to commit such violence due to the attitude of sexual entitlement of men; they think it is their right to have sexual activities with women. Thus, violence is a means by which men construct masculine identities linked to aggressiveness, male honor, superiority, or dominance. The majority of women and some men say that many men use violence as a tool to demonstrate their manliness and to control their female partners or even junior men. In the university, the majority of male teachers, administrators, and senior students try to present themselves as masculine actors. They demonstrate their power, authority, position, and ability and perceive women as powerless, emotional, and weak. On the other hand, when male informants describe university policies, inquiries, and punishments given to males, and when they see women's ability to use their sexuality to advance academically, the male informants then see themselves as in a vulnerable position. These shifting representations evidence the relational construction of gender and the instability of masculine subjectivities (Butler, 1990).

Around 65 percent of the interviewed men and around 40 percent of the interviewed women say that many women like touching, pinching, teasing, and so on. According to them, the notions of masculinity and femininity, gender roles, characteristics, behavior patterns, norms, and values have a direct link to male dominance. This results in the 'natural authority' of the male in decision-making, the notion of male ownership of women, men's aggressive sexual behavior and desire, women's acceptance of violence as a natural activity of men, and the protection of the 'purity' of feminine characteristics by men.

Around 62 percent of female informants state that due to fear of losing the relationship with men or motivation of men, or the trust they have in their partners, they allow men to engage in sexual activities with others. Some of them believe that if the men are not allowed, they will leave the women. Additional root causes are feminine norms such as tolerance or acceptance of gender-based violence and harassment, and the perception of men as protectors and owners of women. Around 54 percent of men and 28 percent of women who participated in the study believe that due to some acts of women, men become violent. In other words, women are also responsible for men's violent acts.

Some respondents, both men and women, point out that many female students and young female academic staff members maintain sexual relationships with senior male colleagues. They willingly do so in order to achieve their aspirations: to obtain good grades on exams, to gain admittance to post-graduate studies, and to gain promotions. These informants point out that some university members view such matters as harassment or violence, but that being born female also has its privileges. As one male student leader puts it: "Some females maintain sexual relations with male teachers mainly for their career advancement." As the case studies demonstrate, these women tend to use their sexuality and gender identities in a beneficial way. Such female academics continue to maintain the Sri Lankan image of 'reputed lady,' while using powerful men to achieve their academic goals and at the same time maintain their family life without any disturbances. They play their traditional motherly role as teacher, counselor, and mentor in the university, but at the same time use their sexual freedom as 'modern women' to continue their extra-marital affairs in a very subtle way. Evidence suggests, however, that such relationships often have violent outcomes if the aspirations are not achieved. Some women even believe that they should endure hardship caused by men, who are stronger and more powerful than they are. The women therefore expect and accept that there are unequal power relationships between men and women. This belief breeds men's dominance and the abuse of women when an opportunity arises.

Evidence suggests that female staff and students are harassed or marginalized inadvertently by some discriminatory policies or social customs and practices within the university, thereby introducing new inequalities or reproducing previously held disadvantageous positions. The university's patriarchal structures have perpetuated structural violence and continue to do women harm.

CONCLUSION

The study concludes that no particular or single factor causes gender-based harassment and violence. Unequal power relations, gender identities and status, gender performance, and doing gender within the patriarchal structure of the University of X have been the main factors for such activities. Since more women and junior men keep quiet about such activities than do senior men, the existing unequal relations, identities, gendered subjectivities, cultural norms, and values are consciously or unconsciously constructed or reinforced by the university community. According to the majority of the respondents, "men mainly justify and rationalize their violence against women, violence is gendered in practice, and the society accepts it as 'normal.'" This study also finds that through violent acts, men show their ability to control their partners, and in this way, to construct their understanding of masculine identities.

Guided by theoretical work that characterizes gender as performance (Butler, 1990, 1993) and doing gender (West & Fenstermarker, 1995), we contend that perpetrators contribute to constructing masculine identities through harassment and violence, while victims, mainly women, contribute to constructing feminine identities through silent acceptance or not questioning violence. In addition, as Hewamanne (2010) says, some women take efforts to negotiate ever-shifting roles and expectations of gender and sexuality. Several educated female staff members, mainly from rural regions, try, on the one hand, to perform as "good, docile, disciplined, nice, caring motherly type teachers," but on the other hand, try to have "secret sexual relations" with powerful male colleagues in the university. They use their freedom to try to climb the academic ladder with the assistance of the more powerful male colleagues. This shows that such women find ways to negotiate in-between identities that allow them to enjoy the benefits and freedom of university life and sexuality.

Combating gender-based harassment and violence is a challenging and difficult task. This may require us to step out of our comfort zones, rethink some of the most fundamental socio-cultural beliefs, traditions, and practices we have embraced, and which have for many years become embedded in ourselves. This requires questioning the very foundation of our understanding of ourselves and our social relations, and changing our attitudes and perceptions that are gender discriminatory. More importantly, it is necessary to develop a university culture in which equality, equity, and human rights are protected, promoted, and fulfilled. Overcoming gender-based harassment and violence requires radical action in terms of building awareness. Clear policies and measures need to be taken to ensure gender equality, and appropriate mechanism should be established to investigate cases and support victims of gender-based harassment and violence. These measures, however, are scanty in the University of X.

REFERENCES

Adkins, L. (1995). *Gendered work: Sexuality, family and the labour market.* Buckingham: Open University Press.

Beninger, C. (2013). Combating sexual harassment in schools in Sub-Saharan Africa: Legal strategies under regional and international human rights law. *African Human Rights Law Journal, 13*, 281–301.

Butler, J. (1990). *Gender trouble: Feminism and the subversion of identity.* London: Routledge.

Butler, J. (1993). *Bodies that matter: On the discursive limits of sex.* New York: Routledge.

Commonwealth Secretariat. (2000). *A Commonwealth vision for women.* London: Commonwealth Secretariat.

Connell, R. W. (1987). *Gender and power.* Stanford: Stanford University Press.

Dziech, B., & Weiner, L. (1990). *The lecherous professor: Sexual harassment on campus.* Chicago: University of Illinois Press.

Gunarathne, C. (2014, January). *Sexual and gender-based violence with special reference to higher educational institutions.* Paper presented at the National Consultative Workshop on Preventing Sexual and Gender-Based Violence in Universities, Colombo, Sri Lanka.

Gunawardena, N., Weerasinghe, M., Rajapakse, L., Wijesekara, P., & Chathuranga, P. W. P. (2011). Romance, sex and coercion: Insights into undergraduate relationships. *Sri Lanka Journal of Psychiatry, 2*(2), 54–59.

Heise, L., Ellsberg, M., & Gottemoeller, M. (1999). Ending violence against women. *Population Reports.* Baltimore: Johns Hopkins University.

Hewamanne, S. (2010). Suicide narratives and in-between identities among Sri Lankan factory workers. *Ethnology, 49*(1), 1–22.

Jayasundere, R. (2009). *Understanding gendered violence against women in Sri Lanka*. Colombo: Women Defining Peace.

Kimmel, M. (2000). *The gendered society*. New York: Oxford University Press.

Leach, F. (2013). Corruption as abuse of power: Sexual violence in educational institutions. In G. Sweeney, K. Despota, & S. Lindner (Eds.), *Transparency international, global corruption report: Education* (pp. 88–98). Abingdon, Oxon: Routledge.

Liyanage, K. (1996). Women in higher education: Perspectives from the University of Peradeniya. In R. A. L. H. Gunawardena, B. R. R. N. Mendis, & M. A. Careem (Eds.), *Proceedings of the annual research sessions* (pp. 21–48). Peradeniya: University of Peradeniya.

Liyanage, K. (2000). Sexual harassment in educational institutions. In *Sexual harassment in Sri Lanka: Women's experiences and policy implications* (Study Series No. 19) (pp. 81–90). Colombo: Centre for Women's Research.

Liyanage, K., Vandort, L., & Paramaguru, M. (2012). A study on gender inequality practices in the University of Peradeniya. In *Conference proceedings, 13th national convention on women's studies* (pp. 1–26). Colombo: Centre for Women's Research.

MacKinnon, C. A. (1979). *Sexual harassment of working women*. New Haven, CT: Yale.

Mawbima. (2016). Weekly Sinhala language newspaper (p. 4). Colombo: Standard Newspapers (pvt.) Ltd.

Perera, J., Abeynayake, S. D., & Galabada, D. P. (2006). Gender based harassment among medical students. In *Proceedings of the 10th national convention on women's studies*. Colombo: Centre for Women's Research.

Sharma, Y. (2013). Harassment, sexual abuse corrupts education worldwide. *University World News*.

Till, F. J. (1980). *Sexual harassment: A report on sexual harassment of students*. Washington, DC: National Advisory Council on Women's Educational Programme. Retrieved March 15, 2016, from eric.ed.gov/?id=ED197242

United Nations. (1995). *Fourth world conference on women: Platform for action and the Beijing declaration*. New York: UN Department of Public Information.

UN Declaration on the Elimination of Violence Against Women. (1993). Retrieved September 21, 2015, from http://www.un.org/documents/ga/res/48/a48r104.htm

Universities Act No. 16 of 1978. (1978). Colombo: University Grants Commission.

West, C., & Fenstermarker, S. (1995). Doing difference. *Gender and Society, 9*, 8–37.

West, C., & Zimmerman, D. H. (1987). Doing gender. *Gender and Society, 1*(2), 125–151.

CHAPTER 5

'Through the Glass Ceiling, over the Glass Cliff?' Women Leaders in Bangladeshi Public Administration

Syeda Lasna Kabir

INTRODUCTION

A large increase in female employment has become the most noticeable social transformational phenomenon around the world. As a result, women have made strides in the public sector, but they continue to face challenges while climbing the management ladder (Sabharwal, 2013; Bowling, Cristine, Jennifer, & Write, 2006; Riccucci, 2009). Different metaphors have been used to document these challenges: sticky floors, a glass wall, a glass escalator, and a glass ceiling.[1] The glass ceiling is most often associated with working women, and research suggests that women are 18

---

[1] 'Glass ceiling' refers to the barriers women are confronted with in their attempt to rise to leadership positions. Glass walls are barriers that hold women in certain types of agencies that are traditionally viewed as 'feminine' in nature. Glass escalators refer to occupational segregation experienced by gender wherein men in female-dominated positions are promoted to leadership positions at a much faster rate than women. Sticky floors hold women down to low-level jobs and prevent them from seeking high management positions.

S. Lasna Kabir (✉)
Department of Public Administration, University of Dhaka, Dhaka, Bangladesh

© The Author(s) 2020
I. Jamil et al. (eds.), *Gender Mainstreaming in Politics, Administration and Development in South Asia*,
https://doi.org/10.1007/978-3-030-36012-2_5

percent less likely to be promoted than are their male co-workers (Pew Research Center, 2018).

Though women in the workforce are shattering the glass ceiling to reach senior management positions in the public sector, there is limited research on what happens to these women once they reach higher leadership positions. Do they continue to face challenges despite breaking through the glass ceiling? It is vigorously argued that women managers in upper-level government services tend to be evaluated less favorably than men, to receive less support from their peers, to be excluded from important networks, and to receive greater scrutiny and criticism even when performing exactly the same leadership roles as men (Sabharwal, 2013). Women in leadership positions face an uphill battle with these challenges. The challenges may set them up for failure, thus pushing them over the edge—a phenomenon called the 'glass cliff' (Sabharwal, 2013).

The glass cliff is a metaphor put forward by Ryan and Haslam (2005, 2007), which relates to the challenges women face in leadership positions. The risk of 'failing off the cliff' is further explained by factors such as lack of influence in policy-making, lack of empowerment, organizational inequity/injustice, and dissatisfaction with the balance between work and family life (Sabharwal, 2013; Naff, 1994). But there can be other factors too, such as a lack of involvement by women executives because of self-imposed barriers and a lack of confidence that they can contribute as much as can men. This points to the ideological power of dominant cultural norms that influences women. One example of an outcome would be women who support patriarchy. The majority of studies on the glass cliff phenomenon focus only on Western countries. Very few address the region of South Asia, and even fewer discuss Bangladesh. Different study findings (Shetu & Ferdous, 2017; IPS, 2019) indicate that women professionals in senior positions in Bangladesh are most likely to face the glass ceiling, and if they achieve elite positions, they will most likely come to the brink of the glass cliff.

This chapter attempts to analyze the factors accounting for women's shattering of the glass ceiling by advancing to top positions in Bangladesh's civil services (BCS), and what those factors may indicate about why women have not made more progress at this level. The chapter is divided into four parts. The first part provides the methodology for the study followed by a theoretical discussion on the above topic by mentioning previous academic research related to the glass ceiling and the glass cliff. The second discusses the status of women in the BCS, some constitutional provisions, and government policy regarding women's advancement in the BCS discussed in the chapter. Part three determines the factors impacting the glass cliff in the BCS context and suggests some policy options for how to cope with it, to improve the employment status of women and their movement up the BCS' organizational ladder. The chapter's fourth part presents concluding thoughts.

METHODOLOGY

This section will discuss the procedures and methods used to investigate whether discriminatory practices in terms of 'glass cliff' exist in senior positions in the BCS and to identify possible measures to address them. To analyze this issue, in-depth face-to-face and/or telephone interviews were conducted. All the interviews were confidential and conducted individually, such that each participant could describe her personal experiences and/or opinions about women's employment conditions in government services as openly as possible. In total, 26 female civil servants from the BCS were selected through purposive sampling.[2] The aim was to map their experiences of seeking advancement to decision-making ranks and, if they already had achieved a senior post, to discover the nature of their experiences there. Respondents are from the BCS cadre and working under three ministries. Given that the majority of participants report having worked in different ministries during their tenure, we may assume that their experiences are not only limited to their current ministry. All of them are married. The average tenure of the participants in the central government is more than 20 years. The interviews were carried out over a six-month period, from June to November 2017. Interview questions mainly dealt with perceived obstacles to career advancement for women bureaucrats as they seek senior positions in the BCS.

Theory: Conceptual Framework for the 'Glass Ceiling' and 'Glass Cliff'

The dominant metaphor that frames the challenges women face in attaining upward mobility has been 'the glass ceiling' (Sabharwal, 2013). The

[2] The small size of the sample may raise concern about a lack of representation of the population. However, respondents often said that they were reporting what they had discussed with their subordinates and colleagues in their workplaces. We can therefore assume that the research findings represent views from a larger body of women in senior positions in Bangladesh's public administration.

metaphor was first used by Carol Hymowitz and Timothy Schellhardt in a *Wall Street Journal* article in 1986, to describe the invisible barriers women face as they approach the top tier of management in organizations. The metaphor was then used by Morrison, White, and Velsor (1987) in their book entitled *Breaking the Glass Ceiling: Can Women Reach the Top of America's Largest Corporations?* The three authors define the glass ceiling as "a transparent barrier that kept women from rising above a certain level in corporations" (p. 13). Since then, the metaphor has been adopted in studies across various disciplines, including public administration (Kerr, Miller, & Reid, 2002). There may be multiple factors that block women's advancement to top positions (Choi & Park, 2014; Naff, 1994), and several competing approaches have categorized them into three models: the human capital model, the socio-psychological model, and the systemic model (Choi & Park, 2014).

The *human capital model* explains that women may stay in lower positions by their own choice (Choi & Park, 2014). In other words, women tend to be less committed to their career and therefore invest less in their human capital, for instance, their education, work experience, resources, and finances (Choi & Park, 2014). This explanation can be deepened by drawing on terms such as 'ideological barrier' or Lukes' 'third dimension of power'. Lukes calls his three-dimensional view the "supreme and most insidious exercise of power", as it allows rulers to shape the preferences and perception of the masses as well as prevent them from having grievances (Lukes, 1974, p. 23). This is because, as Lukes argues, the people will "see or imagine no alternative" to the existing order, "or because they see it as natural and unchangeable, or because they value it as divinely ordained and beneficial" (Lukes, 1974, p. 23). Put simply, ideological power allows some people to influence other people's wishes and thoughts, even making them want things that are opposed to their own self-interest (e.g., causing women to support a patriarchal society). The *socio-psychological model* explains that psycho-social factors such as sex-roles stereotypes may pose strong barriers to women's advancement to managerial positions (Newman, 1993). Women's traditional roles, for instance, taking care of children and serving their husbands, lead society to expect that women will play supporting roles rather than supervising or leading roles. Such roles have created stereotypical perceptions about women, for instance, that they are unqualified for managerial positions. The *systemic model* focuses on barriers embedded in organizational policies and practices that constrain a group's access to top positions. Unequal opportunities and power relations between women and men may impede women from gaining access to important resources (e.g., informal and collegial networks, mentor networks) that may facilitate moving up to top positions (Choi & Park, 2014; Newman, 1993).

The theoretical explanation for why fewer women than men are in leadership positions is provided by many scholars and also well noted in the literature. Leadership is considered a quality mostly associated with men, and most of the traits cited in the literature for an effective leader have been what are considered typically male traits: risk-taking, decisiveness, being direct, assertive, and ambitious (Vinkenburg, Van Engen, Eagly, Mary, & Johannesen, 2011). Theories like 'think-manager-think-male' (Koenig, Eagly, Mitchell, & Ristikari, 2011; Agars, 2004), the social role theory (Eagly, Wendy, & Amanda, 2000), and the role incongruity theory (Koenig et al., 2011) further elaborate the role of men in leadership positions. The think-manager-think-male framework dominates the leadership literature. This theory argues that both male and female managers see the manager's job as masculine and a better fit for males, who are deemed emotionally stable, aggressive, possessing leadership abilities, self-reliant, competitive, self-confident, objective, ambitious, well informed, and forceful. Another theory that builds on the think-manager-think-male framework is the social role theory, which examines differing leadership styles of men and women, with men being understood as more *agentic*, that is, aggressive, assertive, independent, forceful in negotiations, self-confident, and ambitious, while women demonstrate *communal* behavior: they are seen as gentle, kind, affectionate, empathetic, nurturing, sensitive, and helpful (Sabharwal, 2013; Eagly & Karau, 2002). Although these differences form the basis of the social role theory, Eagly and Karau (2002) argue that the role congruity model builds on it and explains the prejudices held against women in their social and leadership roles. The incongruity arises when there is a conflict between the social roles that women hold in a society and the requirements of being in leadership roles. Role incongruity, along with communal and agentic meanings ascribed to leadership roles of women and men (and the perpetuating masculine stereotype), has given way to the more recent glass cliff theory, which aims to explain the challenges women face in leadership positions (Sabharwal, 2013).

Glass Cliff

The 'glass cliff' refers to women being more likely to rise to positions of organizational leadership in times of crisis than in times of success, and men being more likely to achieve those positions in prosperous times. This term was first used in the business literature by Ryan and Haslam (2005, p. 83) and refers to the phenomenon whereby "women may be preferentially placed in leadership roles that are associated with an increased risk of negative consequences. As a result, to the extent that they are achieving leadership roles, these may be more precarious than those occupied by men."

Glass cliffs seem to arise as a result of a combination of social and psychological constructs. The former arises as a form of overt sexism (injustice and inequity issues), whereas the latter is a more subtle dimension reflecting a desire to appoint women to high-risk positions—setting them up for failure (Sabharwal, 2013; Ryan & Haslam, 2005, 2007).

In Ryan and Haslam's analysis, women were being set up to fail, whether intentionally or not. Such failure would reflect poorly not only on the woman in question, but quite possibly on female candidates who followed after them. The American sociologist Glass and his colleague Cook conducted research and found that *white women and people of color are significantly more likely than white men to be promoted to CEO in weakly performing firms.*[3]

Other researchers began looking for evidence of the glass cliff beyond the corporate world. They found it in education, where women are more likely to have leadership positions in failing school districts. They found it in political elections, where women are more likely to run in unwinnable contests; and in political leadership, where women are more often elevated during periods of political instability. There is therefore plenty of evidence for the glass cliff phenomenon. Back in the UK, Michelle Ryan wanted to know why it happened. Was it necessarily driven by discrimination, or

---

[3] Glass and Cook assembled a database of all the CEO transitions in the Fortune 500, male and female, over a 15-year period. Then they looked at the financial health of those firms, not just their stock price. If the female CEOs fail to improve the 'weakly performing firms' then they are often replaced by a man. They *termed this the 'savior effect'. In other words, the firm experimented with this nontraditional leader, perhaps trying to signal that it was headed in a bold new direction or was aggressively going to address a decline in performance. And if that did not happen, these leaders tended to be blamed and replaced, back to normal—bringing in the typically white male leader to navigate the firm out of crisis.*

some other nefarious instinct? To explore this question, Ryan and his colleague set up some lab experiments. They found that *when everything is going well, stereotypically masculine traits are more likely to be seen as desirable. If share prices are up or steady, then people are more likely to want leaders who are ambitious, forceful, and competitive. These are stereotypically masculine traits. This is a finding that has been in the literature since the 1970s, and it is associated with the afore-mentioned think-manager-think-male tendency. When things are going badly, people prefer female managers: 'think-crisis-think-female'.* One explanation for this is that *women might be better leaders in times of crisis, for, as some* research indicates, *someone who is good with people, kind-hearted, a good communicator, tactful, and sociable can be a successful leader when things are going poorly. Now, it cannot be said that all women have these traits, or that no men have these traits, but these are our stereotypically feminine traits.* There is yet another theory regarding think-crisis-think-female which says that the organizations that offer women tough jobs believe they win either way: if the woman succeeds, the company is better off. If she fails, the company is not worse off, for she can be blamed, the company gets credit for having been egalitarian and progressive, and can return to its prior practice of appointing men.[4]

Factors That Cause the Glass Cliff

To examine whether women in senior executive positions in the BCS are more likely to fall off the glass cliff, the study analyzes four factors that create or enhance glass cliffs. The first factor is *influence over policies/decision-making* as an underexplored cause for glass cliffs. Ryan and Haslam (2005, 2007) take note of the fact that despite breaking through the glass ceiling, women continue to have limited leadership opportunities and less authority than men to make decisions. Other studies also indicate that women who exert a relatively large amount of influence on policy-making are less likely to experience glass cliffs than are those who exert less influence at work (Sabharwal, 2013).

The second factor is *empowerment.* Empowerment is usually seen as a goal of attaining equality among group members rather than gaining power and control (Lincoln, Travers, Ackers, & Wilkinson, 2002). There are two approaches to empowerment debated in the literature: the one is

[4]www.cambridgeblog.org/2010/01/glass-cliff.

termed rational, the other psychological. The rational approach takes place when superiors relegate power to their subordinates (House, Umberson, & Landies, 1988), whereas the psychological approach focuses on enhancing feelings of self-efficacy among the parties concerned (Conger & Kanungo, 1988). Various empirical evidence suggest there is a significant relationship between empowerment and job performance, job satisfaction, and turnover (Sabharwal, 2013). The current study will refer to empowerment as the feeling and recognition employees achieve of personal belonging, making a meaningful contribution, legitimate and appropriate status, and encouragement to innovate. It is perceived that empowered women are less likely to experience glass cliffs than do those who are less empowered at work.

The third factor is *organizational justice or equity*. This is the perception about the fairness in treatment that employees receive from their employers. It is a concept that originates from research in social psychology (Greenberg, 1990). Three main forms of organizational justice have been found in the literature: distributive (fairness of outcome), procedural (fairness of process), and interactional (fairness by employee's supervisor). For the purpose of the research, organizational justice and equity refer to fairness in terms of workload, compensation, performance-based rewards, and inclusion in senior leadership positions in the workforce. Inequitable treatment gives rise to negative emotions that can create additional stressors at one's job, resulting in job dissatisfaction and turnover (Fox, Spector, & Miles, 2001). It can therefore be argued that women reporting equitable treatment at work are less likely to experience glass cliffs than do those who experience inequities at work.

The fourth variable is *work/life balance* issues. "By nature it is an all-consuming job and it does take a toll on the family" (Associated Press, 2011; Sabharwal, 2013). These are the words of Michele Flournoy, the most senior female official in the history of Pentagon, when she announced she was stepping down as the chief policy advisor to Defense Secretary Leon Panetta. After spending three years in one of the most demanding jobs, Flournoy, at the age of 51, felt compelled to leave because she was unable to strike a balance between work/life issues. Women opt out of senior management positions when they need to look after their children or elderly family members (Eagly & Carli, 2007). When confronted with a choice between family and career, women often choose the former. Thus, work/life imbalances lead to glass cliffs (Ryan & Haslam, 2007).

Based on the above discussion, we can assume that women reporting higher satisfaction with work/life balance are less likely to experience glass cliffs than those who experience work/life imbalance. Based on this theory and other evidence outlined above, the following section will discuss an overview of the advancement of women in the BCS and factors affecting the glass cliff phenomenon in Bangladesh's public administration.

An Overview of the Advancement of Women in the BCS

The higher-level BCS is horizontally categorized into 27 cadres[5] and vertically into 6 ranks. Appointment to the BCS is at the rank of assistant secretary (or its equivalent in some other cadres). The rank classification system has been in operation since British imperial rule, and recruits are not appointed to specific positions but to ranks. They remain in the civil service doing a variety of jobs until retirement.

Recruitment is through a competitive examination that assesses a candidate's performance in various subjects (both compulsory and elective), a psychological test, and an interview. Scores in each of these components are combined to indicate overall performance. Those who receive a high score normally get into the cadre of their choice (Zafarullah, 2000).

Quota System in the BCS

After independence, the government found that in the public service, not only women, but ethnic groups, religious groups, and some of the regions were under-represented. The Constitution,[6] as a result, indicated its faith

---

[5] Cadre/Non-cadre: The cadre distinguishes the particular occupational group to which a civil servant may belong, either at the time of recruitment or subsequently, through promotion from a lower non-cadre post. A Class I cadre officer has wider promotion prospect within his/her own service, where as a non-cadre Class I officer's promotion prospect is much more restricted. The 27 BCS cadres include BCS administration, education, trade, economic services, and so on. All cadre officers are Class I officers, but all Class I officers are not cadre officers. When counted as a single group, officers of all the cadres comprise less than half of the actual number of Class I officials.

[6] The third section of Bangladesh's Constitution contains provisions for fundamental rights. Rights and opportunities for women are the following (The Constitution of the People's Republic of Bangladesh, 1972, pp. 6, 7, 10): Article 27: Equality of all citizens before law and equal protection under law. Article 28(1): No discrimination on the grounds of religion, race, caste, sex, or place of birth. Article 28(2): Equal opportunity for men and

Table 5.1   Administration of the quota system[a] (until 2018)

Distribution of vacancies	Gazetted posts (Classes I and II) (%)	Non-gazetted posts (Classes III and IV) (%)
Merit	44	Nil
Physically handicapped/mentally retarded (disabled)	1	10
Women	10	15
Freedom fighters	30	30
Tribal people	5	5
General district merit	10	30
Ansar and Village Defence Party (VDP)		10

Source: Khan (2015)

[a]The quota system was introduced through an executive order in 1972 and had been amended several times since. From 1972 to 1976, 20 percent were recruited on merit. Merit-based recruitment was increased to 40 percent in 1976. This percentage of merit-based recruitment continued until 1985, when it was increased to 45 percent. Until the abolition, about 56 percent of government jobs had been reserved for candidates from various quotas. Of this, 30 percent were for freedom fighters' children and grandchildren, 10 percent for women, 10 percent for people from underdeveloped districts, 5 percent for members of indigenous communities, and 1 percent for physically challenged people

in the broad tenets of equal employment opportunities, which were to govern the recruitment and selection of public personnel (Zafarullah & Khan, 1989). In fact, recognizing the urgency of the problem, the government adopted quotas (reservation of posts), which were reflected in the Interim Recruitment Policy of 1972. The government followed this policy, with various modifications from time to time, until 2018. The quota system was designed to achieve greater equity in the representation of all regions and groups in the civil service by reserving positions and giving preference to certain sections of the population (Zafarullah & Khan, 1989). Table 5.1 shows the quota distribution in the BSC until 2018.

Thus, the Government of Bangladesh (GoB) made special arrangements to enhance female participation in the civil service by reserving a

women in all spheres of state and public life. Article 28(3): No discrimination on the grounds of religion, race, caste, sex, or place of birth in providing access to any place of public entertainment or resort, or admission to any educational institution. Article 28(4): Special measures by the state for the development of women, children, and citizens in any backward area. Article 29(1): Equal opportunity for all citizens in respect of employment of office in the service of the republic. Article 29(2): No discrimination on the grounds of religion, race, caste, sex, or place of birth in respect of any employment or office in the service of the republic.

10 percent employment quota for gazetted posts and 15 percent for non-gazetted posts for females. This policy reflects the government's good intention and desire to attain gender equality in the civil service. The gazetted post (Classes I and II) quotas were abolished by the government in 2018,[7] but there are no changes for the non-gazetted post (Classes III and IV) quotas.

Position of women in the BCS[8]

Women's participation in different cadre services is increasing day by day. Since 1982, women have taken the BCS examinations and been recruited in all cadre services on a regular basis. Their recruitment into the police cadre was banned for many years, but this has now been withdrawn, and some female officers have joined the 18th BCS (Kashem et al., 2002). In 1976, women constituted 7 percent of the total public service employment, and after the introduction of a women's quota in 1976, they came to constitute around 8 percent of the total employment strength until 1985 (Khan, 1988). In 1994, it was around 9 percent (Statistical Pocket Book of Bangladesh, 1996), and in 2002, it was 11 percent (Ministry of Establishment, GOB, 2002). By 2008, it had increased to 19 percent, and in 2018, it reached 28 percent (Statistical Pocket Book of Bangladesh, 2008). Compared to 1994, there is a three-fold increase in women's participation in ministries/secretariat posts in 2018. Furthermore, it is

[7] In the last 46 years, Bangladesh has had 218 types of quotas in public services. Because the quota system did not undergo necessary reform, it was often the case that despite having all necessary qualities, many competent candidates were not entering the public services. The country was therefore often deprived of the service of capable manpower. Well-qualified candidates experienced it as a complete waste of their time to prepare themselves for more than three or four years but then not get a job. The quota system was initiated to reduce discrimination between citizens and to facilitate the disadvantaged sections of the society, but this same system eventually ended up developing a new version of inequality. Since this faulty quota system for civil service recruitment could not continue for an indefinite period, it was abolished in September 2018. The discontinuation was abrupt (announced by the prime minister) in the wake of an anti-quota movement organized by frustrated students who claimed that the quota system was unjustified, since most posts were earmarked for freedom fighters (those who were directly involved in the war of independence) and later for their children or grandchildren.

[8] One of the major problems in obtaining data on women's employment in the civil service is that the data are often 3–4 years out of date, and much of it incomplete. It is with these limitations in mind that the data below must be regarded.

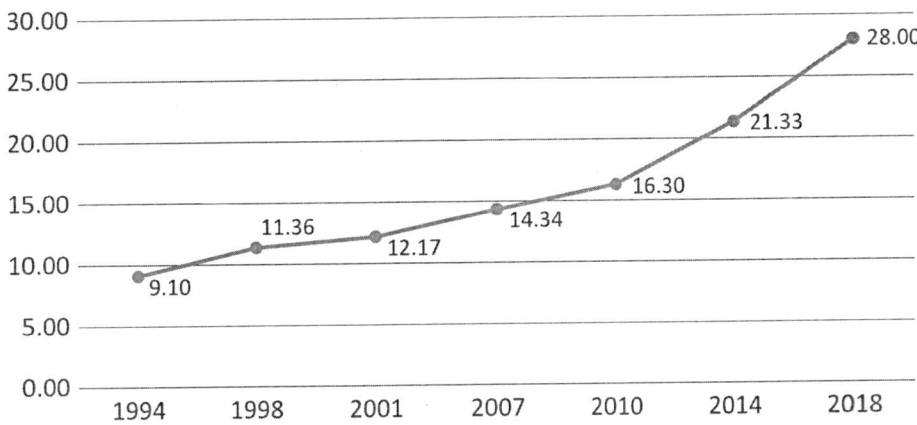

Fig. 5.1 Increase of women's participation in ministries/the Secretariat (%). (Source: Public Administration Computer Centre (PACC), MOPA. (Updated: March 29, 2014 and March 23, 2018))

observed that in the central decision-making arena, the number of female employees is also increasing. In the various ministries, 21.33 percent were females in 2014, and in 2018, it was at 28 percent. Graph 1 shows the percentage of women in the Secretariat (Fig. 5.1).[9]

FACTORS AFFECTING THE GLASS CLIFF PHENOMENON IN THE BCS

The main objective of this chapter is, as stated, to examine the glass cliff phenomenon and its impact on women in senior positions in the BCS, and to propose arguments for why it arises. Now, at the start of this third part of the chapter, it is worth emphasizing that while gender might seem like a significant factor in appointing women to positions of leadership, other factors and realities might also contribute to the success or failure of

[9] The Secretariat is collectively known as the 'nerve center' of the government. The Secretariat consists of ministries and divisions. Some ministries consist of only one division, while others contain more than one division. A secretary is the administrative head of a ministry or division. The Secretariat is dominated by administrative cadre officials, since practically three-fourths of the posts of deputy secretary, joint secretary, and additional secretary are occupied by administration cadre officers. After this distribution, it seems that only one-fourth of such posts are to be shared by officers belonging to the remaining 26 technical and professional cadres.

women in such jobs. The analysis of the glass cliff literature and in-depth interviews offer support for the arguments now proposed.

Influence over Policies/Decisions

Different types of questions were asked to map the perceptions of the respondents regarding their involvement in policy-making. The majority of respondents (20–22 out of 26) think women in senior positions are less than satisfied with their involvement in decisions that affect their work, compared to men. Sometimes they are not given full credit for their contribution to the decision-making process. They also mention that they receive more unfair judgment of their work performance than do their male colleagues. One respondent mentions that it is a common belief in Bangladeshi society that men are natural leaders. In connection to this, if an organization faces problems under a man's leadership, people will look for explanations for the problem instead of criticizing the fact that the leader is a man. By contrast, given that many people in society believe that women do not really belong in positions of authority and are unable to do a good job, if the organization in question encounters any problem under a woman's leadership, people start pointing to her gender as the explanation for the problem.

The BCS has a dual structure: bureaucracy and patriarchy. It is perceived that bureaucracy itself is a construction of male domination (organizational culture built in a patriarchal model), where women in most of the higher-level positions are either ignored (overlooked) or criticized. Some theories also suggest that in organizations where think-manager-think-male and role incongruities by gender are alive and well, the hegemonic masculine stereotype of a leader negatively impacts the ascendancy of women in leadership positions. This is why respondents mention that competitiveness and assertiveness in women's decision-making processes are viewed as negative traits. Several respondents present a similar complaint:

> Older male superiors seem to feel uncomfortable and uneasy about working with female subordinate officials. They tend to prefer male subordinates because they can easily be bullied and given undue instructions. It's harder to do that with a female subordinate. Therefore, male subordinates are preferred and they are given more favorable treatment, such as assigning some important jobs or positions that guarantee faster promotions.

Under such circumstances, women have less opportunities for growth. They exert less influence on decision-making and are less involved in important job assignments, hence more likely to experience a glass cliff (dissatisfaction, withdrawal, less efficacy in performing their assigned job/ responsibilities).

Empowerment

Although there is a strong general perception that women are incapable of making critical decisions, all respondents confirm that they felt personally empowered when posted to a decision-making level. Sometimes they observe that there is less encouragement and recognition for women who come up with a new and better way of doing things. When this happens, their enthusiasm wanes and may lead them to a glass cliff. The lack of support and recognition are also explained by shadow structures, which suggest that women's networks are less resourceful (powerful) than men's networks, even when men and women hold similar positions. Women also report that they feel more excluded than men. Some interviewees say that networking with decision-makers or office politics plays a crucial role in reaching top ranks, and that this is as important as performance. Sometimes networking takes place informally, outside office hours in clubs, but this is difficult for women to attend regularly and be part of. In other words, taking advantage of social networking (e.g., alumni association, regional affiliation) is perceived to be crucial, not only in advancing to top ranks but also in ensuring empowerment.

Another interviewee mentions that the feedback she was given for delays in being promoted to 'additional secretary' was that she did not have enough 'exposure' or 'visibility'.

This supports the proposition that men and women who have equal qualifications have probably not received the same consideration for important position assignments. Research by Sultan (2012) also supports the assumption that at senior levels, there is a feeling that women might not be as skilled as men in 'maintaining liaisons' and networking, which are necessary to secure important policy-making positions and assignments. It is also found that if they have the skill to maintain liaisons, it is portrayed negatively. As respondents from Grade III (additional secretary) mentioned, "Male colleagues (senior or junior) do not like smart, qualified, and intelligent female colleagues because they are afraid of them (the females)."

Organizational Justice or Equity

An important characteristic of glass cliff positions is that they are inherently stressful and often lead to reduced commitment and increased demotivation/turnover. This is certainly true for women in the male-dominated BCS, who experience inequities in their workload, performance appraisal, and promotions when compared with their male colleagues. Involving female civil servants in decisions that affect their jobs and their organizations, empowering them with opportunities to advance the organization's goals and priorities, and providing a fair and just environment at work are important factors that can prevent them from falling off the cliff.

Another issue mentioned by the respondents is subjective discrimination. Subjective discrimination, defined as a person's perception that she (or he) is being discriminated against (not getting equal treatment let alone equity), can be a source of high stress (Naff, 1994) and can cause low self-esteem, withdrawal, resignation, or poor work. The respondents comment that women, more often than men, face an uphill battle in proving their competence to their colleagues. They all agree that a woman must perform better than a man to get an important position. This is an indication that male colleagues often do not want to consider women as equals. This is a clear reflection of Lukes' interpretations regarding the ideological barriers (patriarchy) which women face in elite positions.

The respondents also offer several arguments in support of the view that this kind of stereotyping of women as less competent than men does occur. One respondent who is in a Grade III post mentions, "A working woman has to score twice in the same goal post to win." She adds, "I am in this position because of my ability, education, and experiences from previous challenging jobs. But I have to work ten times more to prove myself." Some batchmates also have professional jealousy, and this has made a negative impact on her career; the jealousy led to her becoming an 'officer on special duty' (OSD).[10]

Another Grade III respondent mentions that the women managing 'hard-core' ministries (which prefer masculine leadership) face more chal-

[10] Being an 'officer on special duty' (OSD) means an officer may be removed from a posting and kept on hold without any assignment. The OSD period may be as long as 5–8 years maximum for some officers. Breaking the status of OSD could be hard, as it may be seen mostly as a punishment, while short-term OSD may be meant for higher education abroad, which may require being absent from work for more than three months. At the same time, an OSD officer may enjoy all facilities as per entitlement.

lenges than do the women who manage 'soft-core' ministries. They must work hard, face lots of political pressure, sometimes feel cornered, and are even threatened with transfer or OSD.

Jobs are often 'sex typed', such that when women do not match the characteristics associated with the job (agentic traits/masculine leadership), it is assumed that they will fail. This can be particularly true when women are in the minority in management positions (decision-making positions).

Furthermore, collectivistic culture, which is characterized by a strong hierarchy, a high level of 'power distance' between seniors and underlings, and an aversion to risk-taking, may have formed strong organizational norms (masculinity) and subcultures that individual members are pressured to follow. Individuals are not allowed (socially/culturally) to take any action to correct any unfair or discriminatory practices in their organization. As one respondent clearly states: "I don't believe that filing complaints would change anything. Rather, I'm afraid of retaliations and harassment by my seniors."

Work/Life Imbalance

The study suggests that balancing family and work is one of the greatest challenges in women's career advancement in the BCS. Most respondents believe that the distinct gender identities and roles in Bangladeshi culture impose greater burdens on working women than on men, as the women pay 'double duty' in their everyday life. For example, when both spouses are working, husbands are not expected to help their wives with household work such as cooking, cleaning, and taking care of young children. One respondent describes the role of women and the burdens associated with it as follows:

> I do not see much differences in career advancement for unmarried women and men, but once married, women are treated differently (unfairly) than their male colleagues... In our (Bangladeshi) culture, women are viewed as the primary caregiver (e.g., raising children, taking care of elderly persons, housekeeping, chores, etc.) in the family, irrespective of whether they work or not.

The lack of organizational support for family values makes it even harder for women to balance between work and family life. Some respondents complain that male superiors are unwilling to take into account women's traditional roles in their family. When women ask to be excused from work on account of family issues, they are viewed as less committed to the job and the organization, which may negatively affect important personnel decisions such as performance evaluations, position assignments, and promotions. Although the GoB provides alternative work arrangements (i.e., six months' maternity leave, husbands and wives getting jobs in proximity to each other, etc.) to promote work/life balance, recent research suggests that those who take advantage of such policies—mostly women—are confronted with unfavorable treatment when it comes to promotions and important assignments. Some respondents mention that female employees who have children and also take care of elderly persons have chosen to be transferred to ministries or departments with less demanding work, thus sacrificing their career development. This is an example of the glass cliff phenomenon. One Grade V respondent mentions that she wanted to quit the job but her mother did not let her. Her mother said: "I did not educate you to do the same job like me, I will help you so you can continue with your job."

At the same time, we see the opposite scenario in a respondent who mentions that her husband, who is an established businessman, offered her money to quit her job. He said: "How much money you are getting from your job? I shall pay you more. You better resign from your job and take care of the family. It is socially unacceptable that you are going out every day."

The above discussion gives us a broad understanding of the factors affecting the glass cliff in the BSC. Table 5.2 summarizes the factors.

Policy Options

Respondents' specific suggestions for how to reduce the risk of falling off the cliff are as follows:

1. Evaluate and reward women's productivity by objective results, not by the number of hours they work. For example, after maternity leave, the female can enjoy flexible office hours (from 8:00 am–2:00 pm at office and from 2:30 pm–4:30 pm back home) or can meet the job responsibilities/requirements within 6 hours instead of staying 8 hours at office.

Table 5.2 Summary of findings: factors affecting the glass cliff in the BCS

Factors affecting glass cliff	Details
Influence over policies/decisions	• Women in senior positions are seldom given full credit for their successful contribution in making right decision.
	• The viewpoint of a women is often not heard at a meeting until it is repeated and reinforced by a man.
	• Women receive more unfair judgments of their work performance (involvement in policy discussion agenda) than men.
	• Competitiveness/assertiveness in decision-making process by women is viewed as a negative trait.
	• Overall, women in senior positions in the BSC have less satisfaction with involvement in decisions that affect their work.
Empowerment	• Women bureaucrats have a feeling of personal empowerment with respect to work while posted at a decision-making level.
	• The general perception of BCS employees is that 'women are incapable of making critical leadership decisions (which is why they are quite often ignored and remain unnoticed).
	• Male-oriented cultures often exclude women from gaining access to social capital (e.g., informal networking, connection to authorities)
	• Women are less encouraged than men to come up with new and better ways of doing things.
	• Women are negatively affected by office politics among men.
Organizational justice or equity	• The workload is unreasonable.
	• Performance appraisal is unfair.
	• Promotions are not based on merit—only on seniority.
	• Subjective discrimination.
	• Cannot disclose a suspected violation of any law, rule, or regulation without fear of reprisal.
Work/life balance	• Women prefer a balanced life more than a highly paid career.
	• Most women avoid careers that involve intense competition with colleagues.
	• Extended work hours and days (e.g., working late at night); being on standby is a challenge for women with family responsibilities.
	• Less satisfaction with childcare, health, and welfare programs
	• Senior leaders demonstrate less support for work / life program. (Policy makers do not often consider women's 'double role' of having both official work duties and family obligations.)

2. Make performance-evaluation criteria explicit, and design evaluation processes to limit the influence of evaluators' biases, as the respondents faced the barrier called the 'maternal wall'. 'Maternal wall' practices include: management using maternity as an excuse to not offer opportunities to mothers; passing mothers over for promotion; eliminating jobs during maternity leave or offering a demotion or less desirable assignments after childbirth and on return to work.

3. Avoid having a sole female member on any team. Outnumbered, women tend to be ignored by men.

4. Acknowledge successful senior-level women as role models.

5. Create and implement leadership-development programs for women, (including international assignments and challenging job experiences) to prepare them for leadership positions. It is badly needed, as there is a lack of senior women at the leadership position who can act as mentors for younger women.

Last but not least, building women's associations and networks (women's caucus) in the civil service is a very important mechanism to prevent women from falling off the cliff. Respondents believe that it is important 'who you know, not what you know'.

A women's caucus takes advantage of 'power-through-alliance', which makes it much easier to gain access to important resources for career success (e.g., informal networks and alliances with peers).

CONCLUSION

While gender equity in employment has been addressed in many countries, in Bangladesh, there is limited scholarly effort in public administration to understand women's working conditions and needs in the workplaces, especially at the higher decision-making level in the Bangladesh Civil Service. This study highlights the importance of protecting women's rights. It should be acknowledged that the implications of the findings may be limited due to the small size of the sample. Nevertheless, when seen in the context of the Ministry of Public Administration's statistical data in 2018 and some other surveys conducted in 2016 and 2017, we can see that the findings of this research are consistent with secondary data and the survey results, which show that women perceive themselves as being treated unfairly in important personnel procedures and practices such as position assignments, decision-making levels, promotion, performance evaluation, and rewards. Furthermore, the findings of this study add more details to the issues raised by survey participants, providing in-depth discussions on why and how women in government services have experienced unfair treatment in their workplace, not only at the entry level but also at the higher level of the decision-making arena.

In this study, the glass cliff phenomenon is explained as another kind of glass ceiling that women face when they ascend to the highest structural levels in an organization. Once they crack the ceiling and are in senior positions, they are unable to exert authority in the same way as men. The findings of this research indicate that dissatisfaction with intrinsic (e.g., involving policy-making, lack of empowerment, and inequality at work) and extrinsic factors (e.g., work/life balance, ideological barriers, or subjective discrimination) leads to the glass cliff. Out of all extrinsic and intrinsic factors, the respondents consider "balancing work and family roles" as a task which is very difficult to accomplish. The difficulty is not only at the entry level but also at the higher level, since more expectations need to be fulfilled at the higher level, both at home and within the family context. Lastly, the respondents also shared some observations regarding reducing the risk of falling off the cliff.

This study is not without its limitations. The data are from a limited source. Future studies should consider using different data sets to test the theory of glass cliffs. In-depth interviews are usually an efficient way to gain deeper insights into women's daily experiences. Using a survey may provide further insights. Hence, the study recommends that researchers diversify their methodologies. Lastly, while Bangladesh is an excellent context outside the Western part of the world to conduct this type of research, other non-Western and Western countries may also provide further insights. The generalization of the findings of the present study should therefore be carefully tied to the particular context of the country. A comparative approach could also be a unique way to bring more insights and shed light on the 'glass prison' and how the glass cliff literature may produce an atmosphere in which practitioners and researchers are convinced that such barriers are determinants of women's career paths (Yaghi, 2017).

References

Agars, M. (2004). Reconsidering the impact of gender stereotypes on the advancement of women in organizations. *Psychology of Women Quarterly, 28*(2), 103–111.

Associated Press. (2011). Michele Flournoy, Pentagon's senior female official, steps down. Retrieved March 28, 2018, from http://www.politico.com/news/stories/1211/70315.html#ixzz2JgiVORNu

Bowling, C., Cristine, K., Jennifer, J., & Write, D. (2006). Cracked ceilings, firmer floors, and weakening walls: Trends and patterns in gender representation among executives leading American state agencies 1970–2000. *Public Administration Review, 66*(6), 823–836.

Choi, S., & Park, C. (2014). Glass ceiling in Korean civil service: Analyzing marries to women's career advancement in the Korean government. *Public Personnel Management, 43*(1), 118–139.

Conger, J. A., & Kanungo, R. N. (1988). The empowerment process: Integrating theory and practice. *Academy of Management Review, 13*(3), 471–482.

Eagly, A. H., & Carli, L. L. (2007). Women and the labyrinth of leadership. *Harvard Business Review, 85*(9), 1–9.

Eagly, A. H., & Karau, S. J. (2002). Role of congruity theory of prejudice toward female leaders. *Psychological Review, 109*(3), 573–598.

Eagly, A. H., Wendy, W., & Amanda, B. D. (2000). Social role theory of sex differences and similarities: A current appraisal. In T. Eckes & H. M. Trautner (Eds.), *The development of social psychology of gender* (pp. 123–174). Mahwah, NJ: Erlbaum.

Fox, S., Spector, P. E., & Don, M. (2001). Counterproductive work behavior (CWB) in response to job stressors and organizational justice: Some mediator and moderator tests for autonomy and emotions. *Journal of Vocational Behavior, 59*(3), 291–309.

Greenberg, J. (1990). Organizational justice: Yesterday, today and tomorrow. *Journal of Management, 16*(2), 399–432.

House, J. S., Umberson, D., & Karl, R. L. (1988). Structures and processes of social support. *Annual Review of Sociology, 14*, 293–318.

Hymowitz, C., & Schellhardt, T. D. (1986). The corporate women (a special report): The glass ceiling: Why women can't seem to break the invisible barrier that blocks them from the top jobs. *The Wall Street Journal*. P.ID, 4D, 5D.

Kashem, M. M., et al. (2002). *Review of quota utilization reserved for women*. Dhaka: Ministry of Women and Children's Affairs, GOB.

Kerr, B., Miller, W., & Reid, M. (2002). Sex-based occupational segregation in US state bureaucracies, 1987–1997. *Public Administration Review, 62*(4), 412–423.

Khan, A. A. (2015). *Gresham's law syndrome and beyond: An analysis of the Bangladesh bureaucracy*. Dhaka: The University Press Limited.

Khan, S. (1988). *The fifty percent: Women in development and policy in Bangladesh.* Dhaka: University Press Limited.

Koenig, A. M., Eagly, A. H., Mitchell, A. A., & Ristikari, T. (2011). Are leader stereotypes masculine? A meta-analysis of three research paradigms. *Psychological Bulletin, 137*(4), 616.

Lincoln, N. D., Travers, C., Ackers, P., & Wilkinson, A. (2002). The meaning of empowerment: The interdisciplinary etymology of a new management concept. *International Journal of Management Reviews, 4*(3), 271–290.

Lukes, S. (1974). *Power: A radical view* (1st ed.). London: Macmillan.

Morrison, A. M., White, R. P., & Velsor, E. V. (1987). The narrow band. *Leadership in Action, 7*(2), 1–7.

Naff, K. C. (1994). Through the glass ceiling: Prospects for the advancement for women in the federal civil service. *Public Administration Review, 54*(6), 507–514.

Newman, M. (1993). Career advancement: Does gender make a difference? *American Review of Public Administration, 23*(4), 361–383.

Parker, K. (2018). *Women in majority-male workplaces report higher rates of gender discrimination.* Pew Research Center. Retrieved March 21, 2018, from https://www.pewresearch.org/fact-tank/2018/03/07/women-in-majority-male-workplaces-report-higher-rates-of-gender-discrimination/

Riccucci, N. M. (2009). The pursuit of social equity in the federal government: A road less travelled? *Public Administration Review, 69*(3), 373–382.

Ryan, M. K., & Haslam, S. A. (2005). The glass cliff: Evidence that women are over represented in precarious leadership positions. *British Journal of Management, 16*(2), 81–90.

Ryan, M. K., & Haslam, S. A. (2007). The glass cliff: Exploring the dynamics surrounding the appointment of women to precarious leadership positions. *Academy of Management Review, 32*(2), 549–572.

Sabharwal, M. (2013). From glass ceiling to glass cliff: Women in senior executive service. *Journal of Public Administration Research and Theory, 25*(2), 399–426.

Shetu, J. F., & Ferdous, C. S. (2017). Glass ceiling and professional women: A study on Bangladesh. *World Journal of Social Sciences, 7*(2), 78–87.

Sultan, M. (2012). *Gender equality and women's empowerment in public administration, Bangladesh Case Study.* UNDP Bangladesh, Unpublished Report.

Vinkenburg, C. J., Van Engen, M. L., Eagly, A. H., Mary, C., & Johannesen, S. (2011). An exploration of stereotypical beliefs about leadership styles: Is transformational leadership a route to women's promotion? *The Leadership Quarterly, 22*(1), 10–21.

Yaghi, A. (2017). Glass cliff or glass prison: Think evil—Think men in organizational leadership. *International Journal of Public Administration, 41*(12), 998–1008.

Zafarullah, H. (2000). Through the brick wall, and the glass ceiling: Women in the civil service in Bangladesh. *International Journal of Public Administration, 7*(3), 197–208.

Zafarullah, H. M., & Khan, M. M. (1989). Towards equity in public employment. In K. K. Tummala (Ed.), *Equity in Public Employment across Nation* (pp. 79–103). Lanham, MD: University Press of America.

REPORTS

Statistical Pocket Book of Bangladesh. (1996, 2008). Bangladesh Bureau of Statistics. Dhaka: Government of Bangladesh.

The Constitution of Bangladesh. (1972, 1998). Dhaka: Government of Bangladesh.

Data on Personnel Management. (2002, 2007, 2010, 2014, 2018). Ministry of Public Administration. Statistic and Research Cell. Dhaka: Government of Bangladesh.

Inter Press Service. Retrieved March 27, 2019, from http://www.ipsnews.net/2017/08/women-slowly-break-barriers-bangladesh/

CHAPTER 6

Emerging Leadership Roles of Women in Rural Local Government: Experiences from Bangladesh

Mizanur Rahman

INTRODUCTION AND CONTEXT

In pluralistic societies, equal political participation by both men and women is the *sine qua non* for ushering in change and transformation, for improving conditions for women, and for strengthening democratic processes. Paxton and Hughes (2007, p. 3) find that in South Asian countries such as India and Bangladesh, women's representation in local government is at an extremely low level (only 2 percent). Women's involvement in politics is deemed crucial because politicians hold power over other social institutions and are thus able to create new laws and modify existing legislations and practices (Martin, 2004). Women's integration into the country's political structure, particularly in the sphere of local government, is therefore essential.

Since achieving independence, Bangladeshi women have made significant strides in almost all sectors. In its wake, in the last four decades,

M. Rahman (✉)
Bangladesh Academy for Rural Development (BARD), Cumilla, Bangladesh

© The Author(s) 2020   111
I. Jamil et al. (eds.), *Gender Mainstreaming in Politics,
Administration and Development in South Asia,*
https://doi.org/10.1007/978-3-030-36012-2_6

women have made remarkable achievements in issues like political empowerment, secured better job prospects, increased opportunities of education and the adoption of new laws to protect their rights despite the fact that policies regarding women's rights in Bangladesh are influenced by patriarchal values (Aurora, 2017, May 21). Infested with patriarchal norms, women have had a limited role in household decision-making, limited access and control over household resources, low level of individual assets, heavy domestic workloads, restricted mobility, and inadequate knowledge and skills that result in women's vulnerability (Sebstad & Cohen, 2000).

In terms of literacy, Bangladesh has made substantial progress, where women are catching up with men in terms of literacy rate. The literacy rate for 15 years and older is 78 percent for men and 71 percent for women (UNESCO, 2018, http://uis.unesco.org/en/country/bd). In the context of Bangladesh, religion is well recognized as playing a major role in sanctioning many cultural norms and practices that underpin women's subordinate status, which includes the patrilineal organization of households, patrilineal inheritance systems, dowry, and early marriage (Kabeer, 2002). Critics argue that women's low or non-participation in the political space is a consequence of a number of factors, including women's responsibilities for family and children, the negative attitudes and discrimination of political parties, patriarchal structures and their implications over political parties, unfair electoral voting systems, high costs of elections, lack of access to training and education, conservative religious and cultural doctrines, discriminatory socio-economic conditions, and the nature of the regime and financial barriers (Reyes, 2001).

In the above context, since 1997, when Bangladeshi women were first elected to the *union parishads* (hereafter UPs), they have striven to consolidate their role in the councils. However, their active and vibrant role needs to evolve and be strengthened. This chapter argues that within the stipulated time span, through their painstaking struggle to play their role in the UPs, some women leaders have initiated important change and social transformation in rural society. With this as background, the study seeks to answer the following research questions: What have women leaders in the UPs done to instigate change in rural society? And how did they do it?

WOMEN'S REPRESENTATION IN THE UNION PARISHADS OF BANGLADESH

The British colonial rule introduced local governments (LG) in this sub-continent with the *Village Chowkidary Act in 1870*, which was the corner-stone of today's union parishad. With the end of British rule in India in 1947, India and Pakistan emerged as two different states. Later, after achieving independence in 1971, Bangladesh inherited the LG system from Pakistan with some modifications in its structure. Since 1870 the functionaries of local government[1] were always in the hands of males (Chowdhury et al., 1994, p. 6) and the right to vote in the local bodies was dependent on educational qualifications, possession of property, tax payment, and so on (Women for Women, 1992). Although women's representation in the political community was allowed by the Government of India Act in 1935 (Forbes, 2002), still, women for the first time took part in the election of rural local bodies in 1956 (Inter Parliamentary Union, 1987). Following this provision, during the Pakistani regime, only one female candidate was elected in the UP election of 1956 and 1969.

After the independence of Bangladesh, in the first UP election of 1973, out of 4352 UPs, only one woman from Rangpur district was elected as UP chairperson (Alam & Begum, 1974, pp. 38–51). Afterwards, women's representation in local government was enshrined by two presidential ordinances, namely the Local Government Ordinance of 1976 and the Municipal Ordinance of 1976, which provided a provision of nomination of two women members in the UPs.

Regarding women's representation in the UPs, an important development took place during the Ershad regime[2] through the passage of the

---

[1] In this research local government connotes the rural local government, more specifically the Union Parishad, the lowest and oldest rural local government body in Bangladesh. In the last 149 years, from 1870 until 2019, the UP has never lost its representative character and elections have continued every five years in the UP, unlike many ups and downs in the Bangladeshi society.

[2] Hussain Muhammad Ershad was one of the military rulers in Bangladesh. While he was the Chief of the Army Staff of the Bangladesh Army, he declared Martial Law following a bloodless coup and became the Chief Martial Law Administrator in 1982. Afterwards he became the President of Bangladesh from 1983 to 1990. During his regime, following the suggestions of the National Executive Committee for Administrative Reform and Reorganization (NICARR), Ershad undertook substantive reform measures in the spheres of civil administration and local government in Bangladesh.

Local Government (Upazila Parishad and Upazila Administration Reorganization) Ordinance of 1982 and the Local Government (Union Parishad) Ordinance of 1983. According to the Local Government (Union Parishad) Act of 1983, a provision of nomination of three women members was introduced (Khan, 2011). A major breakthrough in the representation style of women members in the UPs was made in 1997, which provided reservation of one-third seats for women members. Following this reservation system, a huge number of women were elected in the UPs for the first time in the history of decentralized governance of Bangladesh.

UPs are the lowest unit of rural local government in Bangladesh and cover an area of 10–12 sq. km. They can represent anywhere between 15,000 and 45,000 villagers. They consist of 12 elected members, one of which acts as chairperson. A *union* is divided into nine *wards* (small units of a UP, composed of one or more villages), among which three wards are reserved for a woman member. In each union, nine male members are elected from nine wards and three women are elected from their respective reserved wards. UPs have jurisdiction over a wide range of community services such as maintenance of law and order, public property, huts and bazaars,[3] street lights, records of important statistics, issuing various certificates and licenses, settlement of pretty disputes, construction of physical infrastructure, improving the environment, forestry, disaster mitigation, promoting rural development, administering various safety-net programs, and so forth. UPs must maintain a close relationship with a number of governmental organizations, non-governmental organizations (NGOs), and international donor agencies.

THEORETICAL AND CONCEPTUAL PARAMETERS
OF THE STUDY

Women's participation in pluralistic governance can be analyzed from several conceptual and theoretical angles such as political participation, empowerment, a civic engagement model, political recruitment, political representation, and the critical mass theory. In this chapter, women's involvement and participation in governance and their transformative role

---

[3] In rural Bangladesh, a bazaar is a permanently enclosed marketplace or street where goods and services are exchanged or sold. Hut, on the other hand, refers to the sort of bazaar that is arranged two or three times a week.

in the sphere of UPs have been analyzed in light of theories of political representation and the critical mass theory. These are discussed below.

Understanding the Concept of Political Representation

The concept of political representation is relevant for analyzing the role of women in the UPs. Political representation refers to the political activities undertaken by elected representatives to political office on behalf of their fellow citizens, who remain beyond the purview of political office. Hanna Pitkin (1967), a key exponent for the concept, classifies political representation into four forms of representation: formalistic representation, descriptive representation, symbolic representation, and substantive representation.

Formalistic Representation
Formalistic representation pertains to two types of representation, namely authorization and accountability. 'Authorization' means an individual has been authorized to act on the behalf of another individual or group. 'Accountability' means the individual will be held to account for what he or she does. This implies that a representative is accountable to those he or she represents (Pitkin, 1967, p. 55). In essence, representatives are authorized to act and are held accountable for their actions. These relations serve as a means for democratic control, not only for the representatives, through the authorization principle, but also for those who are represented, through the accountability principle, throughout the representation period.

Descriptive Representation
Descriptive representation implies that a representative "should be an exact portrait, in miniature, of the people at large, as [he/she] should think, feel, reason and act like them" (Christensen & Røvik, 1999, pp. 159–180). According to Pitkin (1967), descriptive representation, alternatively termed as 'standing for,' refers to the idea that the linkage between the representative and the represented is based on shared characteristics or background, such as gender. The rationality behind descriptive representation is that the representatives possess particular characteristics of the group they represent, by virtue of that identity. Therefore, the direct participation of women can be seen as a form of descriptive representation in decision-making bodies.

Symbolic Representation

Symbolic representatives 'stand for' the people they represent as long as those people believe in or accept them as their representative (Pitkin, 1967, p. 174). According to Pitkin, this type of representation is regarded as a kind of 'symbolization.' As symbolic representatives, women in politics may signify women's confidence, abilities, rights, and freedoms. Phillips (1995) states that "when more women candidates are elected, their example is said to raise women's self-esteem, encourage others to follow their footsteps and dislodge deep-rooted assumptions about what is appropriate to women and men" (p. 63).

Substantive Representation

Substantive representation, which is described as 'acting for,' emphasizes whether or not the representative is able and willing to act on behalf of the interests and concerns of those represented (Holli, 2012). It is believed that by holding public office, women play a crucial role in developing gender equality in society. The view of substantive representation upholds that women have special needs, interests, and concerns for which they would like political representation, examples being gender discrimination in social relations, children's welfare, community health services, and the environment. The view of substantive representation thus suggests that women representatives should be experienced and supportive of issues that affect women. In one study, Raaum (1995) finds that women legislators are indeed sensitive to women's interests and the private sphere of women's life.

The above discussion reveals that there are diverse forms of representation. Formalistic representation means representatives are authorized to act on behalf of those they represent in an accountable manner. Descriptive representation suggests that representatives are individuals standing for others whose characteristics correspond to or resemble those who are represented. Symbolic representation signifies individuals who, when standing for others, evoke emotions, feelings, and attitudes about those they represent. With substantive representation, representatives act on behalf of those who are represented, serving their needs and attending to their interests.

Critical Mass Theory

In the firmament of women's political representation and their legislative behavior, the critical mass theory has gained tremendous attention among scholars. The underlying assumption of the critical mass theory is that once a 'critical mass' of elected women is reached, it will lead to changes in political behavior, institutions, and public policy, all of which will radically transform legislation. The theory justifies the rationale for reserving a certain quota of seats for women in political office. Based on the notion that 30 percent constitutes the critical mass needed to favor women-friendly policy changes, many countries have adopted quotas or reservation policies.

A key argument of the critical mass theory is that an increase in women's involvement in politics affects the content, style, and mechanism of politics, as compared to the situation when politics is dominated entirely by men (Holli, 2012). It is argued that when the number of women increases in the political arena, women will be able to work more efficiently to promote women-friendly policy changes (Childs & Krook, 2008). The theory's focus, therefore, is that women should reach a critical mass so that they can affect the political discourse in local governments. Critics note, however, that it is not the quota filled by the women that is important, but that the elected women *act critically*, that is, that they actually promote the interest of women in substantive ways (Holli, 2012).

Scholars have diverse opinions on how the critical mass is formed. According to Kanter (1977), the threshold for critical mass varies from 15 to 40 percent. For Dahlerup (1988), it occurs at 30 percent, while Saint-Germain (1989) and Thomas (1994) suggest that the critical mass exists in the 15–20 percent range. But along with the need for a critical mass, there are also other factors that contribute to strengthening women's role in legislative politics. These include women's willingness and ability to mobilize resources for the organization or institution they think is important, an organized women's caucus, women's role in party leadership and ideology, legislative turnover, education, women's participation in the workforce, voter participation, and cultural attitudes towards gender equality (Dahlerup, 1988, p. 296; Thomas, 1994, p. 154).

It can be concluded that the critical mass theory and the theorization of critical action are both highly relevant for analyzing women's representation and participation in local government in Bangladesh. Using the critical mass theory, we can analyze the representation of women in local government and their impact on political deliberations, whereas by thinking in terms of their critical action, we can examine the substantive contribution of women in local government.

METHODOLOGY

The significance of this study has to do with the general lack of phenomenological studies dealing with woman's political participation in Bangladesh. This chapter is based on a qualitative research approach. A hermeneutical phenomenological approach was therefore adopted and substantiated with case studies and content analysis. The study used a framework of subjective judgment and interpretation to analyze the field data. It was deemed that this qualitative method would help in exploring lived experiences, multiple realities, and the diverse dynamics of the experiences and benefits of women's participation in local government. The perspectives of the woman leaders themselves would hopefully come to the fore, such that the research question would be properly addressed. Sincere efforts were made to collect data through ten in-depth case studies: five concerning women UP members, and five concerning women who were UP chairpersons. These case studies cover different sociocultural zones in Bangladesh.[4] For the phenomenological analysis, the author followed principles of qualitative research to interview woman members and chairpersons of UPs.[5] Before each interview, informed consent was obtained from the participants. Interviews were conducted in the local language, *Bangla*, transcribed, and then translated into English. Observational knowledge gained through prolonged fieldwork is also incorporated into the writing of this chapter. To support primary data and to analyze the textual descriptions obtained from the participants, a method of content analysis was used, and relevant secondary data was consulted through a heuristic search through library materials and online. To analyze data according to a phenomenological method, a thematic analytical approach was employed.

[4] There are 7 divisions, 64 districts, 507 upazilas (sub-districts), and 4498 UPs in Bangladesh. The sampled 23 UP councilors were selected from five divisions and seven districts of Bangladesh: Chittagong, Comilla, Faridpur, Sylhet, Barisal, Bogra, and Gaibandha districts.

[5] In qualitative research, the size of the sample is of secondary importance to the quality of data, as "qualitative research is concerned with smaller numbers of cases with more intensive analysis" (Davidson & Layder, 1994, p. 173). Moreover, in qualitative research, the selection of the sample does not matter much; rather, collecting data from the real world is much more important and even the term 'sampling' is not used.

Change and Transformation by Women Leaders in the UPs

Despite diverse constraints on their participation in the UPs, some women leaders have been able to make a difference at the local political level, and through their socio-cultural involvement, to transform social conditions for women. This will be substantiated in the following sub-sections.

Women Leaders Provided Better Judgment in the Rural Salish[6] System

Women's continued and painstaking struggle for their jurisdictional rights in the UPs has enabled some assertive women to play a limited role in rural society. This is reflected in the words of one woman leader during interview with her:

> I don't know how the general public have benefited by the inclusion of women in the parishad, but I can firmly assure you that women are getting enormous benefit from it. Especially in the village salish, where women UP members are present, the female victim can share her personal experiences or grievances with us, boldly and without hesitation. Previously, when women were not in the UP, the victimized women never dared to open their mouths before the male villagers during the salish. At that time, women were further victimized by the poor judgment given by the male UP members. Now the situation has completely changed due to the involvement of women in the parishad. (Woman member, Khadimpara UP, 28 September 2013)

Women leaders have tried to establish social justice in the UPs, as reflected in the utterance of another female UP member:

> Due to women's entry into the UP, the women folk are getting huge benefit from us because when they experience male oppression and violence, they immediately come to us for remedy and justice. Sometimes we seek advice from the Upazila Women's Affairs Officer, for legal action against violence. (Woman member, Amratali UP, 25 September 2013)

---

[6] *Salish* refers to the informal local arbitration which the UP representatives conduct to resolve people's petty disputes.

Some female UP members play a commendable role in establishing women's right through village courts, called *salish*. Siddiqee (2008) and Amin and Akhter (2005, p. 6), respectively, find that 66 percent and 75 percent of female UP members participate in salish on a regular basis, just as do male UP members. Such participation has helped many village women get proper redress. One male UP member's statement helps explain why:

> When a woman is victimized or oppressed by her husband or anyone else, the female UP member can interview and observe how her husband or others tortured her, personally checking the injury marks on her body. But this was never possible for a male UP member. (Male member, Wahedpur UP, 30 August 2013)

This man's statement implies that before women were included in the UPs, the salish councils passed judgment based on verbal descriptions; after women were included in the UPs and involved in salish processes, they have had the prerogative to observe the evidence of physical torture with their own eyes. Being direct witnesses of the evidence, female UP members have contributed to establishing improved social justice in rural society. Siddiqee (2008) finds that about 74 percent of women leaders respond that they play a role in cases of divorce, child marriage, dowry, acid throwing, women's repression, rape, and so on. Amin and Akhter (2005) find that 76 percent of villagers report that female UP members have been successful in resolving conflicts in the community. This implies that women leaders have provided better judgment in rural society than have male UP members.

A Striking Example of How Women Leaders Provide Suitable Judgment to Rural Women

Fatema Akhter Parul was elected a UP member for two terms (2005, 2011) in Khadimpara UP, Sadar *upazila*, Sylhet. She is 38, has completed grade level 10, and hails from Jahanpur village. In the interview, Parul elaborated that while she attended a village salish, she learned that a young man had raped a young woman. Realizing the significance of such a serious case, she thought she could not leave the salish without passing judgment on the case. She called her husband so that he could accompany her during late hours to finish the judicial procedure. She also requested that some elderly villagers remain present in order to provide valuable input during the judicial process. In the presence of 150 villagers, it took several hours to complete. Judging the contextual reality of Bangladesh, and due to the logic that since the young man violated the woman and she would have to suffer immensely and find it difficult to get married, the jury unanimously decided that the young man had to marry the girl that very night. Then the jury summoned an official matchmaker to register the marriage according to proper religious rituals. When everything was finished, it was 3 am. During the entire judicial procedure, no male UP member was present in the salish. (This case was shared during interview with a woman member of Khadimpara UP, 28 September 2013.)

Empirical Findings

In this section, field data derived from diverse cases and textual descriptions obtained from interviews have been interpreted and analyzed with subjective judgments by the author and with relevant content analysis.

Women UP Leaders Made Culturally Suitable Judgments

From the cases outlined above, it is evident that female UP leaders made culturally suitable judgments. They were sensitive and sympathetic to women's causes, issues, interests, and concerns. Women leaders therefore strove to play a formidable role to safeguard the vital interests of the women in the community. The above cases also reveal that female UP members' participation in the salish has resulted in substantial changes in the outcome of cases. The Khadimpara case shows that the women leader in question was earnestly committed, acted responsibly, and dealt justice with a strong hand, to ensure rule of law in society and an enabling environment. In light of the Bangladeshi culture, the judgments provided by salish committees might be culturally appropriate. However, viewed from the perspective of a substantive rationale, such judgments could also have ominous ramifications for women's lives.

Analytical Implications

The participation of women in UPs has helped rural women achieve social justice and a better life. Before women were elected to the UPs, when women experienced violence in their village, there was little or no opportunity to gather empirical evidence of the perpetrated violence. Now the salish council can provide judgment with evidential proof. When poor women have sought assistance regarding family feuds or violence against themselves or other women, UP women leaders have helped them gain legal support from relevant sources. This was impossible before women were elected to the UPs. Siddiqee (2008) finds that 77 percent of female UP members assist women in their area to gain access to micro-credit from various sources. As Sawer (2002, p. 8) states, all over the world, it was evident that women leaders have a special responsibility to represent the needs and interests of women. Other researchers find that women are more likely than men to prioritize paying bills that are related to children, healthcare for themselves and their family, family policy, care of the elderly, and social services (Thomas & Welch, 1991; Wangnerud, 2000).

Women Leaders Have Rendered Pro-Poor Benefits and Development Services to Rural Society

Field data analysis reveals that women leaders contribute enormously to improving pro-poor benefits in the UPs. A male member of Amratali UP, in response to a question, informs that women are serving society in different ways:

> All three women members are helping in distributing VGD [Vulnerable Group Development] cards, old age pensions and VGF [Vulnerable Group Feeding] cards, birth registration, and many other things. When the beneficiaries of old-age pension schemes withdraw money from the bank, the women members are required to attest the form and sign with their seal. As they represent three wards, when the beneficiaries of all those wards need to withdraw money from the bank, the women UP members need always to be present. This is one way in which they are serving the community. (Male member, Amratali UP, 25 September 2013)

The above quote testifies to the fact that female UP members render immense services to rural communities. Amin and Akhter (2005, pp. 6–7) state that 60 percent of women UP members were involved in distributing VGF and VGD cards, 25 percent had partial involvement, and 15 percent had no opportunity to be involved. Rahman (2014) finds that female UP members not only were associated with the distribution of VGD and VGF cards, but also increased the number of beneficiaries. This can be understood from an account given by one female UP member:

Since we entered the UP, the service delivery has improved a lot. In previous days, the villagers got only 30 VGD cards, whereas now we distributed 120 VGD cards in just one ward, so whether we are doing good to them or not, they understand easily. We select the beneficiary very consciously, if the villagers see any slur to it, they just inform the chairman immediately. We are available for the public as and when necessary, even at midnight. (Woman member, South Durgapur UP, 26 August 2013)

The account of this informant vividly illustrates that female UP members provide pro-poor benefits. They have a sincere and firm commitment to the well-being of society. It was learnt from the villagers of Chandpur UP, Boalmari, Faridpur, that male UP members usually took money (bribes) ranging from 500 to 2000 Taka (between $ 6–24 USD)[7] when they were asked to help villagers apply for various benefits relating to old-age pension, widow allowance, disabled people allowance, succession certificates, and other services rendered by the UPs. Women members, however, rendered these services based on rational judgment.

In line with this, a woman member from Wahedpur UP, Mirsarai, mentioned, "In our society, the government has started a maternal allowance in every village. In such activities, women UP members' help and cooperation are essential for the smooth implementation of this program" (30 August 2013).

The above quote shows some of the ways in which female UP members make immense contributions to improving the management of various safety-net benefits in the local community. Due to easy access to female UP members, their modest approach, and their integrity, villagers find these women leaders enormously beneficial for them. Evidence shows that by ensuring the selection of a fair list of eligible beneficiaries for safety-net programs, local governments have contributed to increasing previously excluded groups' access to social welfare (Sikder, Engali, Byrne, & Tabet, 2011). Nazneen and Tasneem (2010) find that both communities and female UP members value the role the latter play in implementing safety-net programs and development projects, even though the responsibilities of women councilors are not fully demarcated in the legal frame.

---

[7] One US dollar = 83.67 Bangladeshi Taka, as of March 21, 2019.

A Case of a Woman Leader's Role in Development Administration and Gender Equality

Running for election three times, Razia Begum (Mina),[8] a graduate and a widow aged 48, was elected chairperson in Bethkapa UP, Palashbari upazila, Gaibandha. Before she was elected to the UP, she worked in the Grameen Bank. Mina is a bold, skilled, and articulate woman and was able to handle lots of problems created by male UP members. As chairperson, she always tried to distribute development projects to female and male members equally, in line with the legal provision. Due to her practice of gender equality in the UP, all male members verbally threatened her several times, saying they would publish false accusations against her in the press. While telling about her experiences in the UP, Mina notes that through attending salishes, women members provide various services to society. When she herself could not attend a salish, she telephoned a relevant female member to deal with it. In some villages, Mina says, women members conduct salishes themselves and pass judgment. She also states that when a female UP member faces problem, she solves the cases by taking the UP secretary with her. During her tenure in the UP, she achieved crowning success in some areas, especially in setting up a tube well to ensure safe drinking water for poor villagers. Before joining the UP, many villagers practiced open defecation. This led Mina to destroy all bamboo-made open toilets in her territory, and to supply people with low-cost water-sealed toilets. This was a successful initiative. Due to her dynamic leadership, she obtained more than 95 percent sanitation coverage in her UP. Moreover, she solved a long-standing water-logging problem by constructing a drainage system and upgrading most of the important roads in her UP. By bargaining with the local administration, she was also successful in increasing the number of poor beneficiaries of various safety-net programs.

A Case of Civic Engagement and Community-Mindedness by a Women Leader in a UP

Bagging a landslide victory, Nargis Akhter[9] became UP chairperson for a second term, due to her popularity in Machchar UP, Sadar upazila, Faridpur. As a public leader, she needed to attend many ceremonious events in her constituency, for instance, marriages, birthday parties, death

[8] This interview was done on 7 November 2013.
[9] This interview took place on 31 October 2013.

anniversaries, occasions for newborn babies, circumcisions for male children, opening ceremonies for diverse organizations, and so on. When she received a message about any death, she immediately went to the bereaved family to express her sympathy and offer consolation. On all those occasions, she often experienced peculiar phenomena. Once, while attending a marriage ceremony, she noticed that the father of the bride was crying because he could not give anything to his son-in-law. Knowing this, Nargis gave 10,000 Taka ($120 USD) to the wretched father. Sometimes, in connection with a death, she observed that the family could not manage even to pay for the funeral cloth. This would prompt her to contribute some money for that. During her tenure, she once observed that some villagers suffered due to the collapse of a bridge. She immediately helped the villagers by forking out of her own pocket to pay for the construction of a bamboo bridge. In ways such as these, she won love and respect from her constituents. Nargis tried to stand beside her people in all their woes, miseries, adversities, bad days, and happy days. She always had the best interests of her people in mind. Nargis did some excellent work in her UP. As part of her benevolent activities, she personally offered some scholarships to the extremely poor students in some schools. As chair, she was duty-bound to act according to her integrity in the UP. Nargis tried to distribute projects equally between male and female UP members. Based on her straightforward and crystal-clear rationale, she deemed that three female members were tantamount to nine male members. She judged a woman member three times greater than a male member. Thus, she ensured gender equality in her UP. Nargis informed the author that she faced some insurmountable challenges regarding construction of a road in her UP. The villagers informed her that due to the lack of a *pucca*/paved road, they could not market their agricultural products, neither could an ambulance enter the village when anyone became sick. Nargis repeatedly failed to construct that road due to the creation of massive obstacles by some influential elderly villagers and local elites. After receiving help from the chief executive of the sub-district (the upazila) and using some of the managing budget from the government, Nargis successfully completed the road project by employing poor people to construct it. Now everyone was happy—even those who had created obstacles to erect the road—because now the ambulance and other vehicles could enter the village easily. Due to her benevolent leadership, she received an award from the World Mother Teresa Foundation. The Bangladeshi government also gave her the 'Best Chairman Award' in 2012. She felt lucky to be given such a prestigious award from the government.

Summary of Empirical Findings

Women Leaders' Improved Safety-Net Programs

From the grassroots reality of the situations, the women leaders appeared to be pledge-bound to provide services to the community. Their services were better than what the community had previously received. At present, Bangladesh's government is providing various safety-net programs for diverse poor people to improve their situation and reduce poverty, income inequality, malnutrition, and maternal mortality. The safety-net programs implemented by the UPs include the distribution of VGD and VGF cards, old-age pensions, 40-day work assignments, disabled people's allowances, widows' allowances, tax relief, allowances for pregnant mothers, and so on. In distributing safety-net programs, female UP members played formidable roles in selecting applicants based on rational judgments. They strove to enhance the coverage of safety-net programs by bargaining with their male UP colleagues. Through maintaining informal and friendly relations with villagers, women leaders extended those services to the community without any harassment and monetary involvement. This stands in contrast to some cases in which male UP members provided such services only in return for cash.

Women Leaders' Role in Development Administration

From cases such as those of Mina and Nargis, it was evident that some women leaders, especially those who became community leaders using their NGO network, performed in startling ways by undertaking various development projects, improving and extending community services, and demonstrating their integrity in performing their jurisdictional role for rural people. The topmost significance credited to women leaders was that they were able to bring such qualitative changes to local governance while accomplishing their regular household and reproductive role amid challenges posed by the patriarchal social structure.

One Women Leader Had a Strong Community Mentality

Nargis was service minded and had a strong community mentality and attitude. She perceived her political role as that of being a supra-social worker, just as do many women politicians elsewhere in the world. Her community mentality was reflected in many ways, for instance, through her sympathy for the poor father who failed to provide a gift for his son-in-law, and by providing money to construct a bamboo bridge and buy a funeral cloth. Her social activities were expressed when she made provisions for scholarships in the educational institutions. By demonstrating leadership with a strong sense of community feeling, she was able to win a landslide victory in the election for two consecutive terms. By dint of her gifted leadership and community mindset, she was blessing with love and respect from her constituents. Her excellent community service was duly recognized by the international Mother Teresa Foundation and the government of Bangladesh, which gave her the 'Best Chairman Award' in 2012.

Value Judgment in Ensuring Gender Equality
Despite repeated threats from male UP members, Mina opted to practice gender equality in her UP. This value judgment was possible because she was the chairperson. Nargis also provided strong arguments for maintaining gender equality in her UP.

Analytical Implications

Female UP members may have a better-developed community feeling than their male colleagues and may serve women's interests better than do men. There is at least worldwide anecdotal evidence which would supports such a view. According to Childs (2002), female politicians view women as a distinct part of their constituencies, and women leaders have a special responsibility to represent the needs and interests of women. Johnson, Kabuchu, and Kayonga (2003), in their study, found that women participated more than men did in community services at the local government level. This finding is corroborated by Drage (2001), who found that female leaders cared more than male leaders about the social issues, well-being, and welfare of their communities; they contributed in areas such as housing, safety, clean water, sanitation, the environment, education, social implications of policies, health services, childcare, poverty alleviation, and community development. Most women are born and brought up in a highly male-dominated culture, and due to their different socialization and life experience, they think differently from men (Phillips, 1991). Evidence shows that "women bring to politics a different set of values, experiences and expertise" (Phillips, 1995, p. 6). Scholars have found that, in general, male law makers are less likely to initiate and pass laws that serve women's and children's interests, and they often perceive rape, domestic violence, women's health, and childcare differently from women (Childs & Withey, 2004; Schwindt-Bayer, 2006). Women's performance on the basis of qualitative and quantitative indicators was in no way inferior to that of male members. In the context of India, Chathuculam and John (2000, pp. 66–101) found that elected women members of panchayat bodies showed startling performance, particularly in the sectors of health, education, and access to basic services, and in ensuring significant improvement in the living conditions of the communities. Likewise, in Bangladesh, the women leaders who were interviewed provided community service through quality judgment in rural society.

CONVERGING THEORIES AND PRAGMATISM REGARDING WOMEN'S PARTICIPATION IN LOCAL GOVERNMENT IN BANGLADESH

Theory of Representation

Representational government requires representatives to execute diverse activities; the representatives obtain authority from a group of people with whom they share characteristics and to whom they are accountable. From the reality on the ground, it was observed that the formal representation of women has allowed women leaders to be involved in local governance by using their reservation quota. These leaders were held accountable for their actions or inactions in the community. Those who had experience from previous engagements in NGOs and other socio-cultural organizations were better equipped to serve the community amid the difficulties posed by patriarchal society, and many of them were re-elected for a second and third term. Other female UP members also faced severe male domination, and thus failed to play even a minimum role in their UP. They did not try to run for a second term. Despite having been authorized to act on behalf of the community they represented, some women leaders lacked the necessary skills and capacities to face challenges posed by patriarchy; they ended up having no respect whatsoever for their male colleagues and were extremely disgusted by them. It was these women who did not even try to run for a second term.

Elected to local government, women leaders had the characteristics of descriptive representation because they acted on behalf of the women in rural society. Bearing shared characteristics or backgrounds, the women leaders were found to be supportive of women's interest and concerns. Thus, when rural women came to seek help from the women leaders, the leaders tried their level best to solve the problems and satisfy the demands of the women. This was particularly reflected in the rural salish, the administration of safety-net programs, and many other community services in the UP area.

In my opinion, women's leadership in local government is not best characterized as symbolic representation because these women 'stand in' for more than just the women in the community. While being extremely sympathetic and sensitive to the interests, needs, and aspirations of the women, they also attend to the interests and needs of other underrepresented groups. All the empirical findings and data generated from interviewing the women leaders at the grassroots level testify to the fact that they served the basic purpose for which they were elected: to act on behalf of women's own interests and concerns. But viewed from the angle of substantive representation, the women leaders were also found to act on behalf of others, to serve and deliver per their interests and needs as well. In congruence with the principle of substantive representation, some women leaders in the UPs performed their role excellently by favoring the interests of their constituents. These leaders not only rendered support for women, but also provided benefits to the community as a whole. In some cases, a few women leaders implemented many development projects which were better than those of male UP members. Most of the women leaders provided support for issuing birth and death certificates, played a role in school management committees and scheme selection committees, and so on.

Critical Mass Theory

The idea behind the critical mass theory is that an increase in women's involvement in politics affects the quality of women's political participation in a society where patriarchy governs the entire socio-political milieu. It is argued that with an increased number of women in the political arena, women will be able to work more efficiently together to promote women-friendly policy change. The pivotal focus of the theory is thus that women voters and office-holders should reach a critical mass so that they can affect the political discourse in public life in general and in the sphere of local government in particular. On the other hand, the 'critical act approach' focuses not on the number of women who are elected to political office, but on how much they actually promote the interests of those who voted for them.

In line with the critical mass theory, many countries and international organizations advocate that at least 30 percent of politically elected posts should be filled by women, for 30 percent, it is argued, constitutes the point at which women may become a critical mass in favor of women-friendly policy change. Based on this premise, the government of Bangladesh, two decades ago, adopted a 30 percent quota for women in urban and rural local government. Assuming that there is no contention that the basic idea behind the critical mass theory has started to be realized in the UPs of Bangladesh. In my opinion, after these women leaders entered into the trajectory of local government, it was no longer the critical mass theory that was of focal interest, but their critical acts. Many scholars have observed that other factors also contribute to strengthening women's role in legislative politics. These include women's willingness and ability to mobilize resources for the institutions they favor, an organized women's caucus, women's role in party leadership and ideology, legislative turnover, education, women's participation in the workforce, and their attitude towards gender equality.

Likewise, the participation of women leaders in local government in Bangladesh has provided a platform for the collectivization of women, which helps them make a significant contribution to enlarging the definition of politics. In fact, a huge number of NGOs and women's organizations have facilitated a change in women's status in Bangladesh through building awareness, increasing social mobilization, and enhancing political consciousness; they have expanded the scope of women-friendly policies on issues such as population control, health, legal reforms, the participation of women in the political process, and establishing links with NGOs (Khan, Rahman, Islam, & Islam, 1981, p. 7; Jahan, 1995). In the interviews, it was evident that a huge number of women who become UP members and chairpersons had entered the political arena on the background of having been involved in NGOs and other socio-cultural programs and institutions. They had achieved economic emancipation, had been involved in various income-generating activities, and had developed enormous social capital at the grassroots level. All this helped to enhance their women-friendly role in Bangladesh (Gani & Sattar,

2004; Rahman, 2006, 2007, 2014).[10] In sum, female UP members were able to make some differences and initiate change and transformation in the lives of women, and used the prerogatives of their considerable social capital.

Women leaders could perform even better if reservation quotas were not just confined to women. Drawing on evidence from West Bengal and other Indian states, it was found that the Indian government has made provisions for reserving seats in all positions in local government—for chairpersons, vice-chairpersons, and general members—and that these reservation quotas extend to other vulnerable groups in society such as scheduled castes and tribes. In Bangladesh it was observed that in the last UP election (2011–2016), out of 4498 UP chairpersons, only 23 were women. From this, it is clear that the critical mass in women's leadership in Bangladesh has not yet been realized in the truest sense of the term. It is interesting to note at this juncture that in West Bengal, women leaders have been performing excellently in rural local government, in part due to the reservation quota for women having been expanded to 50 percent. Thus most of the women's problems were being addressed by the huge number of women leaders in India. It can therefore be argued that the government of Bangladesh should follow in the footsteps of its neighbor in order to consolidate women's role in rural governance.

CONCLUSION

The basic premise of this chapter was that amid the struggle to ensure women's participation in the UPs, women leaders have been able to make some positive differences and to instigate social transformation in rural governance. With this premise as a backdrop, the chapter aimed to explore two research question: *What did woman leaders do to make a difference in rural society? How did they do it?* To explore these questions, qualitative methods such as phenomenological analysis, case studies, content analysis, and observation methods were used. Regarding the question of how the women leaders brought change and transformation to rural society, it was found that having ensured their limited rights and role in the UPs, some

---

[10] Rahman (2006) found that 64.52 percent, 39 percent, and 72 percent of the women leaders had a linkage with various NGOs and socio-economic development organizations in 2006, 2007, and 2013 respectively (Rahman, 2007), whereas Gani and Sattar (2004) found that 50 percent of the women leaders were involved in NGOs.

women leaders were providing culturally suitable social justice to women through participating in the rural salish or village court system. In this way, they helped the vulnerable segments of rural society. Women leaders were found to be highly sensitive to women's concerns and interests and sought to serve their needs at the community level. Involving themselves in transformative politics, these women leaders were able to provide various development benefits such as social safety-net programs and to improve development administration. Due to their community mentality, some became supra-social workers, and they exercised integrity in the day-to-day affairs of the UPs.

As regards local governance and social change in rural Bangladesh, we observe a slow-motion revolution: The induction of women in local governance is making a difference and benefiting women immensely, especially those who suffer from poverty, exclusion, and violence. Although UPs are elected bodies, they are usually overwhelmed by other local-level institutions as well as elected and administrative bodies at higher levels of government. Being at the bottom of the political and administrative hierarchy, they are often ignored, overpowered, and lack necessary resources to carry out the most basic functions. Historically, the UPs have been dominated by men and have been seen as tools which local and rural elites can use to wield power in local governance. Only on a very limited number of occasions have these male-dominated institutions provided good governance for the poor and women. Now, after the inclusion of women in local governance, we observe that women's representation is making a difference, albeit at an initial and minimal stage. Over time, women's continuous representation in union parishads is likely to result in a critical mass which will transform local governance substantially; from formalistic and symbolic representation, substantial representation would foster more social changes and welfare in rural Bangladesh.

REFERENCES

Alam, B. A., & Begum, R. A. (1974). Violence and union parishad leadership: A few statistics. *Local Government Quarterly, 8,* 1–4.

Amin, R., & Akhter, S. (2005). *Women participation in local government and social integration in rural Bangladesh.* Paper presented in Workshop on Enlarging Citizen Participation and Increasing Local Autonomy in Achieving Societal Harmony held in Beijing, PRC by Network of Asia-Pacific Schools and

Institutes of Public Administration and Governance (NAPSIPAG) Annual Conference 2005, December 5–7.

Aurora, E. (2017, May 21). Patriarchy: The deep rooted cultural beliefs that normalize rape. *The Dhaka Tribune.* Retrieved October 13, 2019, from https://www.dhakatribune.com/bangladesh/law-rights/2017/05/21/patriarchy-kamla-bahsin-obr

Chathuculam, J., & John, M. S. (2000). Empowerment of women panchayat members: Learning from Kerala (India). *AJWS, 6*(4), 66–1010.

Childs, S. (2002). Hitting the target: Are labour women MPs 'acting for' women? *Parliamentary Affairs, 55,* 143–153.

Childs, S., & Krook, M. L. (2008). Critical mass theory and women's political representation. *Political Studies, 56*(3), 725–736.

Childs, S., & Withey, J. (2004). Women representatives acting women: Sex and the signing of early day motions in the 1997 British parliament. *Political Studies, 52,* 552–564.

Chowhdury, N., Begum, H. A., Islam, M., & Mahtab, N., (1994). (Eds.). *Women and politics.* Dhaka: Women for Women.

Christensen, T., & Røvik, K. A. (1999). The ambiguities of appropriateness. In M. Egeberg & P. Lægreid (Eds.), *Organizing political institutions* (pp. 159–180). Oslo: Scandinavian University Press.

Dahlerup, D. (1988). From a small to a large minority: Women in Scandinavian politics. *Scandinavian Political Studies, 11*(4), 275–297.

Davidson, J. O., & Layder, D. (1994). *Methods, sex and madness.* London: Routledge.

Drage, J. (2001). *Women in local government in Asia and the Pacific: A comparative analysis of thirteen countries.* Report for the ESCAP, 34, 2001. Retrieved from http:www.citieslocalgovernments.org/101a/upload/docs/womeninurbanlocalgovernmen. (comparative analysis 13countries.pdf)

Forbes, G. (2002). Women of character, grit and courage: The reservation debate in historical perspective. In L. Sarker, K. Sharma, & D. L. Kasturi (Eds.), *Between tradition, counter tradition and heresy.* Delhi: Rainbow Publishers.

Gani, M. S., & Sattar, M. G. (2004). *Gender and good governance issues in local government of Bangladesh: A baseline report.* Dhaka: Research and Evaluation Division, BRAC.

Holli, A. M. (2012). Does gender have an effect on the selection of experts by parliamentary standing committee? A critical text of "critical" concepts. *Politics & Gender, 8,* 341–366.

Inter Parliamentary Union. (1987). *Distribution of seats between men and women in national assemblies.* Geneva: IPU.

Jahan, R. (1995). *The elusive agenda: Mainstreaming women in development.* Dhaka: University Press.

Johnson, D., Kabuchu, H., & Kayonga, S. V. (2003). Women in Ugandan local government: The impact of affirmative action. *Gender and Development, 11*(3), 8–18.

Kabeer, N. (2002). *We don't do credit: Nijera kori, social mobilization, and the collective capabilities of the poor in rural Bangladesh.* Dhaka: Ruby Enterprise.

Kanter, R. M. (1977). Some effects of proportions on group life. *American Journal of Sociology, 82*(5), 965–990.

Khan, M. M. (2011). *Local government in Bangladesh: Some contemporary issues and practices.* Dhaka: A. H. Publishing House.

Khan, S., Rahman, J., Islam, S., & Islam, M. (Eds.). (1981). *Inventory of women's organizations in Bangladesh.* Dhaka: UNICEF.

Martin, P. Y. (2004). Gender as a social institute. *Social Forces, 82*, 1249–73.

Nazneen, S., & Tasneem, S. (2010). A silver lining: Women in reserved seats in local government in Bangladesh. *IDS Bulletin, 41*(5), 35–42.

Paxton, P., & Hughes, M. (2007). *Women, politics and power: A global perspective.* Los Angeles, London, New Delhi and Singapore: Pine Forge Press.

Phillips, A. (1991). *Engendering democracy.* University Park, PA: Pennsylvania State University Press.

Phillips, A. (1995). *The politics of presence.* New York: Oxford University Press.

Pitkin, H. F. (1967). *The concept of representation.* Los Angeles: University of California Press.

Raaum, C. N. (1995). Women in local democracy. In L. Karvonen & P. Selle (Eds.), *Women in Nordic politics. Closing the gap.* Aldershot: Dartmouth Publishing Company.

Rahman, M. M. (2006, January–June). Socio-economic and political profiles of the women leaders of the grassroots level local governments in Bangladesh and West Bengal, India: A comparative perspective. *Afro-Asian Journal of Rural Development, 39*(1), 37–66.

Rahman, M. M. (2007). Union parishad in Bangladesh: An empirical study on background, linkages, roles and performance of the leaders. *Journal of Public Administration, 16*(2), 83–109.

Rahman, M. M. (2014). *Unheard voices and grim realities of the challenges, coping strategies, and governance of women leaders: The case of the union parishad in Bangladesh.* PhD dissertation submitted to the Graduate School of Public Administration in National Institute of Development Administration (NIDA), Bangkok.

Reyes, S. (2001). *Women in government.* UNDP, Asia Pacific Gender Equality Network (APGEN): The Centre for Legislative Development.

Saint-Germain, M. (1989). Does their difference make a difference? The impact of women on public policy in the Arizona legislature. *Social Science Quarterly, 70*(4), 956–968.

Sawer, M. (2002). The representation of women in Australia: Meaning and make-believe. *Parliamentary Affairs, 55*(1), 5–18.

Schwindt-Bayer, L. A. (2006). Still supermadres? Gender and the policy priorities of Latin American legislators. *American Journal of Political Science, 50*, 570–585.

Sebstad, J., & Cohen, M. (2000). Microfinance, risk management, and poverty. *AIMS Paper*. Office of Microenterprise Development, USAID, Washington, DC.

Siddiqee, M. S. H. (2008). Gender and good governance issues in local government of Bangladesh: A baseline report of extension phase (RETA–6008). Dhaka: Research and Evaluation Division, BRAC.

Sikder, T., Engali, J., Byrne, S., & Tabet, T. (2011). *Socially inclusive local governance-case study: Sharique-Bangladesh*. Dhaka: Inter-cooperation, Institute of Development Studies, the Democratization and Local Government Network.

Thomas, S. (1994). *How Women Legislate*. New York: Oxford University Press.

Thomas, S., & Welch, S. (1991). The impact of gender on activities and priorities of state legislators. *The Western Political Quarterly, 44*, 445–456.

UNESCO. (2018). Retrieved October 14, 2019, from http://uis.unesco.org/en/country/bd

Wangnerud, L. (2000). Testing the politics of presence: Women's representation in the Swedish riksdag. *Scandinavian Political Studies, 23*, 67–91.

Women for Women. (1992). *Women in politics and decision making in the late twentieth century: A United Nations study*. Prepared by the Division for the Advancement of Women, pp. xii–xiii.

CHAPTER 7

Gender Budgeting and Governance Challenges: A Case Study of Bangladesh

Salahuddin M. Aminuzzaman

INTRODUCTION

During the last decade or so, gender has become an important issue in development discourses, but the dynamic interdependence between gender and governance has been overlooked in mainstream theoretical and empirical research (Nussbaum, Basu, Tambiah, & Gopal, 2003). Considerable evidence suggests that enhancing the status of women could lead to a higher rate of economic growth and greater economic stability (UN Women, 2018). Despite this, inequality, discrimination, and violence against women have emerged as serious policy concerns in development dialogues. It is estimated that gender equality has the potential to contribute US$ 12 trillion to global economic growth. A World Bank study estimates that in Bangladesh alone, the economic cost of violence against women is about 2.05 percent of the gross domestic product, that is, about USD $1.8 Billion (Watkins, 2016).

Conceptual discussion identifies two interrelated factors that are crucial for engendering good governance in the context of traditional patriarchal societies: first, dynamic actors, for instance, those involved in women's

S. M. Aminuzzaman (✉)
South Asian Institute of Policy and Governance (SIPG), North South University, Dhaka, Bangladesh

© The Author(s) 2020
I. Jamil et al. (eds.), *Gender Mainstreaming in Politics, Administration and Development in South Asia*,
https://doi.org/10.1007/978-3-030-36012-2_7

movements (with special focus on the nature and extent of their roles), and second, the relationship between the state and civil society (with focus on the nature of that relationship). Gender and governance discourses have been assessed from three dynamic perspectives: access to economic opportunities, professional opportunities, and political opportunities (UNDP, 1995). It is, therefore, generally accepted that the interface between gender and governance must be understood and analyzed in a wider perspective than that of the customary approaches (Nussbaum et al., 2003).

A country's public policy regime and legislative framework have significant influence on fostering and/or hindering gender-based rights and their inclusion in the development agenda. Factors such as political commitment, professional competence and skills, mobilization and allocation of resources, technical assistance, and a supportive institutional infrastructure provide the most important foundation for the implementation and enforcement of a progressive women's development policy.

It is also empirically verified that without sufficient focus on the importance and the role of public policy and legislation, the necessary mechanisms to effectively promote gender issues are almost impossible to establish. Empirical findings further suggest that cultural, structural, and interactional influences in dysfunctional and ritualistic policy regimes have further bred gender discrimination and, in some cases, lead to disempowerment (Bobbitt-Zeher, 2011).

Over the last decade and a half, Bangladesh has made some noticeable policy interventions to address gender equality issues and women's empowerment. In order to ensure financial allocations and distributive justice, the Government of Bangladesh (GoB) has, since 2009, introduced gender budgeting with a focus on gender-specific allocations. The prime purpose of gender budgeting is to make public expenditures more gender responsive and gender friendly, thus to enhance women's social dignity (Siddique, 2013).

Given the context, this chapter attempts to assess some of the procedural and institutional challenges that affect the formulation and implementation of gender budgeting of selected ministries in Bangladesh.

Context

During the last decade, conditions for women in Bangladesh have significantly improved on some selected social indicators, for instance, those of the Gender Equity Index (GEI). Bangladesh stands now in the top position amongst the South Asian countries and second in Asia (after the Philippines) (Global Gender Gap Report, 2018). Nevertheless, the status of women and their participation in the political process, the economic sphere, and in decision-making structures are still poorly visible and inadequate.

The Seventh Five Year Plan (SFYP) of the GoB duly recognizes that "women in Bangladesh are under-utilized, underpaid, and under-appreciated" (GoB, 2015, p. 46). The plan sets the gender budget target at 29.5 percent (at least) by 2020. In order to institutionalize gender-based planning approaches, the SFYP further asserts the need for a "responsive budgeting system." Similarly, the GoB's Vision 2021 foresees "a society that sustains gender parity and laws relating to gender inequality and makes those gender sensitive" (GoB, 2012, p. 11).

Gender balance is one of the core principles of the state policy of Bangladesh. In order to promote gender balance, over the years a number of policy measures have been taken to institutionalize a gender-sensitive planning and budgeting system. The SFYP recognizes the need to expand women's participation in the productive engagement process from about 29 percent at present to 40 percent by 2021. The SFYP also asserts that "all laws relating to gender inequality are to be reviewed to ensure gender sensitivity, with due respect for personal laws and community-specific customs" (GoB, 2012, p. 213).

Against this backdrop, this chapter presents an overview and assessment of Bangladesh's gender budgeting and its allocation pattern. It assesses the methodological approaches to preparing the gender budget. It also explores the extent to which the gender budgeting has been able to shape and prioritize the gender-responsive and need-based redistribution of public resources.

The quantitative data for this research have been collected from the Ministry of Finance and the selected line ministries/agencies in the fiscal year 2015–2016. The budget documents—annual development-plan books, the Department Project Proforma, Annual Development Program allocation, notifications/circulars, orders, and relevant documents of the Ministry of Finance and line agencies—have been reviewed. Senior officials in the Ministry of Finance and line ministries have been interviewed. Furthermore, data and descriptive narratives have been discussed with and validated by strategic stakeholders including senior policymakers. Key civil servants in the respective ministries, particularly those assigned to monitor and review the gender-related activities of the ministries (called 'gender focal points'), have been interviewed to understand and assess the perspectives of the ministries. In addition, some professionals of selected civil society organizations have been interviewed to capture their perspectives.

THE CONCEPT OF GENDER BUDGETING

Up until the early 1980s, macro-economic policies in general and fiscal policies in particular were gender-neutral if not gender blind (Zuckerman, 2000). Researchers since the early 1980s have noted that the macro-economic policies of governments in general lacked an appropriate gender perspective. Some researchers have further observed that "the prescriptions for cuts in social spending and ambitious growth targets spell disaster for nearly 60 percent of women," and that those who are poor usually "gain nothing from the formal market economy" (Taylor, 1997, p. 13)

Gender budgeting is a normative framework for ensuring distributive justice and transformative change in the allocation of public resources. It aims to develop a rational allocation of public resources based on an appropriate application of gender analysis (O'Hagan & Klatzer, 2018). A standard definition of gender budgeting refers to "a budget, incorporating a gender perspective at all levels of the budgetary process and restructuring revenues and expenditures in order to promote gender equality" (COE, 2009, p. 7). Gender budgeting is thus a policy instrument to mainstream gender in budgetary processes. It is based on the premise that a budget is a gateway and key determinant of policy formulation and modulation. Along with this is the assumption that a responsive budget could have a significant impact on distributive justice and gender-focused public expenditures.

Gender budgeting has gained prominence in recent years, and was given additional impetus by the Fourth World Conference on Women, held in Beijing in 1995, which called for ensuring the integration of a gender perspective in budgetary policies and programs (Sarraf, 2003). There has been an increasing trend to use a 'gender lens' when allocating public funds. More precisely, gender budgeting has come to be recognized as an important tool for allocating funding and for measuring the impact of public investment on citizens, based on their gender identity. As a formal mechanism, the introduction of gender budgeting has enabled governments to restructure revenues and spending in order to reduce socio-economic inequalities between men and women (Stokey, 2006).

Gender budgeting is essentially an instrument that attempts to ensure gender mainstreaming in the budgetary system and process (Kuosmanen, 2016) and to ensure that budget allocations at all levels are made with a gender perspective. It, therefore, demands a new system of arranging revenues and expenditure structures in budgetary systems. This unique type of budget primarily attempts to utilize resources to reduce the gender gap in various strategic sectors and make them gender responsive and sensitive, so that various development projects and government programs will channel resources to meet vital gender needs. Gender budgeting broadly attempts to address the gender gap in opportunities and outputs, and ultimately to empower women both socially and economically.

Nevertheless, gender budgeting does not necessarily imply specific and separate allocations for women. It simply presents an analysis and calculation of a country's national budget from the viewpoint of gender sensitivity in the various development and non-development activities of the government. It could, therefore, also be described as an effective instrument for assessing and understanding the extent of gender responsiveness in public policies and programs. In broader term, this is a budget system that aims to ensure greater gender responsiveness in public budgets, while more specifically, it aims also to promote equity, efficiency, and effectiveness in government policy and implementation, to develop an alternative perspective and set of values and principles that prioritize the socio-economic needs of women.

Drawing on the positive outcomes worldwide, gender budgeting can be summarized as follows: (a) it is a policy framework that leads to fiscal policies more oriented toward gender equality; (b) it initiates various types of tax restructuring; (c) it introduces a new perspective in analyzing public spending; and (d) it is a transparent approach for budgetary allocation in favor of women and, most importantly, it ensures allocative justice and gender equality.

Discourses on Gender Budgeting

In development studies literature, several researches focus on critical issues of inclusive growth within a gender perspective. Kabeer (1994) argues that 'class analysis alone is insufficient for assessing the priorities and problems of the poor, while a 'gender analysis' uses a perspective that could reveal the true and in-depth assessment of the challenges of women's subordination and exclusion.

Drawing on Indian experiences, Das and Mishra (2006) reveal that gender budget preparation is based on a set of assumptions related to the scheme-based allocations assumed to be directly benefiting women. However, such assumptions seem to be based on the unrealistic assessment that eventually weakens the relevance and spirit of such a budget. For example, the distribution of contraceptives and support for family planning are treated as a women-specific allocation, which is highly questionable. Experiences from India further reveal that the government apparently considers budget allocations for child development, family planning, and rural housing as part of the gender budget. Such assumptions are contrary to the very spirit of gender budgeting and merely measure allocation differences without considering the overall impact of the given budget.

Since the mid-1980s, gender budgeting has been introduced in many countries, and efforts have been made to understand and challenge the macro-economic theorizing and inclusive policy regimes (Cagatay, 2003). Unfortunately, despite the introduction of gender equality and a pro-poor budget framework, there is no evidence of a visible and tangible impact of public spending through gender-responsive tools (Cagatay, 2003). It is, therefore, strongly argued that there is a need to develop a comprehensive gender framework for fiscal policy, and to do research which could lead to creating a meaningful gender budget (Stewart, 2017).

Actual gender budget implementation in some cases seems to suffer from a process of 'evaporation' (Kusakabe, 2005), especially at the lower levels of government. Such evaporation partly occurs because of a lack of political commitment to gender mainstreaming as well as misconceptions about gender issues at different levels of policy making. Thus, Kusakabe (2005) notes that the concept of gender mainstreaming remains vague and unaddressed.

Mishra and Navanita (2012, p. 28) observe that the process and manner in which gender-responsive budgeting in India has been implemented is "a classic case of putting the cart before the horse." The authors note that there is theoretical and applied asymmetry between gender budget statements and the actual gender budgeting process. Similarly, Mishra and Jhamb (2007) observe that the gender-based programs and allocations remain plagued by 'mistakes,' where several schemes have been incorrectly listed as being gender focused. In some cases, gender budgeting is merely seen as a routine form-filling exercise and based on hypothetical and/or assumed data filled into a standard format. The impact of the budget is not measured by real evidence (Siddique, 2013). Kapungu (2008) therefore concludes that gender budgeting has created a new hype and a new policy wave, but that there is still room for a strategic shift to ensure the actual design and implementation of gender-sensitive policies.

The global and regional evidence tends to suggest that the effectiveness of gender budgeting depends on a host of factors (Frey & Kohnen, 2012). These include: (i) a clearly spelled-out gender policy with sector-specific interventions; (ii) setting realistic targets; (iii) technical preparation and capacity building; (iv) taking a learning-by-doing approach; v. internal and external monitoring; and (vi) public accountability and transparency.

The State of Women in Bangladesh—An Overview

Over the last decade, Bangladesh has made significant progress in the area of gender equity. It scored a value of 0.55 in the Gender Equity Index (GEI) 2012 and is ranked 114 out of 168 countries. For specific sectors such as education, Bangladesh scored a GEI value of 0.81, which indicates medium-level status, while for economic activities, the score is 0.65. The lowest score is 0.18 for women's empowerment. In the Social Progress

Table 7.1 Gender gap: South Asian scenario 2018

Country	Position
Bangladesh	48
Sri Lanka	100
India	108
Nepal	105
Maldives	113
Bhutan	122
Pakistan	148

Source: Global Gender Gap Report (2018), World Economic Forum

Table 7.2   Gender distribution of economic participation and opportunities

	Score	Average	Female Male Ratio
Economic participation &opportunity	0.4410	0.586	0.42
Labor force participation	0.425541	0.669	0.55
Wage equality for similar work	0.5805	0.645	0.54
Estimated earned income (US$,PPP)	0.489	0.510	0.49
Legislators, senior officials managers	0.1207	0.329	0.12
Professional and technical workers	0.421	0.753	0.42

Source: Global Gender Gap Report (2018)

Index 2014, Bangladesh scored 52.04, which is a little higher than the scores of Nepal, India, and Pakistan, but lower compared to Sri Lanka (59.71). However, it is noteworthy that the Global Gender Gap Report 2016 places Bangladesh at the top of the South Asian countries in gender equality for two consecutive years.

Macro-level data, meanwhile, indicate a gross rise in the income of women and the poorer section of the community, but the Gini coefficient remains the same. Furthermore, the gender-disaggregated data show an increasing level of disparity between men and women.

Table 7.1 presents a snapshot of the gender gap scenario in South Asian countries.

In the global gender ranking, Bangladesh has moved forward, especially in terms of health and political empowerment. However, the comparative data on the global gender gap further reveal that Bangladesh's ranking has slipped in some selected indicators. For economic participation and opportunity, it appears, from the recent comparative data, that women in Bangladesh are still relatively low in senior, managerial, and professional positions. Table 7.2 shows that the economic participation, estimated income, and professional and managerial engagement of women are relatively low compared to men in Bangladesh.

OVERVIEW OF POLICY FRAMEWORK OF BANGLADESH: GENDER PERSPECTIVE

As regards the GoB's macro-level planning documents, the need to empower women and to address gender issues is well recognized. As the SFYP duly recognizes, "Women make up almost half of the population of Bangladesh; however, they remain one of the most at risk social groups of the country. Although steps have been taken to advance women's position in society, they continue to have lower economic, social and political opportunities" (GoB, 2015, p. 718). The SFYP further notes that "one other obstacle to empowerment lies in the persistence of gender disparities—in higher education, access to work, and in wages. It is a fact that women in Bangladesh are under-utilized, underpaid, and under-appreciated" (GoB, 2015, p. 101).

The SFYP sets the targeted gender budget as a percentage of the total budget, from 28.2 percent in 2014 to 29.5 percent by 2020. The GoB emphasized the importance of gender equity in the health sector and more equitable and gender-friendly access to health services. In terms of educational attainment, gender parity has been strongly emphasized for female enrollment in primary and secondary education.

In fact, "empowering women and reducing gender inequality" is the SFYP's strategic approach to addressing gender issues. One of the core objectives of the SFYP is to ensure women's advancement as self-reliant human beings and to reduce discriminatory barriers by taking both development and institutional measures. Thus, the plan asserts that empowerment strategies to enhance women's capabilities and access to resources and opportunities should also address the barriers in structures and social norms. The plan thus attempts to ensure gender equality, income equality, and social protection. The SFYP emphasizes the following strategic principles of women's empowerment and development: (i) enhancement of human capacity; (ii) increased engagement in economic development activities; (iii) enhancing voice and accountability; (iv) creating an enabling environment for women's advancement; and (v) more access to and opportunities for economic engagement.

Vision 2021 is a perspective plan of the GoB that aims to transform the country from a relatively low-income economy to the primary stage of a middle-income country by the year 2021. The prime aim of the 2021 Vision is to eradicate poverty and make the society "full of caring and educated people living healthy and happy lives." The vision, therefore, foresees "a society where '*gender equality*' would be assured."

BUDGETARY REFORM AND GENDER

Gender budgeting as a policy commitment of the GoB started with the Medium Term Budgetary Framework in 2008. This framework started a piloting process to enhance budget efficiency and responsiveness and to introduce the Gender Responsive Budgeting System with performance indicators. This system was meant to be the foundation for promoting gender equality. In 2009, the government initiated the Recurrent, Capital, Gender, and Poverty Model to ensure a percentage of allocation dedicated to benefiting women and addressing poverty. Accordingly, the Ministry of Finance set guidelines for the allocation of gender-responsive resource and aligned them with the identified priority areas based on a set of 14 criteria that addressed gender development and equality. In summary, we may recognize the three sets of policy drivers that address gender issues in Bangladesh: Vision 2021, the SFYP, and gender budgeting.

Assessment of Gender Budget of Selected Ministries

Bangladesh's gender budgeting started with a piloting of a gender-disaggregated beneficiary assessment of community health services provided by the Ministry of Health. After reviewing the findings of this piloting, the GoB decided, in principle, to incorporate gender into the mainstream budget. The Ministry of Finance introduced a working manual to explain different generic examples of activities of various ministries/divisions having potential implications on women's advancement and rights. Over the years, the number of ministries with gender budgeting increased substantially. As of today, all ministries and divisions of the government have been brought under the gender budget system. Figure 7.1 shows the trends of overall gender budget as the percentage of the total

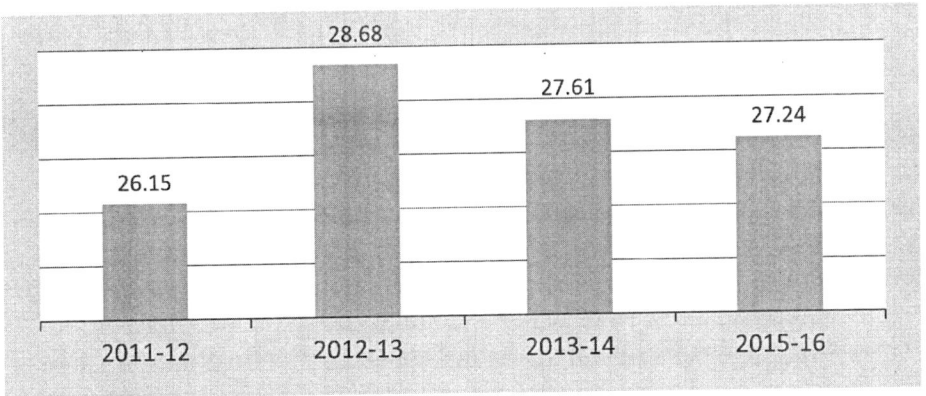

Fig. 7.1 Annual allocation of gender budget (as % of total budget) 2011–2016. (Source: Ministry of Finance Database)

national budget. Starting with about 26.15 percent, it grew to 27.24 percent, with an average allocation of 27.42 percent over the years.

Figure 7.1 presents the gender budget allocation of 25 different development ministries for the financial year 2015–2016.

Some General Observations on Gender Budgeting

Various case studies and country experiences reveal that gender budgeting is stalled, ineffective, unsuccessful, and dysfunctional. This is due to several factors: inadequate class analysis (Kabeer, 1994); wrong or inappropriate and unrealistic assumptions on women's issues (Das & Mishra, 2006); the lack of a comprehensive gender framework for fiscal policy, and a weak conceptual understanding of gender mainstreaming (Cagatay, 2003); and incorrect allocations and scheme selections (Siddique, 2013). There are also a host of other factors that distort the effectiveness of gender budgets, for instance, inappropriate interventions and unrealistic targets, weak technical design, the absence of effective internal and external monitoring, and the lack of external accountability and transparency (Frey & Kohnen, 2012). Unsurprisingly, Bangladesh's experiences with gender budgeting seem to be similar to experiences elsewhere in the world.

Figure 7.2 shows the gender budget allocations of the 25 most relevant and strategic ministries for the fiscal year 2015–2016. A detailed review and analysis of the budgets lead to the following broad observations:

1. Out of the 25 ministries that are reviewed, the highest allocation (76.98%) is in the Ministry of Women's and Children's Affairs, and the lowest (7.27%) is in the Ministry of Home Affairs.
2. The Ministry of Home Affairs, by virtue of its mandate, is supposed to play a vital role in maintaining law and order. With the increasingly high rate of violence against women, gender-insensitive attitudes amongst a section of the community, and women's limited scope to exercise their rights, women are still being marginalized and suffer from insecurity. Moreover, citizens' trust in the police force is relatively low on the whole, and especially low amongst women.[1] A very recent study indicates that women appear to have

[1] Research Monographs of 8th Semester PA 414, "Institutional Trust of Service Agencies—Does gender matter?", Department of Public Administration, University of Dhaka, 2016.

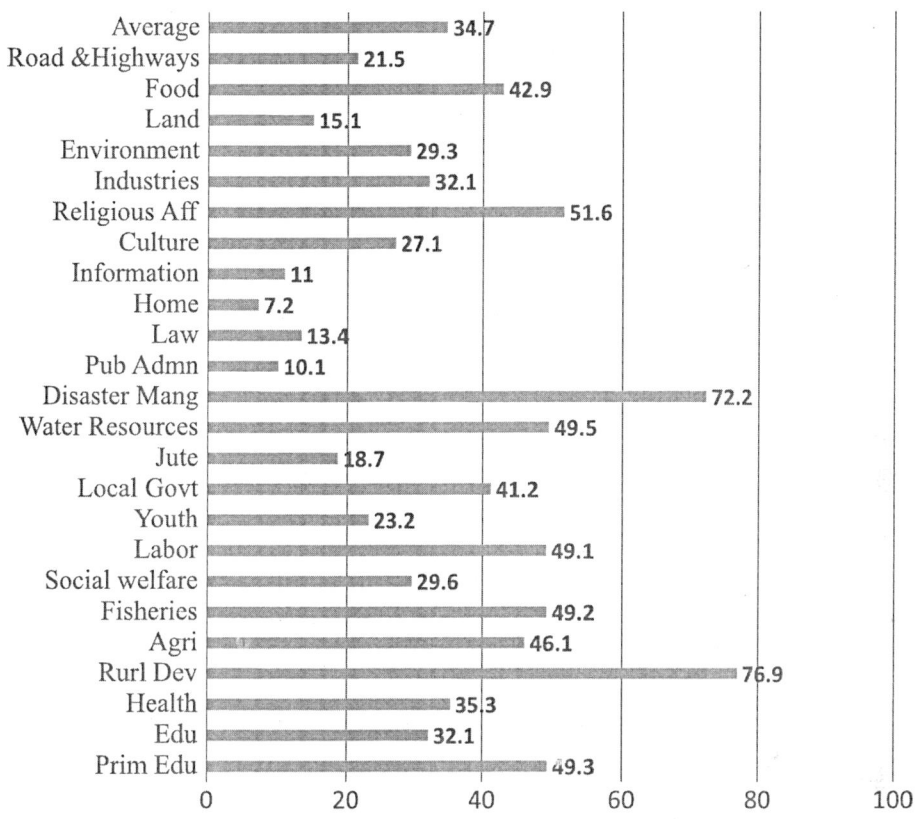

Fig. 7.2 Gender share as % of the total budget of selected ministries 2015–2016

low access to, and low trust in, the police force (Rahman, 2018). Considering its role, and institutional importance, and scope for extended pro-active engagement, the lowest percentage (7%) of the gender budget allocation of the Ministry of Home Affairs appears to be surprising and unanticipated.

3. The second largest contribution goes to the Ministry of Disaster Management (72.2%). This allocation appears to be realistic, as available empirical data indicate that women are usually the "critical and worst victims of disaster." However, there is hardly any detail in

the gender budget on the nature of the projects that have been implemented to address the needs and priorities of women.

4. The third largest gender budget contribution goes to the Ministry of Religious Affairs (51.6%). This allocation appears to be very high. Due to the conservative religious and cultural context, women's access to the mosques is restricted in rural Bangladesh. Such a high allocation is therefore ambiguous and not target specific.

5. It is notable that some of the strategic ministries such as Education, Health, Social Welfare, and Information, have a relatively low gender budget allocation (on average 29.6%), even lower than the average for all ministries combined.

6. An overall average of the allocation for all 25 ministries is 29.52 percent, however, if the average is calculated without the Ministry of Women's and Children's Affairs, the percentage slides down to 27.61 percent.

7. It, therefore, appears that in addition to snags in design and implementation, the average gender budget allocation is meager when compared with the total sectoral budget.

Further in-depth reviews of the gender budget reports prepared by the respective ministries do not specifically mention what has actually been achieved during the last fiscal year. The reports do not provide any information on what specific areas of change were to be made through the allocations for gender in the assigned sectors. The ministerial gender budgets tend to produce a set of "wish lists" for the officials in the ministries, yet without having specific targets and output indicators.

There is no body at the national level that can monitor the effectiveness of gender-based budgeting and oversee whether the allocations are being spent in the right track and result in any change. None of the gender budgeting documents, specifically the Development Project Proforma of the selected ministries specifically, mention the disaggregated budgetary allocations, and there are no precise indications as regards the number of beneficiaries and the potential development outcome.

The gender budget reports prepared by the concerned ministries do not provide any information as to what specific changes would be made through the gender allocations for the sector. Furthermore, based on the categories outlined in the gender budget for the Ministry of Women's and

Children's Affairs,[2] the evidence tends to suggest that all ministerial budgets seem to be 'gender blind' and/or 'gender neutral.'

UNDERSTANDING GENDER EQUALITY—LESSONS LEARNED

The global and regional evidence tends to suggest that the effectiveness of gender budgeting depends on a host of factors (Frey & Kohnen, 2012). These include: (i) a clearly spelled-out gender policy with sector-specific interventions; (ii) setting realistic targets; (iii) technical preparation and capacity building; (iv) adopting a learning-by-doing approach; (v) internal and external monitoring; and (vi) public accountability and transparency.

A number of critical factors could be identified that affect the preparation and implementation of gender budget processes in Bangladesh:

- *Absence of more in-depth gender analyses.* A prerequisite for mainstreaming gender equality is to understand how and why gender inequalities affect the productivity of an organization, and how to find appropriate opportunities that support greater equality between women and men.
- *Gender-disaggregated data are critical.* The availability and effective use of gender-disaggregated data and statistics can ensure effective and responsive gender-based interventions. The lack of such data hinders proper evaluation. Oftentimes the available data on which to make judgments are poor and out of date.
- *Inadequate institutional preparedness.* Policy commitments to gender budgeting are not always backed by good gender distribution strategies of the government agencies. There may also be inadequate methodological preparedness and a lack of sufficient funds to fulfill the policy commitments. Line agencies seriously lack an appropriate conceptual and practical understanding of a gender-based budgeting system.
- *Ownership of the agenda.* Most importantly, gender budgeting as a concept is seen as an externally imposed agenda—a top-down initiative which is not attended by 'real' commitment on the part of the

---

[2] The categories are *gender blind*—projects that do not directly cater to or address women's development; *gender neutral*—projects in which both men and women are likely to be benefitted equally; *gender specific*—projects exclusively formulated for the development of women; *gender responsive*—projects/policies sensitive to gender parity.

implementers. This is in spite of the fact that there seems to be a strong political will. Policy planners seem to have a ritualistic commitment, hence follow-up actions are often delayed and in some cases are not even made.

Gender-allocation analysis in the ministries' own budget documents is generally not rigorous enough for assessing the allocations and their outcomes. In most cases, the ministries often claim to have achieved the target. They tend to insist that there has been a notable positive impact on women's advancement and rights. Such claims, in almost all cases, are not supported by any substantive and real evidence.

The key performance indicators of the ministries simply present the progress and achievements being made by the allocated resources, but they do not provide any gender-disaggregated indicators. In fact, the project-monitoring plans of such interventions do not have any gender-disaggregated database.

The planning documents of each of the ministries reveal that the ministries have not yet professionally spelled out their mission statements as regards gender and resource allocations to promote gender equity. These mission statements of the line agencies are still based on the standardized Rules of Business and Allocation of Business of the Government, which are largely identical and generally formulated without considering gender-related issues. In some cases, the gender-related programs and projects of ministries are not complementary to, or coordinated with, the SFYP's own gender-related goals. This disconnection at times breeds confusion and even inconsistencies between the program/project design and priorities of a given ministry and other sectoral ministries.

In summary, an objective review of gender budgeting in Bangladesh reveals that: (i). there is a general lack of conceptual clarity and understanding amongst the officials on gender budgeting as a concept and its purpose; (ii). ministries in general do not follow a standardized and appropriate methodology for preparing gender budgeting; (iii). none of the ministries and line agencies have any monitoring mechanism with specific, objectively verifiable indicators (OVI) to follow up or track the gender budget; (iv). the *gender focal points*[3] of the ministries that are supposed to

---

[3] A gender focal point of a ministry is the assigned officer who monitors and reviews the gender-related activities of the concerned ministries, with particular responsibility to follow the gender-budget implementation and its implications.

track gender budget process management are in most cases inactive, and in some cases, not even assigned; and (v). none of the ministries covered in this study have any comprehensive database, nor do they maintain an appropriate gender-segregated data bank.

There appears to be a gross lack of conceptual clarity on gender budgeting amongst professionals working in the different ministries. Almost no ministry has disaggregated data or an information bank with gender-sensitive indicators. There is also a shortage of skills in designing gender budgets and responsive planning in the ministries. None of the ministries covered in the study has ever used a gender audit system as a supportive monitoring tool, and none of them seem to be fully aligned with the broad sectoral policy of the ministries. More surprisingly, measurable gender-specific indicators for the sectoral policy are also missing.

CONCLUSIONS

Bangladesh introduced the gender budget system in 2008, as a policy framework for making the fiscal policies more oriented toward gender equality. However, the country has neither been able to initiate a substantive gender-responsive tax restructuring nor adopt an objective approach to budgetary allocations in favor of women. Many of the gender indicators mask significant economic disparities.

There is hardly any credible evidence to suggest that the introduction of gender budgeting has fostered a noticeable reduction in inequalities between women and men in Bangladesh. Nor can we find evidence of noticeable improvement in the quality and efficiency of public services in line with the gender-specific interventions. It is, therefore, difficult to assess to what extent the introduction of gender budgeting has ensured allocative justice and gender equality.

Gender budgeting in Bangladesh is a significant policy intervention, but the method for allocating and prioritizing project interventions does not seem to be based on a sound framework or gender analysis. The introduction of gender budgeting has not been able to respond to the needs and priorities based on objective analysis of gender implications. The evidence therefore suggests that budget-making processes are still gender-neutral in their effects.

This prompts two questions: Why is Bangladesh doing so well with regard to gender parity compared to other South Asian nations? Why has gender budgeting not been effectively formulated in the ministries despite it being a priority of the GoB?

Way Forward

The line ministries need to have specific and objectively verifiable indicators (OVIs) on gender-specific interventions and to devise standardized monitoring tools. During the design phase of programs and specific projects, gender-disaggregated monitoring indicators should be in place. In-house capacity of the planning unit of the respective ministries also needs to be developed to monitor gender-focused projects. The ministries also need to develop a data bank for sex-disaggregated data/information with measurable gender-specific indicators. Furthermore, the GoB should actively consider the introduction of a gender audit system as a monitoring tool for programs and projects.

In order to assess the impact of gender budgeting and to address the inadequacies of the sector-specific policy interventions, there is a need for regular measurement of gender inequalities. The Gender Development Index may be used to assess the gaps between men and women and identify and address sector-specific policy imperfections.

The ministries' rules of business and allocation of business need to be revised and to have new clauses to address gender disparities. The Ministry of Planning may issue circulars to ensure that the rules of business, allocation of business, sectoral policies, and national policies are coherently linked and synchronized with the respective five-year plan of the sector.

Furthermore, such specific indicators need to be added and aligned to project documents such as the Technical Assistance Project Proforma (TAPP) and the Development Project Proforma.

The government may seriously consider the active involvement of grassroots-based local government, civil society organizations, and women's development networks in the conception, planning, design, and implementation of gender budgets.

The Ministry of Finance, with active support from local think tanks, should independently assess the gender-budget implications and their impact on the concerned ministries. Furthermore, capacities should be developed within the ministries to undertake gender-disaggregated beneficiary assessments of the major interventions.

REFERENCES

Bobbitt-Zeher, D. (2011). Gender discrimination at work: Connecting gender stereotypes, institutional policies, and gender composition of workplace. *Gender and Society, 25*(6), 764–786.

Cagatay, N. (2003). Gender budgets and beyond: Feminist fiscal policy in the context of globalization. *Gender and Development, 11*(1), 15–24.

Council of Europe (COE). (2009, April). *Gender budgeting: Practical implementation.* Handbook, Council of Europe, Directorate General of Human Rights and Legal Affairs.

Das, S., & Mishra, Y. (2006). Gender budgeting statement: Misleading and patriarchal assumptions. *Economic and Political Weekly, 41*(30), 3285–3288.

Frey, R., & Kohnen, M. (2012). *Guidance gender budgeting in public administration.* Vienna: Bundesministerin Für Frauen und Öffentlichen Dienst.

Global Gender Gap Report. (2018). World Economic Forum, Geneva.

Government of Bangladesh. (2012). *Perspective plan of Bangladesh 2010–2021: Making vision 2021 a reality.* General Economics Division, Planning Commission, Government of the People's Republic of Bangladesh.

Government of Bangladesh. (2015). *7th Five Year Plan 2016–2020: Accelerating growth, empowering citizens.* General Economic Division, Planning Commission.

Kabeer, N. (1994). *Reverse reality: Hierarchies in development thought.* London: Verso.

Kapungu, R. (2008). The Zimbabwe gender budgeting and women's empowerment programme. Issue: Engendering national & global economic policies. *Agenda, 22*(78), 68–78. https://doi.org/10.1080/10130950.2008.9674985

Kuosmanen, J. (2016). Human rights, public budgets and epistemic challenges. *Human Rights Review, 17*(2), 247–267.

Kusakabe, K. (2005). Gender mainstreaming in government offices in Thailand, Cambodia, and Laos: Perspectives from below. *Gender and Development, 13*(2), 46–56.

Mishra, Y., & Jhamb, B. (2007). What does budget 2007–08 offer women? *Economic and Political Weekly, 42*(16), 1423–1428.

Mishra, Y., & Navanita, S. (2012). Gender responsive budgeting in India: What has gone wrong? *Economic and Political Weekly, 47*(17), 50–57.

Nussbaum, M., Basu, A., Tambiah, Y., & Gopal, J. N. (2003). *Essay on gender and governance.* New Delhi: Human Development Resource Centre, UNDP.

O'Hagan, A., & Klatzer, E. (2018). Introducing gender budgeting in Europe. In A. O'Hagan & E. Klatzer (Eds.), *Gender budgeting in Europe* (pp. 3–18). London: Palgrave Macmillan.

Rahman, M. (2018). *Policing mega city—A study of metropolitan Dhaka.* Unpublished PhD dissertation, University of Dhaka.

Sarraf, F. (2003). Gender-responsive government budgeting. *International Monetary Fund Working Paper 03/83*. International Monetary Fund, Washington, DC.

Siddique, K. (2013). *A case study of gender responsive budgeting in Bangladesh*. London: Commonwealth Secretariat.

Stewart, M. (2017). Gender inequality in Australia's tax-transfer system. In M. Stewart (Ed.), *Tax, social policy and gender: Rethinking equality and efficiency*. Canberra: ANU Press.

Stokey, J. G. (2006). Gender budgeting. *IMF Working Paper No. 06/232*. International Monetary Fund (IMF), Washington, DC.

Taylor, V. (1997). Economic gender injustice: The MACRO picture. *Agenda, 13*(33), 9–25. https://doi.org/10.1080/10130950.1997.9675600

UN Women. (2018). Facts and figures: Economic empowerment. Retrieved May 5, 2019, from http://www.unwomen.org/en/what-we-do/economic-empowerment/facts-and-figures

UNDP. (1995). *Human Development Report 1995*. New York: Oxford University Press.

Watkins, R. (2016, January 1). The road to 2030: Development challenges in Bangladesh. *The Daily Star*.

Zuckerman, E. (2000). *Macroeconomic policies and gender in the World Bank*. Background paper for integrating gender into the World Bank's Work: A strategy for action. Washington, DC: World Bank.

CHAPTER 8

Empowering Women Through e-Governance in the Indian Province of Odisha: Capacity Building as an Enabling Measure

Sangita Dhal

INTRODUCTION

Women's empowerment, emancipation, and gender justice have been the focus of global concern for many years. Situating women in the new global economic order raises a few important questions with regard to gender distinctions and inequalities. There have been momentous changes in the world in the past few decades; some of them are transformational in nature, while others, due to a host of factors, have warranted immediate attention from the global community to redress the damages caused. Women are a vulnerable category in the demographic profile of any society, not just in the underdeveloped world. Being the greatest victims of

This paper is a part of my post doctoral research on 'Emprical study on information and communication technology practices in Odisha' and was funded by University Grants Commission, New Delhi, India.

S. Dhal (✉)
Department of Political Science, Kalindi College, University of Delhi, Delhi, India

© The Author(s) 2020
I. Jamil et al. (eds.), *Gender Mainstreaming in Politics, Administration and Development in South Asia*,
https://doi.org/10.1007/978-3-030-36012-2_8

knowledge deficit today, women suffer from inbuilt weakness vis-à-vis men. One way to help women overcome this problem is to build their capacities. In fact, capacity building is considered an essential precondition for the successful implementation of policies and programs meant to ameliorate and emancipate women (Stivers, 2002; Jaggar, 1983). To ensure greater benefits, it is essential to empower women through guaranteeing their constitutional rights, and, in particular, to give them easy access to knowledge and information that act as catalysts in the process of such empowerment (Young, 2000). Women's capacity building is facilitated by new measures and initiatives such as training programs and electronic governance (henceforth e-governance). The enabling effects of e-governance are measured in terms of economic development and democratic dividends, which strengthen democracy through inclusive governance and citizen participation. Experience shows that e-government applications have benefited India's marginalized communities, which now have access to better service delivery and various entitlements, thereby overcoming numerous hurdles they previously faced. Through its application, e-governance can also provide a democratic space and equal opportunity to women, and contribute to their economic and social empowerment (Boraian, 2008).

The last decade has witnessed the emergence of powerful liberal and eco-feminist positions that challenge the view that women share an uneasy relationship with technology. Pippa Norris (2001, pp. 82–84) rightly observes that technology can be an important solution in building women's economic, social, and political capabilities so that they do not suffer the stigma of discrimination imposed by patriarchal structures in society. Apart from introducing progressive legislation, the state also needs to provide enabling tools for building the capacities of the hitherto technologically challenged and deprived segment of the society (Kapur & Crossman, 1999). It is believed that through enhanced capacity-building measures, women would make a significant contribution to society, for instance, by having a positive impact not only on the household income but also on encouraging inclusive development in the country as a whole (Rajneesh, 2008). The need for capacity building emerges from the federal framework of Indian polity. The nature and scope for the e-governance initiatives undertaken by the last few governments envisage standardization and consistency of rules and principles across the various states of India. It is therefore important to build human capacities in terms of knowledge, training, and skills to implement and sustain the various e-governance projects for good governance and inclusive economic development goals (Prakash & Singh, 2008).

There is a paucity of research on gender and technology, and most existing studies have been guided by a Western lens with regard to the impact of technology on gender relations in society. Gender and ICT (information, communication, and technology) projects in developing and under-developing countries are much more challenging than those in developed countries. The challenge of enabling both men and women to enjoy the fruit of the ICT sector's revolution is exceedingly complex. Most literature available on gender and technology is based on the Western idea of technology as a 'given' to the citizens, as an enabler and instrument of empowerment, irrespective of gender considerations (Fox, Johnson, & Rosser, 2006; Gill & Grint, 1995). The situation in India presents a contrast to this Western idea: under the prevailing socio-cultural eco-system in which technology is considered the privilege of the few and access to it is limited to the miniscule minority, gender relations and their impact on the society need be critically analyzed. In other words, technology does not automatically come as a 'given', nor is it necessarily an enabler or facilitator for empowering women, economically, socially, or in other ways. Rather, it has to be seen through the prism of complex socio-cultural bias and gender discrimination. This chapter will, therefore, examine the relationship between gender and technology from the perspective of deep-seated patriarchal prejudices that work against women, which tend to discriminate against them, and deny them access to the technology that has the potential to connect them to a world of diverse opportunities and pave the way for their substantive emancipation.

Acknowledging the importance of women's empowerment at the grassroots level, this chapter attempts to examine the significance of e-governance and analyze its impact through the functioning of the Common Service Centers (CSCs, *Jana Seva Kendras*) or rural tele-centers, which facilitate women's empowerment through ICT tools along with participative models of governance. The CSCs were introduced as a sustainable business model for the entrepreneurs to earn a living by providing the common citizens access to services through a digital framework. The state of Odisha in its attempt to ensure good governance percolating down to the grassroots level has initiated many such endeavors in the last one decade. The purpose of bringing good governance to the target population who are beneficiaries of the state-sponsored social welfare schemes is to ensure that the desired outcome of such plans and programs meet the expectations of the policy makers.

Good governance as an enabling process is seen as the only way to go forward in this mission by using certain best practices of administration and delivery mechanism. From this perspective, governance is seen to be an effective tool to not only make governance transparent, accountable and responsive but also make the delivery system work faster and convenient for woman to avail and access government schemes and claim their entitlements without much human interface and logistic constraints.

The present study is an attempt to analyze governance activities which offers both opportunities and challenges that women are exposed to due to the changing nature of the economy. These changes and constraints often translate into real-life hardships and even violence due to their exposure to a new work environment where they are constantly fighting for their dignity and rights. This chapter also explores how e-governance tools are helping to create a level-playing field for women in the Indian state of Odisha. It also examines the prospects and possibilities that a new generation of women have as they face myriad challenges while trying to avail themselves of the growing opportunities and make informed decisions on issues that affect their lives.

The concept of e-governance is explored in this study as a major outcome of new public service reforms in Odisha. These have had a tremendous impact on the functions of the government and its administrative policies. One of the pioneering initiatives of the rural entrepreneurship model in Odisha—the *e-gramaproject* (e-village project) implemented in the Ganjam district—was conceived as a pilot project to bring the benefits of ICT to the district's entire population and to government offices situated at the block and district levels. In some parts of the district, the e-gramakiosks were entirely and efficiently managed by all-women self-help groups (WSHGs). Computer training programs and their applications were taught to the literate members of these groups through the e-grama project. Studies have shown that this IT-enabled project not only helped bridge the growing digital divide between men and women, but also increased computer literacy among the women living in rural areas and helped generate more employment opportunities in these regions (Dash & Naik, 2006).

OBJECTIVES

This chapter explores how e-governance tools are helping to level the playing field for women in Odisha. As intimated in the introduction, it also examines the prospects and possibilities which younger women have as they try to take advantage of the growing opportunities and to make informed decisions on issues that affect their lives. There are two specific objectives which shape the contours of the study. First, an attempt is made to develop a conceptual framework for understanding the relationship between women's empowerment and ICT. Here the focus will be on the importance of rural women's skill development and capacity building, which enable them to apply for jobs such as running the CSCs. It is believed that imparting certain 'soft' skills and increasing computer literacy amongst young women in rural areas will open up opportunities for them to become self-sufficient. Inasmuch as this creates self-employment and raises their self-esteem, there is a need for such skills and education amongst the rural woman. The government should therefore set up skill-enhancement programs for woman in rural areas, to contribute to their ability to earn a living.

Second, the study seeks to find out whether technology in itself is sufficient for empowerment, or whether a socio-cultural eco-system needs to be created to compliment technology as an enabler. The scope of the study includes critical analysis of gender bias in Indian society, which results in discrimination and the exclusion of women from entering newly established CSCs where they can seek self-employment that would lead to their economic empowerment. The study also tries to identify the structural impediments, bureaucratic hurdles, societal pressures, patriarchal domination, and gender stereotypes that are often seen as roadblocks to women's empowerment and self-reliance.

The present chapter addresses women's empowerment through their involvement in the common service centers (CSCs), a new entrepreneurship venture based on digital technology. The development of CSCs in the rural areas has contributed significantly to the employment expansion and economic development that addresses the pertinent problems of unemployment and inclusive growth among the rural youth in general and the educated rural women in particular. Enabling women through capacity-building measures and by creating an eco-system of informed choices and requisite technology will definitely create the foundational base of:

- Financial autonomy for women through involvement in income-generating activities
- Educational and skill development
- Participatory model of governance

This framework provides the hypothetical base of the present chapter and forms the basis of the productive indicators for women's empowerment.

RESEARCH METHODS

To make a comparative assessment of CSCs and to increase the value of the findings, two districts of Odisha were chosen for the study, based on their ethnographic profile and socio-economic development indicators. Ganjam, located in the southern revenue division of Odisha, represents an urban and progressive district. It was chosen as a sample district because it is where CSCs were first introduced in Odisha in 2011. Keonjhar represents a rural district with a predominantly tribal population, and it is located in the northern revenue division. The study provides an empirical analysis of the working of two CSCs in Ganjam and Keonjhar, exploring how women entrepreneurs use ICT in CSCs to facilitate governance and provide services to the rural people. The chapter further examines how self-employed woman in the CSCs have contributed to the growth of their household income, thereby improving the quality of life of their children and family in general.

Primary data for this study was collected from the CSCs. The respondents include women entrepreneurs but also other categories of people. The study used both random and purposive sampling methods in the selection of the respondents from the two districts. Separate interview schedules were prepared for village users, CSC operators, women respondents, and government and project officials. Secondary data were collected through reading-related documents, articles, and books. This chapter is organized into several sections. The next section provides an overview of the origin and development of the CSCs.

COMMON SERVICE CENTERS: AGENCIES FOR CITIZEN ENGAGEMENT

CSCs are envisaged as the grassroots agencies for social change in rural areas, providing e-governance in the fields of employment, education, tele-medicine, agriculture, and entertainment. They have been popularized by the concept of reaching 'the bottom of the pyramid' (London & Hart, 2004; Prahalad & Hart, 2002). The CSC project, which is a strategic component of the National e-Governance Plan, was approved in September 2006 to address the major issue of delay in public service delivery and to ensure citizen-friendly governance among India's rural population. Addressing the challenge of bridging the rural-urban divide, a network of CSCs all over India aims to take the processes of digitization, financial inclusion, and entrepreneurship to the 50,000,000 villages and to impart information technology skills to 5.25 million people across the country. There are at present nearly 300 services provided by the 2,070,000 CSCs; these include employment for hundreds of thousands of young people in the rural areas, 40,000 of whom are women CSC operators. The most common method of reaching out to the rural areas through the CSCs has been through ICT, Internet, and the service providers. Recently, the private sector has been involved in the IT for development, financing, and the operation of such systems. In such cases, a nominal fee is charged for providing government services and official certificates. The objective of involving the private sector and non-governmental organizations (NGOs) in CSC projects is to make the CSCs, NGOs, and the private sector partners in developing rural India.

CSCs are an integral part of the Digital India mission established under a public-private partnership model. They are managed by computer-literate entrepreneurs who are CSC operators (village-level entrepreneurs) and who are instrumental for the success of CSC operations. An efficient village-level entrepreneur (VLE) has a strong social commitment and enjoys respect within the community. He or she can provide citizens with an *Aadhaar* card (a unique identification number), banking services, insurance, and can promote digital literacy in rural India (see Fig. 8.1). Many studies have shown that there is a direct correlation between the quality of services offered at CSCs and the entrepreneurial abilities of the VLEs operating them (http://apna.csc.gov.in). Thus, CSCs have emerged as a strategic cornerstone for delivering various electronic services to villages in India, thereby contributing to a digitally and financially inclusive

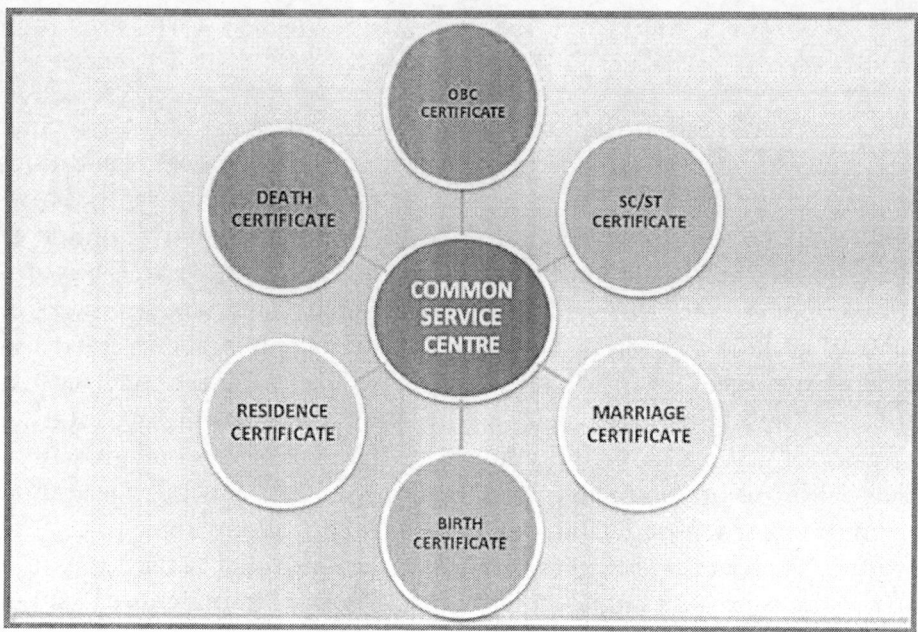

Fig. 8.1 Types of services offered through CSCs. OBC: Other Backward Caste, SC: Scheduled Caste, ST: Scheduled Tribe. (Source: Author)

society (Sangita & Dash, 2008). As per the CSC guidelines outlined by the Government of India, there should be one CSC for every six census villages. With 51,349 census villages in Odisha, the target of establishing 8558 CSCs in the state is yet to be achieved. So far, 6647 CSCs have been set up in Odisha, covering around 6234 villages (http://ocac.in/Content/3/13/12/39). Their experience reveals that unemployed men and women in rural areas can create a niche for themselves by becoming CSC operators; they can take charge of their work and their lives through extensive use of ICT, which provides new opportunities for them to improve their lives economically and socially. The district administration, the state, and the central government departments often delegate the responsibility of providing services to the rural citizens at convenient locations through the CSCs (http://www.ocac.in/).

Figure 8.1 outlines the list of government-to-citizen services provided by the CSCs at a low cost, for instance, issuing government certificates (e.g., for birth, income, caste, residence, legal heir, solvency, employment), and thereby ensuring efficiency and reliability to satisfy the basic needs of ordinary citizens. The process involves simple procedures wherein the citizen has to apply in a CSC, pay a nominal fee, provide supporting documents, proof of identity, and photographs. The CSC operators point out that the demand for residence, income, and caste certificates is mostly in connection with school and college admissions, and when people apply for various jobs.

In the era of the market economy, however, the CSCs also deliver business-to-citizen services. People come to CSCs to pay television licenses, recharge their cell telephones, take computer classes, do money transfers, and book trips (air and rail), all for a nominal service fee. In addition, people can pay utility bills for electricity and water. They can do online banking transactions, pay insurance premiums, and even apply for college admission. Through their operation, CSCs thus function as the service providers for government, NGOs, and the rural population through web-enabled interface. This idea is based on the public-private partnership model, which is executed by the village-level entrepreneurs.

It was observed during the field survey that Ganjam has 927 functioning CSCs whereas Keonjhar has only 186. This significant difference in the sample districts is due to the fact that Ganjam has the added advantage of being a high-profile district and the constituency of the chief minister. According to the e-governance district manager of Ganjam, 14,450,113 e-certificates were issued to the citizens from 927 CSCs from August 2011 to the end of 2018. By contrast, the e-district governance manager of Keonjhar claims that his district's 186 CSCs issued 8,230,273 e-certificates from November 2013 to the end of 2018. As these statistics illustrate, the CSCs, through the application of ICT, help bridge the trust deficit between the government and the citizens and are found to be useful. The CSCs have proven to be highly beneficial to the common people by providing them with essential and utility services at an affordable price, thereby improving the quality of governance in the rural areas.

The district authorities in Ganjam and Keonjhar have recognized that to ensure the effective implementation of the e-governance projects, they need to strengthen their own technical and IT capabilities significantly. Technology has proven to be an enabler and game changer for government officials by enhancing and building their capacities, and in the age of knowledge and information, the best way to ensure service delivery to stakeholders is by creating an efficient and transparent administrative system that serves their needs.

For the smooth delivery of services and for promoting a citizen-friendly administration, India launched the ambitious and pioneering *e-district project* under the National e-Governance Plan in 2008. With the advent of the mission mode e-district project, the survey has revealed that increased ICT and connectivity have bridged the knowledge gap among women and encouraged their informed and active participation in society. Women CSC operators are said to be enthusiastically participating in this knowledge dissemination process, patiently dealing with the queries of students, pensioners, farmers, women, panchayat-level workers and so on. Most of these customers are illiterate and technologically challenged. But beyond the specific scope of women, the findings of the study reveal how e-governance projects and the CSCs are instrumental in bridging the digital divide by enhancing capacity-building measures in the rural areas as a whole. The common perception among the respondents is that e-governance initiatives and projects have facilitated the much-desired *connectivity* among the citizens and the government, which was missing earlier.

EMPOWERMENT THROUGH SELF-HELP GROUPS: WOMEN–GOVERNANCE INTERFACE

One of the ideas of women's empowerment rests on the premise that liberalization, privatization, and globalization have brought about a paradigm shift in the approach to economic development, with women being perceived as having equal status to men and as being an important part of the productive workforce (Phillips, 1995). Examining women's empowerment within a capability framework, Kabeer (2000) interprets empowerment as well-being and the ability to make choices that will facilitate women's increased participation in society, thereby enabling them to have decision-making authority. From our study, we link women's empowerment with technology, which can prove to be a great leveler *if* social and cultural prejudices are removed through progressive ideas and gender-sensitive policies. In recent years, women have started entering India's workforce in increasing numbers, contributing significantly to expanding employment and alleviating poverty. Innovative models and positive steps like Internet and television broadcasts, knowledge networking, gender sensitization, education for girls, and greater employment options for women, will eventually address women's issues and the challenges to their empowerment in the state (Coonrod, 2011). This is illustrated by the crucial role of the more than 46,500 women entrepreneurs who work in the CSCs nationwide and serve as agents for social change under the Digital India program.

Another instance of the proactive role of CSC women operators is witnessed in the ambitious scheme of 'Women's Self-Dignity'(*Stree Swabhiman*), which aims to create a sustainable model for giving adolescent girls and women access to affordable sanitary products. Under this project, sanitary napkin micro-manufacturing units are set up at CSCs across Odisha, particularly those run by women. This exemplary initiative, driven by awareness, enables women entrepreneurs to produce and market the affordable sanitary napkins themselves. Besides promoting women's health and hygiene, the initiative also provides employment opportunities for women in rural communities, as each facility center has nearly ten women workers. The sanitary napkins produced by these units are not only easily available to the girls and women in marginalized communities but also biodegradable and thus environment friendly.

In order to build effective and sustained group identity, the Odisha government has introduced concrete measures for the provision of livelihood security through self-employment programs, entrepreneurship, and enrolment in women's self-help groups (WSHGs). The number of WSHGs existing in Odisha today has almost exceeded 600,000, with a total of 67,600,656 members. WSHGs prepare mid-day meals for school children and distribute food to poor people. They are engaged in developing the livelihood opportunities that are provided through different social welfare schemes. Promoting WSHGs is one of the key strategies in Odisha for achieving women's empowerment, for they help women overcome negative social pressure and gender bias. The district administration in the state has encouraged the WSHGs to enhance the capacity building of its existing groups and encourage new groups to engage in income-generating and remunerative economic activities by providing them with the necessary technical support, ICT applications, and market and credit linkages (Mohanty, Das, & Mohanty, 2013).

The experiences of the WSHGs have shown that their members use the Internet in various ways to achieve their goals of empowerment and rapid socio-economic change in rural India. For instance, multimedia compact disks are made available to the female service providers on nutrition, health, education, pickle making, and jam making. As stated, students frequently visit these rural CSCs when they require various certificates while applying for jobs. This has fostered rural development, provided a good opportunity to earn revenue from the rural CSCs, and improved the prospects of the many rural women who run them (Rath, 2007). The field study also reveals that ICT is promoted among the WSHGs in Ganjam and Keonjhar, for marketing their products and services at locations convenient to the rural people. Another empowering application of ICT has been e-commerce, which has benefited women entrepreneur significantly in both rural and urban areas. However, the path has not been easy for the women CSC entrepreneurs and the WSHGs, as their successes have generated new social situations and triggered opposition to inclusive gender practices, as illustrated in the next section.

GENDER PROFILE OF CSC OPERATORS

In general, this chapter section illustrates that women's presence in society is best promoted through measures that make space for them in the inclusive development model and participatory governance, both in a substantive and a symbolic sense (Nath, 2001). The establishment of the CSCs as new hubs for information dissemination and for providing quick solutions to citizens' needs in rural areas of the state has no doubt created new job opportunities for rural youth, yet it is still far from achieving gender justice for rural women. The field survey reveals that in both of the sample districts, male CSC operators far outnumbered female CSC operators, a trend coinciding with the prevailing tradition of gender disparity in e-governance projects. This trend hampers women's inclusion in many areas of society. Table 8.1 demonstrates the trend of significant gender imbalance in the public domain in the sample districts. During the survey, a few women CSC operators pointed out that although they have the necessary technical skills for effectively managing their CSC, they face discrimination from their male counterparts. So, although the CSCs play a

Table 8.1 Comparative analysis of women and men CSC operators in Ganjam and Keonjhar districts, 2016–2018

Serial no.	Name of the sample district	Number of women CSC operators		Number of men CSC operators	
		2016	2018	2016	2018
1	Ganjam	59	72	128	885
2	Keonjhar	46	66	147	170

Source: e-Governance district manager, Ganjam and Keonjhar, 2018

vital role in envisaging and ensuring women's empowerment, the challenge lies in sensitizing the stakeholders—a group which includes male CSC operators, officials, and the rural society at large—to highlight the need to eradicate discrimination and harassment against women at all levels. Unless this happens, no attempt toward implementing technological enablers for development will succeed in achieving the larger goal of inclusive socio-economic development.

No major difference can be noticed between the two districts as regards the number of women operators. Nor can the increase in their number over the years be considered significant. As Table 8.1 shows, the number of women CSC operators is higher in Ganjam district, as it increased from 59 in 2016 to 72 in 2018. This stands in contrast to Keonjhar district, where the number of women CSC operators increased from 46 in 2016 to 66 in 2018.[1] But although the number of women managing the CSCs may be increasing, they still constitute a small percentage of the total number of CSC operators. Nevertheless, many women respondents point out that ICT provides new opportunities for them to improve their quality of life, despite the fact that they have to constantly negotiate with the existing challenges that emanate from the larger socio-cultural milieu governed by deeply entrenched patriarchal norms and values. This may be seen as a new-found confidence and determination to succeed at any cost, not only for sake of earning a living, but also to ensure their overall empowerment and self-dignity in the socio-economic domain.

CSCs: An Alternative Occupational Choice for Earning a Living with Dignity

The field study in Keonjhar district, which revealed that there were 46 women CSC operators (24%) versus147 male CSC operators (76%) in 2016, and 66 (28%) female CSC operators versus 170 (72%) male CSC operators in 2018, reflects the chronic issue of women's underrepresentation in the workforce and the historical marginalization of women as a group. These figures do not portray an encouraging trend for women's empowerment because women as citizens have a right to representation in the social, political, and economic spheres. In contrast, Ganjam district had a slightly increased women's presence in 2016, with

---

[1] State e-Governance Mission Team (SeMT), OCAC, Directorate of Electronics and IT Department, Bhubaneswar, Odisha, December 2018.

59 women CSC operators (33%) versus 128 male CSC operators (68%), but the situation changed dramatically by 2018: now there were only 72 (8%) women CSC operators versus an overwhelming 885 (92%) male CSC operators. Table 8.1 reflects a seven-fold increase in male CSC operators in two years (700%), whereas for women CSC operators, the increase was abysmally low (little more than 25%). The data shows a greater degree of reliance on such alternatives for unemployed youth in the rural areas, where unemployment is considered a stigma for men. This proves that young unemployed men have seized the opportunity for self-employment through starting a CSC, thus achieving financial independence to some extent, at the same time as they are saved from the social stigma. It also reflects the influence of the 'male first' syndrome that is deeply embedded and pervasive in social structures, processes, and behavior in patriarchal society. Under such circumstances, ambitious women confront the challenges of 'exclusion' that perpetuate gender disparity in the public domain. But in addition to social prejudice and male dominance, there is poverty, which also hinders women from becoming ICT savvy. This is one of the main reasons for women's exclusion from the CSCs (Lal, 2015). A third reason for the gross imbalance in male and female CSC operators may be that women's access to opportunities is constrained by limited mobility and restrictions on their ability to exercise their freedom of choice.

As the above paragraphs show, CSCs are a new avenue for job creation at the rural level, providing employment to rural young people, some of whom are women, who find it suitable to their existing situation. The centers are close to home and the women do not need much education to work in them, so they provide a convenient source of income. The nature of working with ICT enhances the women's self-esteem and financially empowers them in their further choices, for instance, to become active members in the gram panchayat (village administrative units) and other public institutions. Through having direct contact with the local people and addressing their issues in a receptive and sympathetic manner, the women CSC operators tend to be highly appreciated. This enhances their social status, helps decrease the trust deficit, boosts their confidence level, uplifts their morale, and ultimately leads to a new social equation between these women entrepreneurs and the villagers, which is based on trust and mutual dependence. It is the sense of satisfaction that they get from serving their fellow villagers at the same time as contributing to the process of good governance that makes them feel empowered.

SITUATING WOMEN IN THE PUBLIC DOMAIN: EMERGING CHALLENGES

This section presents the case studies of woman CSC operators who have embarked on the digital journey with the support of district and block-level officials and local NGOs. As mentioned earlier, in a male-dominated patriarchal society, women are often discouraged from entering the public domain; institutional and social norms prevent them from contributing to economic development as a productive force equal to men. This is both unfair and violates the principle of equality. A few women CSC operators have complained about false and frivolous charges being leveled against them by people with vested interests, who try to spread false and malicious claims with the intention of isolating the women and inducing people not to visit the women's CSCs. This demoralizes the women CSC operators, who are committed to working sincerely and honestly. Faced with such adverse situations, much of their energy and time are wasted on salvaging their image at higher official levels than on spending their time working at the CSC. But in combination with this problem, there are yet other challenges which affect women's ability to work in CSCs: primarily family obligations, economic considerations, insufficient education/training, and geographical distance. These challenges are highlighted by the case study of Dipika Sahu and Madhusmita Barik, woman CSC operators in Ganjam and Keonjhar districts, respectively.

Case Study of a Woman CSC Operator in Ganjam District of Odisha

Under the ambit of the e-governance project, several government-to-citizen (G2C) services were introduced in 2009 in the Ganjam district (Odisha). One of them was the creation of the CSCs where public utility services are provided for nominal fees.

Ms. Dipika Kumari Sahu, 22 years of age, is pursuing an M.Phil while simultaneously working as a village-level entrepreneur at the CSC in Hinjli-2, Ganjam. Through her endeavors, she has provided services to those who seek them at the center where she works. She makes a decent monthly amount of rupees 4500–5000/(US$1 = Indian rupees 70) through her efforts. Due to a staunch patriarchal set-up, Ms. Sahu has faced tremendous discrimination aimed to thwart the successful operation of her CSC. She was at the receiving end of malicious rumors, which often caused the local people to boycott her services. To lodge complaints against the male CSC operators who spread the false statements, she approached the district revenue officer, who suggested shifting her CSC to a busy locality.

After initial successes, she experienced resistance from her junior staff and faced threats to her life from her male CSC counterparts. She was even forced to vacate her premises by the unyielding property owner. Meetings with the block development officer proved fruitless, as he was under tremendous political pressure. Frustrated with the attitude of the corrupt block officials, she approached the district magistrate who addressed her grievance promptly. Since she was popular amongst some locals who appreciated her sincerity and work ethic, she managed to receive ample support. Her CSC has finally re-started operations and is presently functioning successfully. Dipika's services were also acknowledged by the minister of information and technology at the National Conference of Women CSC Operators held in New Delhi on February 20, 2016. Thus, Dipika has successfully delivered IT-enabled services through her CSC to the rural people in her local community.

Case Study of a Woman CSC Operator in Keonjhar District of Odisha

A native of Keonjhar district in Odisha, Mrs. Madhusmita Barik, a CSC operator, was found to be a classic case of a proxy operator in whose name a CSC was sanctioned. The survey revealed that in reality, her brother-in-law ran the CSC and provided government services to the people in areas, for instance, tele-law and tele-health services. Madhusmita explained that this arrangement was different from the stereotypical explanation given under such circumstances, which points to patriarchal domination or family pressure. Her brother-in-law, being computer literate, had strong entrepreneurial traits and knowledge of dealing with online transactions, so was more competent and suitable to run the center than she herself is. She is a 'mere graduate' and lacks technical knowledge related to working with a computer. She further explained that financial needs sometimes force women to compromise their family obligations. This also applies in her case: she chose to handover responsibility for running the CSC to her brother-in-law, whose earnings ensure financial stability in the family, while she concentrates on meeting family obligations. Thus, the dual aim of makings ends meet and fulfilling family responsibilities on the domestic front is achieved through a mutual arrangement by which Madhusmita claims that she commands credibility and respect in the village community. Further, she appreciates the government's effort to remove the middle-men, as this has reduced corruption to a significant extent.

Women's Emancipation: A Continuous Struggle

Recent discourses on gender representation have highlighted that women are mostly under-represented in India's economic activities, particularly in the rural areas, barring the agricultural sector (Chaudhuri, 2011). This has been primarily due to the twin challenges of social constraints and capacity deficit, which women constantly grapple with. For a host of socio-economic reasons, women face serious handicaps in terms of their qualifications and capabilities to perform as skilled workers. Until recently, Odisha lacked a congenial environment for women's participation in the public sphere, and this came to expression through their low participation in the workforce. When it comes to the issue of gender parity in the socio-economic domain, Odisha also has a low record of inclusive growth. The suppression of women has been based on biological differences and male dominance. Women have been disadvantaged by remaining economically dependent on men and by having little say in the distribution of benefits in the society. However, in the current situation, women are being exposed to new technology and receiving vocational training, both of which offer them opportunities to discover their hidden talents (Panda, 2005).

This study also reveals that socially constructed notions of gender often determine the way in which men and women participate in the workforce, in financial matters, and in political sectors in society. Gender disparity in a deep-rooted patriarchal system manifests itself in various structural inequalities and a culture of violence and silence, which are reflected in power relations and the distribution of economic resources. New opportunities for women's economic empowerment and gender equality pose new challenges to their safety and security. While participating in the survey, many respondents pointed out that marriage and family pressures often discourage women from becoming CSC operators, and that in addition, there can be considerable mental, physical, and financial strain. Another challenge pertains to taking the culture of administration to a new level where the role of women as critical partners in progress needs to be acknowledged (Gurumurthy, 2004). So, while we today deliberate on a multi-pronged strategy to achieve double-digit growth in India's economy, we cannot ignore the potential of women as vital stakeholders, who, with their increased participation in society, strive to bring about the desired change of inclusive development. It is a politico-economic imperative for any society to recognize the role and contribution of women in public life and to give them their rightful place in it. Gender-friendly policies are essential to make this happen: such policies enhance the capacity of women and empower them to address the negative socio-economic situations they face in society, also when the situations are by-products of the globalization process. In order to create an enabling environment and to support women's social and economic empowerment through ICT, various actors must take action at local, regional, national, and international levels, to enable women to pursue sustainable livelihoods.

From the above account, it is observed that there has been an exponential growth in the number of CSCs across the country between 2014 and 2019. The total number of CSCs in India as on December 2014 was 1,40,833 which increased to nearly double in December 2016 with 2,90,150 CSCs across the country. It shows that due to its popularity amongst the common people for delivering faster and cost-effective access to government schemes and services through digital means, the state governments have opened more such CSCs Centers in their respective states. Therefore, the two-fold increase of such CSCs between 2014 and 2019 proves their effectiveness and credibility amongst the common people and the corresponding impact of e-governance on them. This has also resulted in an unprecedented four time increase in the volume of transactions through the CSCs during the corresponding period 2014–2019 (2014— 4.5 crores & 2019—17.5 crores), in the number of transactions at the CSCs (*www.csc.gov.in*). This goes on to prove that on the one hand in the pursuit of good governance, the state governments are not only moving toward digital governance (e-governance) but also are increasingly showing positive results in terms of accessibility and productivity of government schemes and programs for the welfare and convenience of the general population (Aghi, 2015). The increase in the number of CSCs and the quantum jump in e-transactions have also revealed a new trend in participation and inclusiveness in governance and empowerment of women.

More women are seen to be involving themselves in the CSC activities as these centers have spread their geographical base into the remote areas of every state, the impact of which can be observed in the two-way model of participation and empowerment where one group of women are being benefited by having convenient, easy access to the welfare schemes of the government which empowers them socially and politically to avail the opportunities and entitlements. On the other hand, there is another set of women who are being benefited from these CSCs by directly getting self-employment and greater exposure to services provided by the center which contributes toward their economic empowerment and financial inclusion in the digital economy and e-governance framework.

Indicators of women's empowerment through engagement in e-governance activities:

- *Financial inclusion*: The common service centers as an enabler provide the women CSC entrepreneurs' an incentive for financial empowerment through applications of digital technology. Through the self-employment and earning model, they make their living by providing e-services and charging a nominal fee for business-to-consumer services [B2C] they are able to create a sustainable business model. This in the long run will have a positive impact in the growth potential of the rural economy.
- *Skill development*: Women in general are availing new frontiers of opportunity by way of their interactions with technology at the CSCs. This interface has resulted in their skill development which has enhanced their employability, access to resources, income-generation, increased awareness and better livelihood options.
- *Education opportunities*: Education for employment purposes has been the focus area of the digital literacy mission. This also enables women in the rural areas to have access to education information regarding higher studies, MBA program, law course and other online courses through designated websites, similar to what is available in the urban areas.
- *Participative model of governance*: Through this collaborative framework, women are interacting with government officials at the block and the district level. This practice establishes a two-way communication with the government and the governed that is now possible due to digitalization. A continuous and seamless connect with the rural women happens through online interaction which has led to the enhancement of Internet usage. This has changed the lives of the rural women and impacted the lives of thousands of villagers residing in the rural areas.
- *Health and nutrition*: Digital rural service centers also addresses the issue of digital divide. The rural women are getting access to infor-

mation and government aid on health and nutrition. ICDS and SHGs are networking, collaborating, and communicating with the buyers and sellers of the agro-based products, selling and marketing of these products have now become easy for them.

- *Family-level empowerment indicators*: With education and professional degree, woman are financially independent, they stay connected with their families with the use of mobile phones. Women are now having access to power, public space, are self-sufficient, the benefits of which will percolate to the family at large. This also positively impacts the household income as a result of which children are provided with good education and better healthcare facilities. Income in the hands of women boosts her economic strength and instills confidence in her to participate in the family affairs of decision-making.

CONCLUSION

While acknowledging that the road to gender equality will continue to be challenging, information and communication technology (ICT) offers solutions to a variety of shortcomings and obstacles faced by women in their day-to-day life. The ICT revolution in the last two decades has opened windows of opportunity for women and proved to be an effective enabler in terms of providing strategic information. The successful functioning of the CSCs reduces the economic dependency of women and promotes their financial autonomy as they are engaged in sustainable productive activity. The field survey revealed that with the advent of e-governance projects, connectivity has increased and improved the life of the people in the sample regions. Yet, although the role of ICT in empowering women is quite commendable, it is not a panacea for all the problems women face. Nevertheless, if women succeed in managing the adverse socio-economic challenges, the use of ICT will positively contribute to their empowerment in future.

A silent but significant revolution is taking shape through the ubiquitous rural tele-centers, which are geared toward ensuring good governance and providing social and financial empowerment for women at the grassroots level. What matters for the sustainability of CSCs, however, is the administrative context and the technological readiness within which they operate. The larger socio-cultural environment, in which women operate in a male-dominated society like Odisha in particular and India in general, requires more reforms than mere technological inputs to bring about the real emancipation of women. Strengthening grassroots institutions, implementing gender-sensitization policies, and creating awareness amongst both men and women to respect the larger issue of human dignity would help the government bridge the gap in gender disparity in adopting technology.

REFERENCES

Aghi, M. (2015, December 11). Delivering on the digital promise. *The Hindu*, New Delhi.

Boraian, M. P. (2008). *Empowerment of rural woman: The deterrents and determinants*. New Delhi: Concept Publishing Company.

Chaudhuri, M. (Ed.). (2011). *Feminism in India*. New Delhi: Kali for Women.

Coonrod, J. (2011). Status of women in Odisha: Investing in women's leadership in panchayats. The Hunger Project in India. Retrieved February 2, 2019, from https://thpind.wordpress.com/2011/02/11/broad-issues-affecting-womens-leadership-in-odisha/

Dash, R. K., & Naik, N. K. (2006, January). E-grama. The rural information gateway of Orissa: The community passed information technology for rural mass. *Orissa Review*.

Fox, M. F., Johnson, D. G., & Rosser, S. V. (Eds.). (2006). *Women, gender and technology*. Champaign, IL: University of Illinois.

Gill, R., & Grint, K. (Eds.). (1995). *The gender technology relation: Contemporary theory and research*. Bristol: Taylor & Francis.

Gurumurthy, A. (2004). *Bridging the digital gender divide: Issues and Insights on ICT for women's economic empowerment*. New Delhi: UNIFEM. Online. Retrieved December 14, 2018, from http://www.itforchange.net/resources/Pat.htm

Jaggar, A. (1983). *Feminist politics and human nature*. Brighton: Harvester Press.

Kabeer, N. (2000). Resources, agency, achievements: Reflections on the measurement of women's empowerment. In S. Razavi (Ed.), *Gendered poverty and well-being* (pp. 27–56). Oxford: Blackwell Publishers.

Kapur, R., & Crossman, B. (1999). On women, equality and the constitution. In N. Menon (Ed.), *Gender and politics in India: Themes in politics*. Delhi: Oxford University Press.

Lal, S. (2015, December 17). Common service center: The bridge for the rural-urban digital divide? *Hindustan Times*.

London, T., & Hart, S. (2004). Reinventing strategies for emerging markets: Beyond the translational model. *Journal of International Business Studies*, *35*(3), 350–370.

Mohanty, S. R., Das, B., & Mohanty, T. (2013). Empowerment of women in rural Odisha through micro-enterprises. *IOSR Journal of Humanities and Social Sciences, 12*(1), 1–8.

Nath, V. (2001). *Empowerment and governance through information and communication technologies: Women's perspective.* Academic Press. Online. Retrieved February 2, 2017, from http://www.cddc.vt.edu/digitalgov/gov-menu.html

Norris, P. (2001). *Digital divide: Civic engagement, information, poverty and the internet world wide.* Cambridge: Cambridge University Press.

Panda, S. (2005). *Political empowerment of women.* New Delhi: Raj Publishers.

Phillips, A. (1995). *The politics of presence: The political representation of gender, ethnicity and race.* Oxford: Oxford University Press.

Prahalad, C. K., & Hart, S. L. (2002, January 10). The fortune at the bottom of the pyramid. *Strategy and Business, 26.*

Prakash, G., & Singh, A. (2008). A new public management perspective in Indian e-governance initiatives. In *Critical thinking in e-governance.* Delhi. Online. Retrieved April 24, 2017, from http://www.iceg.net/2008/books/1/(vi).pdf

Rajneesh, S. (2008, October–December). Gender budgeting to gender mainstreaming. *Indian Journal of Public Administration, 54*(4), 904–906.

Rath, B. (2007). Post evaluation study of the scheme of micro-credit help to women self help groups (WSHGs) in KBK districts of Orissa. Retrieved October 10, 2018, from http://www.odisha.gov.in/pc/Download/WSHG_Final_Report.pdf

Sangita, S. N., & Dash, B. C. (2008). ICT, governance and service delivery in India: A critical review. *Indian Journal of Public Administration, 54*(1), 45–67.

Stivers, C. (2002). *Gender images in public administration.* Thousand Oaks, CA: Sage Publishers.

Young, I. M. (2000). *Inclusion and democracy.* Oxford: Oxford University Press.

Web Addresses

www.csc.gov.in (accessed October 15, 2019).

http://apna.csc.gov.in (accessed December 25, 2018).

http://articles.economictimes.indiatimes.com/2015-03-14/news/60111605_1_centres-entrepreneurs-csc (accessed February 22, 2019).

http://eodisha.eletsonline.com/2014/ (accessed March 20, 2019).

http://ocac.in/Content/3/13/12/39 (accessed March 11, 2019).

www.ocac.in (accessed March 21, 2019).

http://ordistricts.nic.in/district_home.php?did=kjr (accessed February 25, 2019).

http://www.edistrictorissa.gov.in/edistrict/index.php (accessed March 20, 2019).

http://www.ordistricts.nic.in/district_home.php?did=gnm (accessed March 22, 2019).

http://www.unifem.undp.org/conferen.html (accessed March 10, 2019).

www.deity.gov.in (accessed March 21, 2019).

www.odissaonline.gov.in (accessed March 17, 2019).

http://www.ogip.in/literacy.html (accessed February 14, 2019).

CHAPTER 9

A Paradigm Shift in Women's Turnout and Representation in Indian Elections

Sanjay Kumar

INTRODUCTION

The pronounced gender gap in electoral participation in India remains an untenable dilemma of democracy in the country. Women constitute close to half of the total Indian electorate, yet remain underrepresented at the polling booth. Political representation and participation are two of the most effective ways to represent women's interests and voices, and their involvement in the process is therefore particularly important. Despite this, the Indian democracy grapples with an inadequate representation of women in the political arena and a gender gap in voter turnout. These are undeniably discouraging aspects of Indian elections. In recent years, however, there has been a considerable change on both these accounts, especially with respect to voter turnout.

This chapter seeks to examine these changes and the various factors that surround them. There are two parts to the chapter: the first deals with the rise in women's turnout on the election day, while the second looks at

S. Kumar (✉)
Centre for the Study of Developing Societies (CSDS), New Delhi, India
e-mail: sanjay@csds.in

I. Jamil et al. (eds.), *Gender Mainstreaming in Politics, Administration and Development in South Asia,*
https://doi.org/10.1007/978-3-030-36012-2_9

181

other forms of women's participation in politics, primarily in the form of political representation.

WOMEN'S TURNOUT

Even though Indian elections have consistently witnessed a reasonably higher turnout than what is the case in the most advanced democracies, a gender gap in voting continues to exist. And yet, the country has also made some substantial gains in electoral participation. Although, India continues to fare poorly on gender parity, as reflected in its 87th rank in the latest Global Gender Parity Report (2016) of the World Economic Forum,[1] major changes seem to be occurring in the political arena. Recent trends in women's turnout in Indian elections indicate that the country could soon witness a gender reversal in electoral participation. The analysis of gender-wise turnout and voting for various elections (data from the Election Commission of India) over the last four decades indicates that there has been a significant decline in the gender bias in voting in recent years. The decline could be attributed to a higher level of participation among women, as the change in the gender ratio of voters is higher than the change in the gender ratio of the electors. An intriguing dimension of this emerging story is that the change has been sharp in most of the so-called backward states (Kapoor & Ravi, 2014). Considering how an increase in women's turnout makes an impact on the overall turnout and the larger process of democratization, it becomes crucial to dissect this change and understand the factors behind it.

It is widely believed that orthodox social norms in India have limited the role of women in mainstream electoral politics, restraining them from emerging as independent voters, and reducing the importance of gender issues in policy discourses. However, one witnesses an increase in women's turnout figures in the state assembly elections held in recent years, and in the recently concluded 2014 *Lok Sabha* election.[2] In many states, not only has the turnout among women voters increased compared to previous elections, but they have also outnumbered men in voting. What explains this dramatic shift in voting among women voters in India? Does it result

[1] The Global Gender Parity Report provides an overall ranking of countries based on a composite index, which includes variables on gender differences in various arenas. The World Economic Forum releases the report annually.

[2] The *Lok Sabha* is the lower house of parliament, and the *Rajya Sabha* is the upper house.

from a weakening of traditional barriers and their hold on women? Is this trend made possible because of an increasing level of educational attainment among women voters? Is or can it be attributed to greater exposure of women voters to the media? Is it an affirmation of the distinctness of women voters' issues? Has improved security around polling stations made it more conducive for women to come out and vote? Alternatively, is it as result of women's increased participation in the third tier of the electoral system, namely the Panchayats, by way of reservation?

Recent Upsurge in the Participation of Women

There has been a decrease in the gender gap in turnout for both national and state assembly elections. During the 2014 Lok Sabha elections, the gender gap in the turnout was almost negligible: from nearly 17 percent in 1957, it dropped to less than 2 percent in 2014. Barring a period of stagnation from 1984 until 2004, there has been a consistent decline in the gap, falling from 8 percent in 1999 to 4.4 percent in 2009, and to 1.46 percent in 2014. In fact, many states have recorded an all-time high turnout for women and the lowest-ever gender gap in the recently concluded Lok Sabha elections (Figs. 9.1, 9.2 and 9.3).

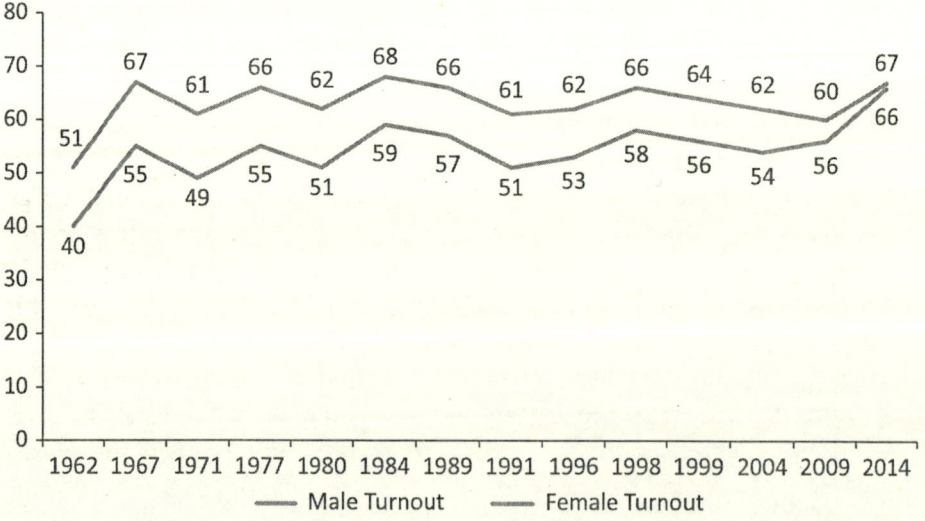

Fig. 9.1 Electoral participation: Men's and women's turnout, 1962–2014 (%)

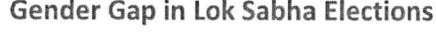

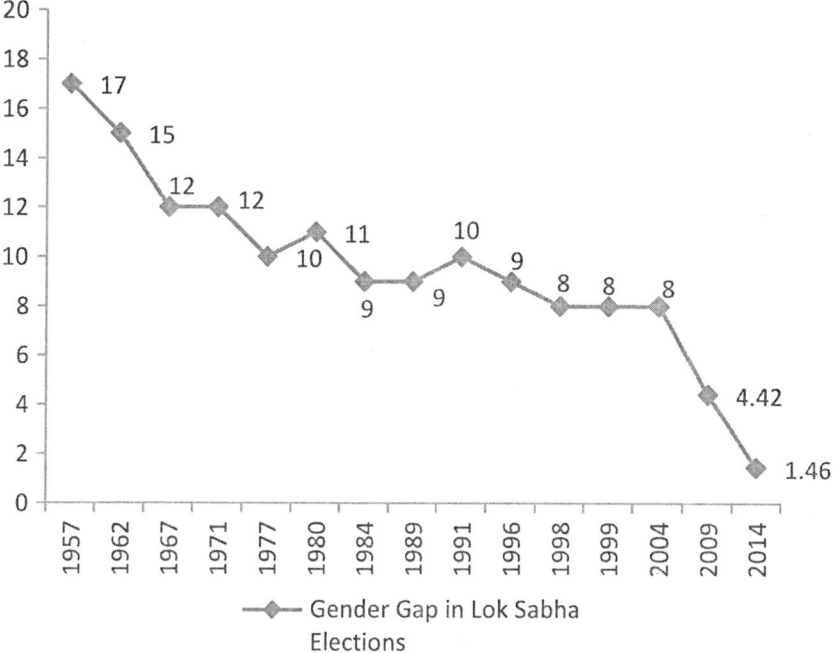

Fig. 9.2 Gender gap in turnout: Lok Sabha elections (1957–2014) (%). (Note: Calculated as the difference between men's turnout (%) and women's turnout (%) for the Lok Sabha election. Source: Authors' analysis of data released by the Election Commission of India)

The analysis of the aggregate data released by the Election Commission of India on turnout in various assembly elections held in India between 1990 and 2016 suggests that the gender gap in turnout did not change much between 1990 and 2001. The turnout among women voters begins to increase in earnest from 2002 onward; in most assembly elections held after that, the women's turnout continues to increase. We notice this change in most of the states in varying degrees. While some change in the turnout among women voters began in the mid-1990s, the most significant change in women's turnout happened from 2008 onward. In fact, the states that had witnessed a very narrow gender gap in men and women's turnout in 1990s saw the trend move in the opposite direction: during the period 2008–2016, these states witnessed a higher turnout among women voters compared to men (Table 9.1).

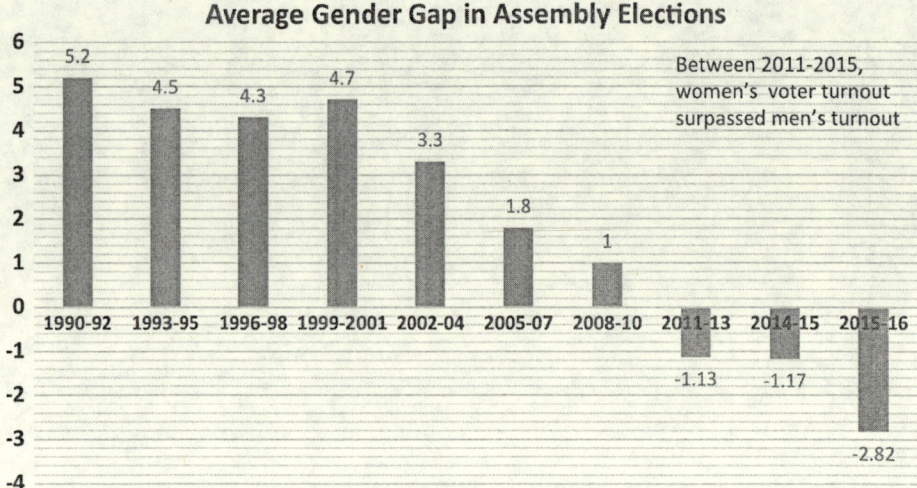

Fig. 9.3 Gender gap in turnout: State assembly elections 1990–2016 (%). (Note: Calculated as the difference between the men's turnout (%) and women's turnout (%) for the state assembly election. Source: Authors' analysis of data released by the Election Commission of India)

Table 9.1 Difference in gender gap in turnout in different states: Assembly elections 1990–2013 (%)

	Category 1 states: high gender gap	Category 2 states: moderate gender gap	Category 3 states: low gender gap
1990–1995	10.48	4.81	0.68
1996–2001	10.94	4.39	1.74
2002–2007	6.09	3.86	−0.45
2008–2013	0.94	0.76	−2.64

Source: Authors' analysis of data released by the Election Commission of India

Note: States with a high gender gap are Bihar, Madhya Pradesh, Rajasthan, Uttar Pradesh, Odisha, and Gujarat. States with a moderate gender gap are Andhra Pradesh, Chhattisgarh, Delhi, Karnataka, Maharashtra, Tamil Nadu, Tripura, Sikkim, and Haryana. States with a low gender gap are Arunachal Pradesh, Assam, Manipur, Meghalaya, Mizoram, Nagaland, West Bengal, Himachal Pradesh, Kerala, Goa, and Uttarakhand

What May Affect Gender Gap in Turnout?

The narrowing gender gap could have four algebraic explanations: first, that the women's turnout remains the same, while the men's turnout reduces; second, that both male and female turnout falls, but the male turnout witnesses a sharper decline; third, that both rise, but the rise in women's turnout is higher; and fourth, that there is a decline in men's turnout and an increase in women's turnout, with the latter greater than the former.

Based on the magnitude of the gender gap in the early years in the period under analysis (1990 onward), the states have been classified into three categories: (1) states with a high gender gap, (2) states with a moderate gender gap, and (3) states with a low gender gap. Interestingly, a broader regional pattern emerges in this classification: the BIMARU states of North India, along with Odisha and Gujarat, fall in the high gender-gap category, while the second category of states primarily includes all the South India states except Kerala. The third category mostly includes the states in North-East India such as West Bengal, Kerala, and some of the hill states. The unique thing about the states in this third category is that most of them are small. The gender gap remained almost constant during the first two periods (1990–1995 & 1996–2001, see Table 9.2) in all three categories of state grouping, but this gap narrowed substantially in states with a high gap during the period 2002–2007. During the last five years, the gender gap in turnout has reduced in all the three categories of states, but the sharpest decline took

Table 9.2 Declining gender gap in turnout in different kinds of states: Assembly elections 1990–2013 (%)

	States with high gender gap		States with moderate gender gap		States with a low gender gap	
	Men turnout (in %)	Women turnout (in %)	Men turnout (in %)	Women turnout (in %)	Men turnout (in %)	Women turnout (in %)
1990–1995	64	53.5	72.1	67.3	79	78.3
1996–2001	65.1	54.2	69.6	65.2	76.7	74.8
2002–2007	61.3	55.2	70.9	67	73.6	73.8
2008–2013	67.6	66.3	73.8	73	79	81.5

Source: Authors' analysis of data released by the Election Commission of India

place in the states where the gap in turnout was highest. Table 9.3 indicates how men and women's turnout has changed over the years in the three groups of states. The average overall turnout seems to be higher in states with a lower gender gap. While the decline in the gender gap in the period 2002–2007 in category 1 states could be attributed to a fall in men's turnout, the decline in the latest period has been due to a relatively high increase in women's turnout, which is true across categories. However, it is interesting to see that there is no uniform trend across all

Table 9.3 Turnout among men and women voters: Assembly elections since 2010 (%)

Election	Year	Men turnout (%)	Women turnout (%)	Difference (%)
Bihar	2015	53.32	60.48	−7.16
Kerala	2016	75.97	78.14	−2.17
Assam	2016	81.95	83.24	−1.29
Tamil Nadu	2016	74.16	74.33	−0.17
West Bengal	2016	82.23	83.13	−0.9
Uttarakhand	2017	61.11	68.72	−7.61
Uttar Pradesh	2017	59.15	63.31	−4.16
Punjab	2017	75.88	77.90	−2.02
Manipur	2012	76.94	81.36	−4.42
Himachal Pradesh	2012	69.39	76.20	−6.81
Gujarat	2012	72.94	69.50	3.44
Goa	2012	78.6	84.57	−5.97
Tripura	2013	90.73	92.4	−1.67
Rajasthan	2013	74.67	75.4	−0.73
Mizoram	2013	79.50	82.1	−2.6
Meghalaya	2013	85.17	88.44	−3.27
Madhya Pradesh	2013	73.86	70.9	−2.96
Karnataka	2013	72.40	70.47	1.93
Delhi	2015	67.63	66.49	1.14
Chhattisgarh	2013	76.93	77.32	−0.39
Andhra Pradesh	2014	74.22	74.18	0.04
Arunachal Pradesh	2014	63.23	66.76	−3.53
Haryana	2014	76.59	75.59	1
Jammu & Kashmir	2014	64.85	66.27	−1.42
Maharashtra	2014	64.33	61.69	2.64
Nagaland	2013	89.09	91.33	−2.24
Odisha	2014	72.95	74.42	−1.47
Sikkim	2014	80.31	81.31	−1
Jharkhand	2014	65.90	67.00	−1.1

Source: Results from the ECI

states. In some states, the change in the gender gap has taken place without any substantial increase in women's turnout. Take for example the case of Bihar, which is a 'high-gap' state: although the 2010 election in Bihar is often cited as an instance of the gender gap's substantial contraction, the decrease in the gap was primarily due to a decline in the men's turnout. The women's turnout in the 2010 election (52.7%) was almost equal to the average in the state from 1990 onward (52.3%), while the men's turnout was 51 percent, which is much lower than the post-1990 average of 61.1 percent. In the second category of states, women's turnout increased as compared to earlier years in around two-thirds of the states. In the third category, it has either remained constant at threshold levels, or declined.

At a preliminary glance, we can see that the increase in women's turnout could be witnessed more in relatively poor and socially backward states. The regional epicenter of this surge in women's participation is the 'Hindi heartland,' and the magnitude of the increase is such that there would definitely be factors other than the low base. The intriguing aspect of the story is that all these states except Gujarat rank low on the Human Development Index (HDI) for Indian states. Even Gujarat, despite its relatively higher per capita income, has a moderate HDI score.

The aggregate analysis above clearly establishes the rise of female participation in the voting process. Many social scientists and political commentators have attempted to understand the broader implications of this rise in women's turnout. Oftentimes, larger sociological and demographic changes lie behind trends and patterns in the aggregate data. The objective of this chapter is to move beyond recent work on political participation among women in India by trying to discuss why these changes are taking place. The idea is to identify possible factors behind this recent upsurge in their political participation and delineate various macrocosmic and regional factors behind it. The analysis is based on aggregate data from various government sources, survey data from the National Election Studies series conducted by the Centre for the Study of Developing Societies for the years 2004, 2009, and the 2014 general elections, and data from the Census of India for 2001 and 2011. The rise in women's turnout, particularly in states that have traditionally lagged behind in various social indicators and measures of gender parity, cannot be explained through a single factor. Rather than one factor playing across the heterogeneous populace of the country, an interplay of multiple factors must be examined. This chapter attempts to identify a set of possible factors and tries to understand their role in causing this upsurge in women's participation.

THE SELF-EMPOWERMENT ARGUMENT

The self-empowerment argument is based on the belief that more women are voluntarily turning out to exercise their right to vote due to greater awareness and a deepening political consciousness. Counter to this argument, there is a common belief that a large proportion of women do not have the independence to participate in public life; many women, both as voters and representatives, participate as proxies of male family members. In an interview, former Union Minister and Chief Minister of Bihar, Lalu Prasad Yadav has dismissed the political relevance of the increased women's turnout, as he felt that they simply vote for whomever the men tell them to vote for (Mishra, 2010). At the outset, it must be understood that a substantial proportion of voters take into account the opinion of others before deciding whom to vote for. Deciding whom to vote for is not always a solitary decision, given that voters discuss politics with family members, friends, colleagues, local elites, and so on. Survey data from national polls has consistently shown that more than 40 percent of voters admit that they did not decide entirely on their own and that the opinions of others mattered while making up their mind. Still, one must note that there is a gender gap in the proportion of voters who voted independently. While more than two-thirds of the men claimed to have decided without taking anybody else's opinion into consideration, the same figure was a little more than one-half for women (Tables 9.4 and 9.5).

Even among those who took others' opinions into consideration while deciding who to vote for, there is a gender difference in terms of whose opinion mattered most. Men tend to interact with a broader group of

Table 9.4 Proportion of voters who voted without taking anybody else's opinion into account: Lok Sabha elections 2004–2014 (%)

Year of election	All	Men	Women
2004	63	71	53
2009	58	65	50
2014	63	69	56

Source: National Election Studies 2004, 2009, and 2014 conducted by the Centre for the Study of Developing Societies (CSDS)

Table 9.5 Whom do voters normally consult while voting? Lok Sabha elections 2009–2014 (%)

Voters who consulted	Year	All voters	Men	Women
Spouse	2009	30	13	45
	2014	21	11	30
Other family members	2009	30	30	31
	2014	34	31	37
Local political leader	2009	16	24	9
	2014	17	22	13
Caste/community leaders	2009	12	17	8
	2014	16	21	12
Friends, co-workers and colleagues	2009	8	11	4
	2014	9	13	6

Source: National Election Studies 2009 and 2014 conducted by the CSDS

Note: The rest said that they consulted others

people, as more than half of the men who did not vote on their own consulted individuals outside their immediate household—friends, colleagues, caste leaders, or local leaders. On the other hand, for more than two-thirds of the women who did not vote entirely on their own, the opinion of their husbands or other family members mattered most. Socialization and independence in decision-making should not be understood as an either/or situation, that is, of either relying solely on one's own opinion or solely following the opinion of someone else. An individual who interacts with a wider range of people and discusses politics outside the household would be considered to have a greater degree of political socialization. In addition, it would be safe to assume that even in a discussion on politics within the household, women, especially younger ones, would have the least say.

The self-empowerment hypothesis would explain women's higher turnout as a result of women's increased socialization and independent decision-making with lesser influence from other family members. The analysis of survey data from the National Election Studies in 2009 and 2014 indicates mixed results for eight states which have seen a significant fall in the gender gap due to an increase in women turnout: the BIMARU states (Bihar, Madhya Pradesh, Rajasthan, and Uttar Pradesh), plus Assam, Chhattisgarh, Jharkhand, and Odisha. In four of these states—Rajasthan, Uttar Pradesh, Assam, and Chhattisgarh—there was a sizeable increase in the proportion of women who voted without taking anybody else's opinion into account. In other states, however, the proportion has either remained constant or in fact decreased. Looking at this data alone is difficult to corroborate the hypothesis that women voters have become more empowered.

A broad self-empowerment hypothesis cannot be accepted or refuted completely based on mixed evidence of changes in the proportion of women voting on their own. One must look at other dimensions of the concept before drawing a larger conclusion. Let's try to see if voter issues are different between men and women, and if that could have any implication on the turnout (Table 9.6).

Figures in Table 9.7 indicate that there is no significant gender-based difference when it comes to the most important issue for voters. The most important issue has been the same for both men and women: drinking water in 2009 and a price rise in 2014. On the other hand, corruption and unemployment seem to be more important for men than for women. This could simply be attributed to men's greater public participation and involvement in the work force. Clearly, there is almost no difference in the concerns or the issues, which motivate the women and men to vote. What is noteworthy is that the issue of crimes against women remains a non-issue for both men and women.

Table 9.6 State-wise analysis of proportion of voters who voted without taking anybody else's opinion into account (%)

State	Increase in women's turnout between 2009 and 2014	Gender gap in voting		Change in proportion of women voting without taking anybody else's opinion into account
		2009	2014	
Rajasthan	16.6	6.7	3.2	27
Uttar Pradesh	13.2	6.5	1.7	22
Assam	12.4	5.3	−4.8	11
Chhattisgarh	16	6	2.7	9
Madhya Pradesh	12.7	13.7	9.5	2
Jharkhand	15.8	6.2	0.7	1
Bihar	15.1	6.5	−2.6	−1
Odisha	10.4	1.5	−2.4	−8

Source: National Election Studies 2009 and 2014, conducted by the CSDS

Note: The gender gap is estimated as the difference between the men's turnout (%) and women's turnout (%)

Table 9.7 Gender-wise opinions on issues which influenced voting decisions: Lok Sabha elections 2009–2014 (%)

Issue	2009		2014	
	Men	Women	Men	Women
Price rise	8	9	18	20
Road, electricity, water and development	31	33	24	22
Corruption	1	1	13	9
Unemployment	15	10	9	6
Women's issues and crimes against women	1	1	1	3

Source: National Election Studies 2009 and 2014, conducted by the CSDS

Note: An open-ended question was asked to all respondents and the responses were coded later. Others either gave different answers or had no opinion

If the increase in women's turnout was indeed a result of women emerging as a separate political constituency, then one would also expect them to emerge as a distinct voter bank, as in the case of various caste identities and young people as a distinct voter bank. Research on gender voting in India has primarily demonstrated the existence of a gender gap in the support base of the principal national parties—the Bharatiya Janata Party (BJP) and the Congress Party. The Congress Party has traditionally been known to have a slight gender advantage among women. The proportion of votes it receives from women has normally always exceeded the proportion of votes it gets from men (Yadav, 2003). This difference for the Congress Party narrowed in 2014, as the party received almost the same proportion of votes from both men and women (Fig. 9.4). The BJP, on the other hand, has been known to have a gender disadvantage, since more men are likely to vote for it as compared to women (Deshpande, 2009).

Rajeshwari Deshpande, in her analysis of voting behavior in the 2009 general election, indicates that gender was not a major social cleavage determining voting patterns, and women did not always vote as gendered beings (Deshpande, 2009). This can be seen through post-poll data from the Study of Developing Societies (CSDS) as well as by the fact that the gap in support among men and women for both the BJP and the Congress Party is marginal if compared with the uneven support for the parties among religious groups, castes, and other social groups and classes.

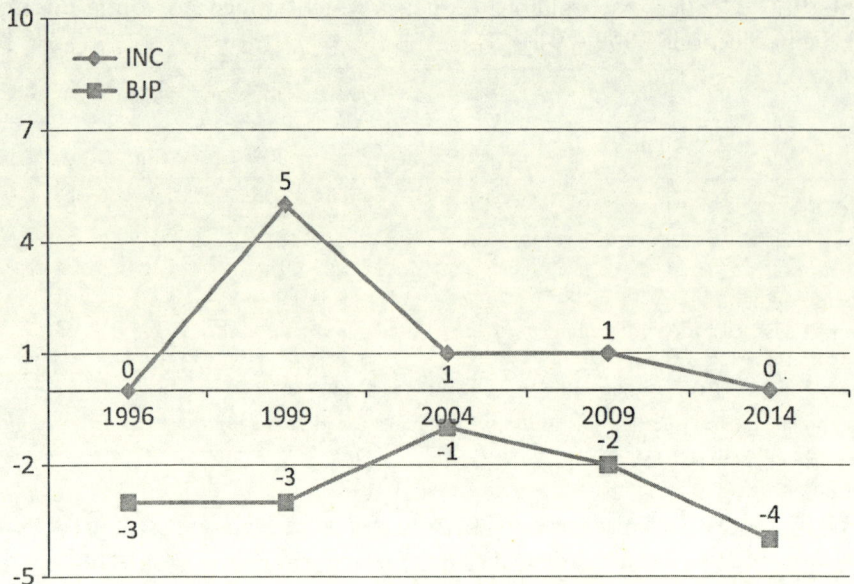

Fig. 9.4 Gender gap in voting for Congress and BJP (%). (Note: Difference in the percentage vote among women voters and men voters. Source: National Election Studies 2009 and 2014, conducted by the CSDS)

TESTING THE ARGUMENT OF WOMEN'S HIGHER LEVEL OF SOCIO-ECONOMIC DEVELOPMENT

There are two possible factors for the historical deficit in women's political participation. First, women have had relatively less access to the information and knowledge that is necessary for participation in political life. Second, women have traditionally been subject to restrictions on participating in activities outside the household sphere. The rise in literacy among women and the rapid spread of information (a natural consequence of the development process post-liberalization) could perhaps have led to a moderation of patriarchal norms and an improvement in the position of women in households. This could partly explain the higher female turnout. It is also possible to draw a connection between women's turnout and their increased level of literacy (Giné & Mansuri, 2011). This association cannot, however, be simplistic. Globally, there is mixed evidence for the relationship between education and turnout. A few studies in the Americas have shown how the level of education affects turnout by raising the political skill level of voters and lowering their cost of voting. On the other hand, Fornos, Power, and Garand (2004) used pooled data from presidential and legislative elections in Latin American countries to show that there was an insignificant relationship between literacy and voter turnout.

Analysis of the data presented in Table 9.8 indicates the lack of any clear association between education levels and voting turnouts. There seems to be a sharp difference in the turnout if one compares the middle and lower category. Basic literacy is important because it does provide an increased political awareness, but education must not be treated as the ultimate panacea for voter participation. If that were the case, the most educated would also be the most participative, which the data disputes. Factors such as class come into play there, as turnouts have traditionally been lower among the upper class, across gender. There are, however, some linkages between education/literacy and the probability of turning out to vote, which I now try to match with the rise in women's turnout in various states.

Data from the 2001 and 2011 Census of India suggests that in category 1 states (high gender-gap states), no clear relationship exists between changes in women's turnout and literacy. Improvement in women's literacy was considerably higher than the national average only in Uttar Pradesh and Odisha. While Gujarat performed at par with the national average, improvements in Rajasthan and Madhya Pradesh were slightly lower. Interestingly, there has been no major long-term increase in women's turnout in Bihar, which had recorded very high improvement (61%) in the literacy rate among women. Except Tripura, in all category 2 states, the improvement in literacy was lower than the national average. Low improvement in Tamil Nadu and Delhi is not surprising, since these states had limited scope due to their high literacy base. Even though there seems to be no uniformity in the quantum of change, one must not ignore the substantial increase in female literacy rates. Thus, while one must be careful not to over-emphasize the role of education in higher voter participation, one must also resist discounting this fact completely (Table 9.9).

Table 9.8 Level of educational attainment of women voters and turnout: Lok Sabha elections 2009–2014 (%)

Level of educational attainment	2009	2014
Non-literate	53.2	65.2
Up to metric	58.3	67.4
College and above	55.1	63.2

Source: National Election Studies 2009 and 2014, conducted by the CSDS

Table 9.9 State-wise pattern of increased literacy rate among women and declining gender gap in literacy (%)

State	Gender gap in literacy		Increase in literacy rate among women (2001–2011)
	2001	*2011*	
All India	21.6	16.6	22
States with traditionally high gender gap in turnout (Category I states of above-mentioned classification)			
Uttar Pradesh	26.6	19.9	40.5
Odisha	24.8	18	27.5
Rajasthan	31.9	27.8	19.8
Madhya Pradesh	25.8	20.5	19.3
Gujarat	21.9	16.5	22.3
States with traditionally moderate gender gap in turnout (Category II states of above-mentioned classification)			
Tripura	16.1	9	28.2
Chhattisgarh	25.5	20.9	16.8
Delhi	12.6	10.1	8.3
Haryana	22.8	18.6	19.9
Tamil Nadu	18	12.9	14.8

Source: Census of India 2001 and 2011

Alongside the increase in literacy, the last decade has also witnessed rapid technological progress, which has led to a major increase in media exposure in the country. Newspapers, television, and radio are sources of information for people nationwide. The media plays an important role in inducing political participation by generating awareness about rights and issues. It also aids various civil society organizations and the Election Commission of India that use it as a platform for voter-awareness campaigns. Similar to education, there seems to be a sharp difference if one compares turnout among women who lack exposure to media with those who have limited exposure. Lower turnout in the top category could again be a reflection of the class and locality effect. The exposure to media has been estimated based on the frequency with which women follow news through the three main sources: television, newspaper, and radio. Comparing data from the 2011 census with the previous round shows that there has been an increase in TV ownership, from 32 percent in 2001 to more than 47 percent in the latest census.[3] Data from the National Election

[3] Census 2011 and 2001: Household ownership of assets.

Table 9.10 Level of media exposure and turnout among women voters: Lok Sabha elections 2009–2014 (%)

	2009	2014
High media exposure	58.1	69.2
Moderate/low media exposure	61.8	66.7
No media exposure	54	63.4

Source: National Election Studies 2009 and 2014, conducted by CSDS

Table 9.11 Declining proportion of voters (men and women) not exposed to media: Lok Sabha elections 2004–2014 (%)

Not exposed to media	2004	2009	2014
All	57	53	30
Men	49	43	22
Women	67	65	39

Source: National Election Studies 2004, 2009 and 2014, conducted by the CSDS

Studies show that there has been a massive upsurge in media exposure in the last half decade. Figures reported in Table 9.10 indicate the proportion of voters who had no or very low exposure to media. It is quite evident that there has been an overall increase in the exposure to media, and now more than half the electorate seems to be following news through television, newspapers, and/or radio with different frequency. In the last five years, there has been a massive increase in media exposure among both men and women, and the proportion of women with very low or no media exposure has dropped sharply from 65 percent in 2009 to 39 percent in 2014. The trend continues nationwide. Table 9.11 shows that in most of the low-income states except Assam and Rajasthan, there was a huge rise in media exposure among women.

An interest in politics also influences the voting behavior of women (Table 9.12). Out of those women who had an interest in politics, only 9 percent did not vote, while 20 percent of those women who had no interest in politics did not cast their vote (Table 9.13).

ROLE OF THE ELECTION COMMISSION OF INDIA

One of the principal objectives of the Election Commission of India is to ensure maximum electoral participation of voters in all the state assembly elections and national elections. In the last few years, most of the

Table 9.12   State-wise analysis of change in level of media exposure and gender gap on voting: Lok Sabha elections 2009–2014 (%)

State	2009		2014	
	Gender gap in turnout	Proportion of population with no media exposure	Gender gap in turnout	Proportion of population with no media exposure
Rajasthan	6.7	50	3.2	43
Uttar Pradesh	6.5	79	1.7	30
Assam	5.3	59	−4.8	58
Chhattisgarh	6	79	2.7	57
Madhya Pradesh	13.7	72	9.5	31
Jharkhand	6.2	85	0.7	37
Bihar	6.5	89	−2.6	56
Odisha	1.5	66	−2.4	39

Source: National Election Studies 2009 and 2014, conducted by the CSDS

Table 9.13   Interest in politics and voting

Factor	Vote	Do not vote
Interest in politics	91	9
No interest in politics	80	20

commission's activities for voter awareness and ensuring maximum participation have been integrated and conducted under the Systematic Voters' Education and Electoral Participation (SVEEP) program. The program focuses on information, motivation, and facilitation, all of which have been identified as the key drivers of participation. To implement the program nationally, the commission has collaborated with various civil society organizations and media houses. A formal agreement has been made with the National Literacy Mission Authority of India for electoral literacy in rural areas, and with the charity ASHA and Anganwadi childcare centers. Female field workers have also been involved at the local level. Apart from the voter-awareness programs, the Election Commission of India (ECI) should also be credited for its concerted efforts to clean the electoral rolls. The deletion of ghost voters from electoral rolls would naturally increase the turnout (Kumar, 2013). While there is some indication that this move by the ECI has helped to increase the enrolment of voters and resulted in higher turnout among all voters, which should normally apply to women voters as well, there is no evidence to suggest the extent to which this effort of the ECI has helped to increase the turnout among women voters in recent elections in India.

REPRESENTATION OF WOMEN IN LEGISLATURES AND LOCAL BODIES

Although, the proportion of women in the Lok Sabha (lower house of parliament) has increased marginally between 1996 and 2014—from 7.4 percent to 11.2 percent—there has been a significant rise in the number of women candidates. A study of women's participation in state assembly elections in India has shown that the victory of women candidates only leads to an increase in the share of the women candidates in subsequent elections and has no effect whatsoever on women's turnout or spillover effects to neighboring seats (Bhalotra, Irma, & Lakshmi, 2013). No correlation has been found between the vote share of women candidates and voter turnout among women (Chari, 2011). Yet, some of the studies may suggest a minimal relationship between female legislators, female candidates, and higher vote shares for female candidates at the local level (Panchayat level). At this level, there seems to be some evidence for a positive impact of women's increased political representation through reservation, especially with respect to the participation of women in the activities of the Gram Sabha (village councils) (Chattopadhyay & Duflo, 2004). Findings reported in Table 9.14 indicate how the number of elected women representatives in local bodies has increased over the years. Given

Table 9.14 Increasing number of elected women representatives in gram panchayats: 2001–2014 (%)

Year	Total number of elected representatives	Number of women
2001	2,739,666	685,155
2002	1,630,327	548,794
2004	2,065,882	838,227
2006	2,656,476	975,116
2008	2,645,883	975,057
2009	2,645,880	974,255
2014	2,916,000	1,271,050

Source: Ministry of Panchayati Raj

that in many states, the reservation of seats for women has been increased from 33 percent to 50 percent, the proportion of elected women representatives has increased even more after 2009. Bihar was the first state to introduce 50 percent reservation for women in Panchayats. Now, barring Gujarat, Haryana, Tamil Nadu, and Uttar Pradesh, which still have a system of 33 percent reservation, most of the other states have followed Bihar and increased women's reservation to 50 percent in Panchayats.

Though it is reasonable to expect that the entry of more than a million women into public life would have an impact on the socialization of women, it is important to exercise some restraint and not to draw larger conclusions without adequate empirical evidence.

Women's Representation

Of all the possible factors for the positive surge in women's participation, we have seen that the increase in women's representation at the local panchayat level has had the clearest association with voter turnout. Hence, it becomes important to examine the issue of women's representation in elections at a more macro level. While there has been a significant reduction in the gender gap in voter turnout since independence in 1947, the same cannot be said about representation in Parliament and state legislatures. The Women's Reservation Bill, which was first introduced in Parliament in 1996 by the H. D. Deve Gowda government, still has not been passed. The current version of the bill, the 108th Amendment, which seeks to reserve for women 33 percent of all seats in governing bodies at the center, state, and local level, has been passed by the Rajya Sabha, but has been stalled by the Lok Sabha. This reflects an inadequate commitment of the Indian legislature to women's political representation.

Despite this discouraging reality, it cannot be said there has been no change in this domain since independence. There has been a quantitative increase in the number of women candidates as well as the number of women legislators. Since 1957, there has been an increasing trend in the number of women running for office in the Lok Sabha elections. While only 45 women stood for election in 1957, this number rose to 668 in 2014 (Fig. 9.5). Though the increase has been largely gradual, a sharp rise was seen in 1996, when 599 women ran for election. However, in the following two elections, there was a decline in this number as well. The failure to pass the Women's Reservation Bill and the disenchantment that

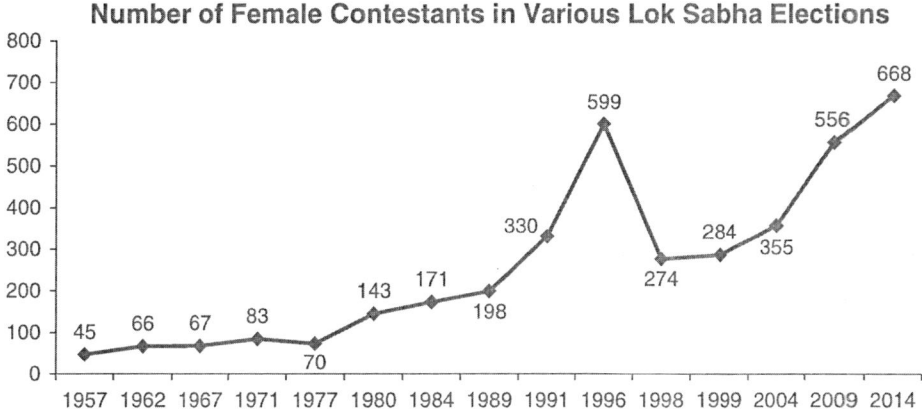

Fig. 9.5 Number of female candidates in Lok Sabha elections (1957–2014)

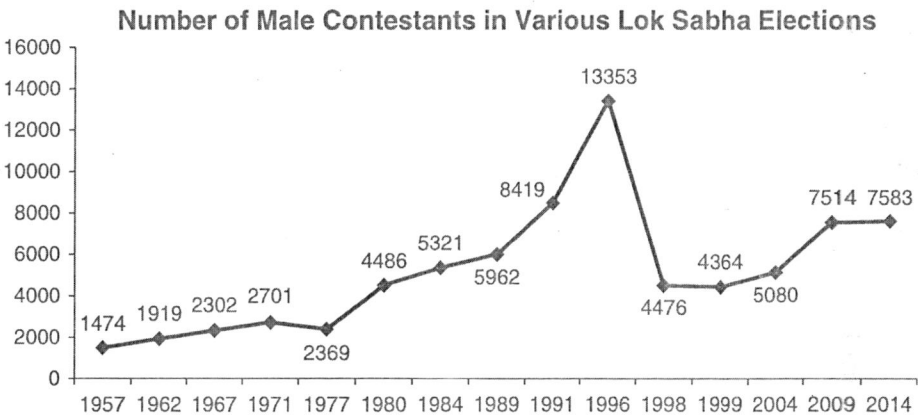

Fig. 9.6 Number of male candidates in Lok Sabha elections (1957–2014). (Source: https://i0.wp.com/factly.in/wp-content/uploads/2015/02/Number-of-Male-Contenstants-in-Various-Lok-Sabha-Elections.png?ssl=1)

followed can be a reason behind the same. However, since then, a steady increase in the number of women candidates has resumed.

The number of male candidates has consistently been much higher compared to female candidates. While only 45 women ran for office in 1957, the figure for men was 1474, and in 2014, 7583 men stood for elections in contrast to 668 women (Fig. 9.6). The gender gap is clearly very large. However, in terms of proportion, the increase in the number of female candidates is much greater than that of male candidates (Fig. 9.7).

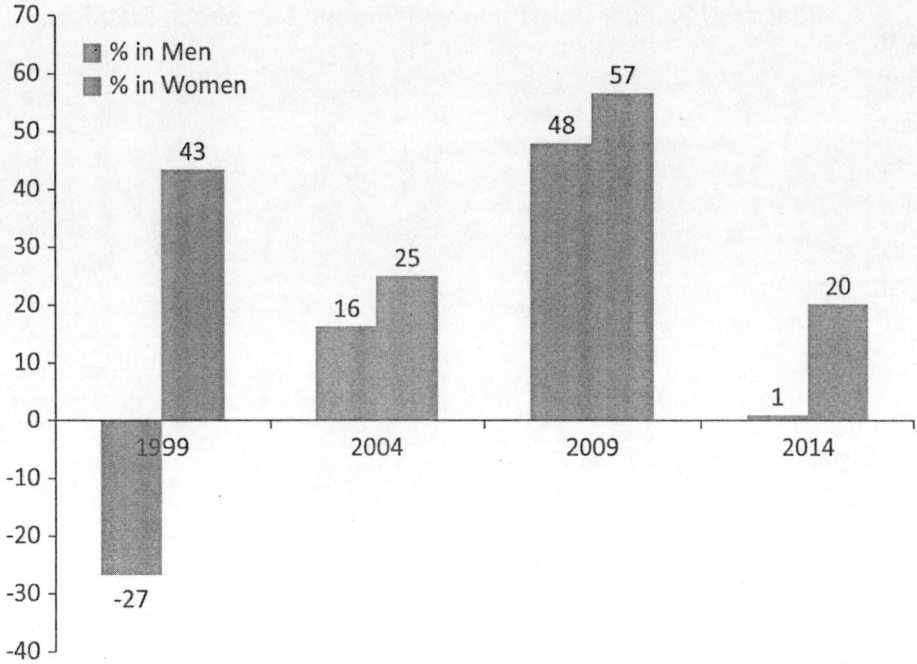

Fig. 9.7 Proportion of increase in male and female candidates

This fact does not necessarily mean that the gender gap in this respect is dwindling. In fact, by examining the absolute values, there is a wide gap between the two. One possible reason for this significant difference in proportion is that the base value for the number of male candidates is already very high.

Interestingly, one can observe that the success rate of female candidates winning their seat has always been higher than that of male candidates. In 1957, the success rate of female candidates was considerably higher than that of male candidates, 49 percent as opposed to 32 percent. This gap has reduced since then, with 2014 having a difference of only 4 percent between the two success rates (Fig. 9.8). This data can give the impression that the electorate does not vote in a gender-biased manner, however, it is important to examine the data more closely before reaching that conclusion. One reason for the consistently higher success rate of female contestants is the fact that fewer women stand for elections as compared to men; therefore, it appears that women have a higher chance at winning the election if they stand for it. It can also be observed that there is a decline

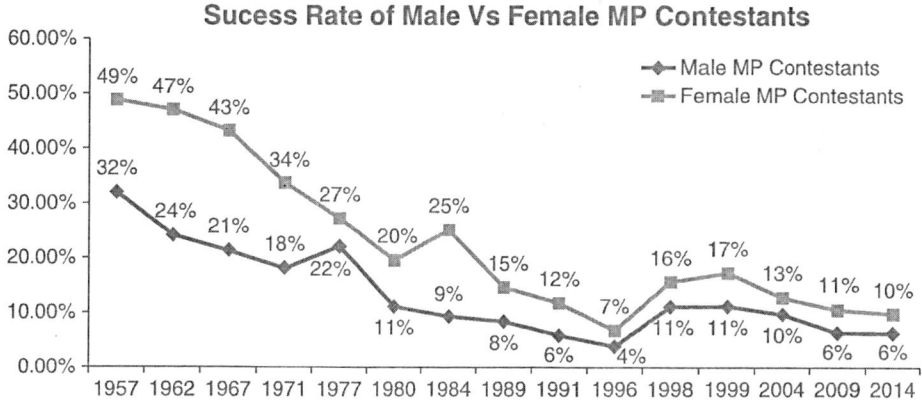

Fig. 9.8 Success rate of male vs. female MP candidates (%)

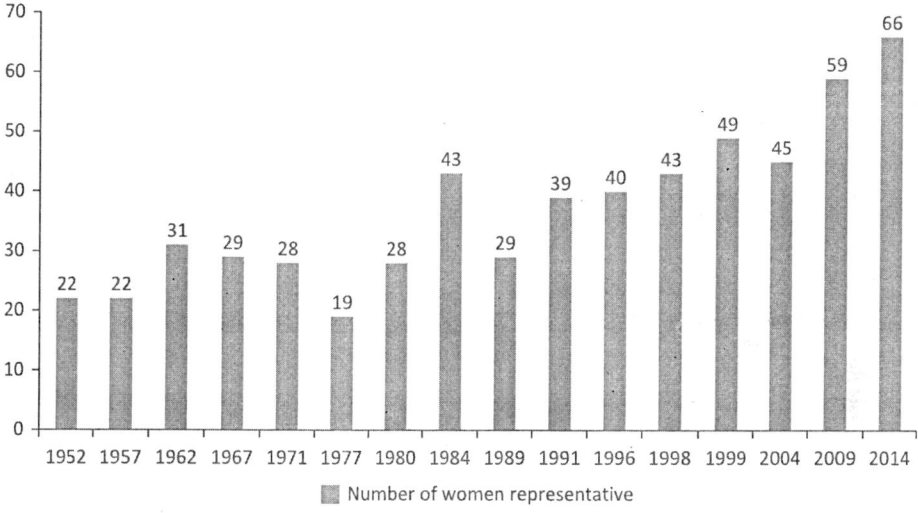

Fig. 9.9 Number of women MPs in the Lok Sabha (1952–2014)

in the success rates for both men and women; this is because the number of candidates in both categories has increased over the years, thereby reducing the chance of victory.

Despite an increasing trend in the number of female candidates and a high female success rate, women's representation in parliament remains abysmally low. Out of 545 seats in the Lok Sabha, women (Fig. 9.9) hold only 66. This is a meager 11 percent of the total number of MPs in the

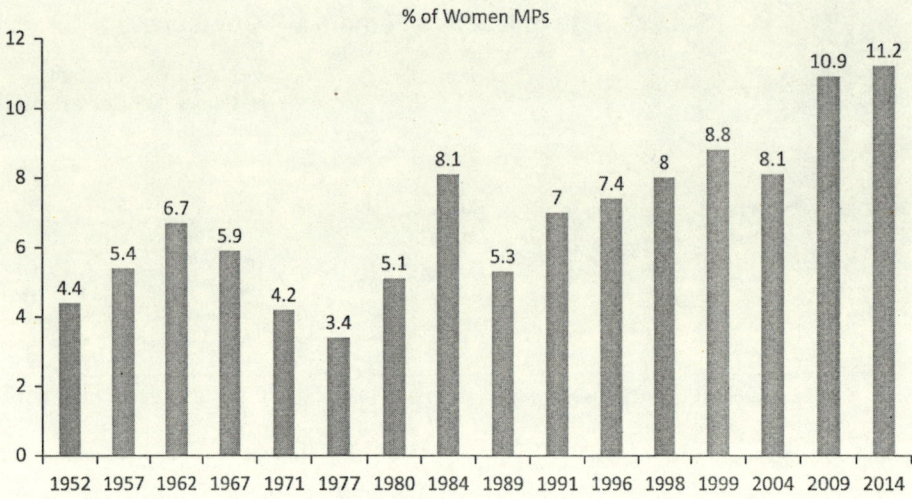

Fig. 9.10   Proportion of women's representation in the Lok Sabha (1952–2014) (%)

Lok Sabha (Fig. 9.10). Though there has been an increase in the proportion of women's representation in the Lok Sabha, from 4.4 percent in 1952 to 11.2 percent in 2014, India still ranks very low in terms of women's representation in parliament, with a world ranking of 147.

Even among other South Asian countries, India's ranking in terms of women representatives has been very low; only Sri Lanka, the Maldives, and Bhutan have a lower rank than India. These nations are opposed to reservation policies for women. All the South Asian countries that have a policy for reserving a number of seats for women in parliament have secured a considerably higher rank. Nepal was ranked the highest, at 47, with nearly 30 percent of the total MPs being women. Its recently instated policy of 33 percent reservation for women candidates in parliament has played a part in this achievement (Table 9.15). Afghanistan, a nation riddled with rampant oppression of women, was ranked at 53. Here again, 27 percent of the seats in the lower house, *Wolesi Jirga*, are reserved for women. This has drastically improved the representation of women's interests and given women a strong political voice. Pakistan too has done better than India, with a world ranking of 89. Pakistan has a policy of reserving 17 percent of the seats for women in the National Assembly, and in its last general election in 2013, 21 percent of the seats were won by

Table 9.15 Women's representation in parliaments of South Asian countries

Country	Afghanistan	Bangladesh	Bhutan	India	Maldives	Nepal	Pakistan	Sri Lanka
Year of last general election	Lower house: 2010 Upper house: 2015	2014	2013	2014	2014	2013	Lower house: 2013 Upper house: 2015	2015
Percentage of seats held by women in the parliament	Lower house, House of the People, Wolesi Jirga: 27.7% Upper house, House of elders, Meshrano Jirga: 26.47%[a]	20.3%	Lower house, National Assembly: 8.5% Upper house, National Council: 8%	Lower house, Lok Sabha: 11.8% Upper house, Rajya Sabha: 11.1%	5.88%	29.6%	Lower house, National Assembly: 20.6% Upper house, Senate: 18.3%	5.8%
No. of seats held by women/total number of seats	Lower house: 69/249 Upper house: 18/68	71/350	Lower house: 4/247 Upper house: 2/25	Lower house: 64/542 Upper house: 27/244	5/85	176/595	Lower house: 70/340 Upper house: 19/104	13/225
World ranking in women's representation in parliament	53	91	169	147	177	47	89	178

[a]The Upper has 102 seats but in 2015, elections only took place in 68 seats

women candidates, a significantly higher proportion than that in India. Bangladesh earned a much higher rank than India as well, at 91. Bangladesh has also introduced a reservation policy whereby 50 out of the 350 seats in parliament are reserved for women. By gauging the performance of all these neighboring states of India, a direct correlation can be seen between reserving seats for women in legislature and the country's performance in reducing the gender gap in political representation.

The representation of women in state assemblies also remains low—below 10 percent in most states. On average, the proportion of women in state assemblies is 6–7 percent, and in Kerala, this proportion is as low as 5 percent. There have been instances in which no women are in state assemblies, examples being Puducherry in 2001, Nagaland in 2003, and Mizoram in 2003. In some states, for instance, Manipur and Goa, there has been only one woman representative. These facts highlight the extent of the gender gap in political representation in India, and that there has hardly been any change in the pattern of women's representation in legislature. This calls for further steps to be taken to correct the problem.

Participation in democratic process is not limited merely to voting and standing for office, but also extends to participation in election meetings, processions, door-to-door canvassing, and so forth. Here we can see an increase in women's participation in election meetings and rallies, from 9 percent in 2009 to 15 percent in 2014 (Table 9.16). Women's increased involvement at the grassroots level can thus be seen as a positive change. With respect to *nukkad nataks*, processions, and door-to-door campaigning, there has been a meager change or no change between 2009 and 2014. We, therefore, need to do more research to get a holistic picture of women's political participation at the local level.

Table 9.16   Electoral participation beyond voting and running for office

Forms of electoral participation	2009		2014	
	Women (%)	Men (%)	Women (%)	Men (%)
Election meetings/rallies	9	28	15	34
Participation in processions/*nukkad natak*, etc.	5	20	6	15
Participation in door-to-door canvassing	6	17	6	14

CONCLUSION

This chapter is simply an exercise in identifying the factors behind the surge in turnout numbers of women voters. The increase in women's turnout in state assembly elections and Lok Sabha elections held in India during the last few years calls for a specialized inquiry. This could help delineate and encourage the processes involved. Possible hypotheses were tested to figure out the probable factor(s) contributing to the higher electoral participation of women in recent years. The analysis of the data does indicate some positive correlations between these factors and a higher turnout and helps in finding some answers to this big question, but more research is needed to understand the other latent factors involved. More than this, however, detailed and systematic research is required to find out if this higher turnout among women voters has made any impact on the life of the Indian women outside their household domain. The trend of higher women's turnout is only a recent phenomenon (last five years). Stability in this trend could indeed be an indicator of a possible structural change in political participation in India. Studies are required to throw light on whether this has had a positive effect on the social and cultural life of women.

Overcoming the gender gap in turnout is indeed a landmark moment in the democratization process in India, as in any other country. If the gap continues to remain low and differences in the quantum of change in men's and women's turnout are eliminated in most states, India would join a group of established democracies such as some of the Nordic countries (Seppälä, 2004), United States of America, and Britain (Norris, 2002) which achieved a gender reversal in electoral participation more than three decades ago.

There has been an increase in female candidates in elections, and their success rates have also consistently been higher than that of male candidates. While this presents a positive image for gender parity, one must desist from making such a conclusion because the number of seats held by women still remains very low. Further, we observed the trends in women's representation in the parliament and compared India's performance in this domain to that of other South Asian nations. This was in order to understand where India stands in terms of gender parity in the political representation of women as well as to find out whether there is a relation between policies on reservation and a narrowing of the existing gender gap. Examining the above as well as seeing the poor level of women's representation in state legislatures, there seems to be a need for active political intervention to increase women's representation and give greater political accessibility to women in legislative bodies. Women do not gain representation in legislative bodies because political parties do not nominate a sizeable number of women as candidates for elections. Nor do women hold important positions within the parties. Women's representation and participation in politics are vital, but they must be accompanied by an integration of gender concerns in the political discourse. Only having some women in a few positions of power does not lead to a transformed society; rather, women need to be represented at all levels and in spheres of the political process.

Although the representation of women remains low, the rise in their voter turnout is significant: the marginal increase in their representation in parliament, the positive change in the representation of women in gram panchayats, and their increased involvement in other electoral activities must not be discounted, for these demonstrate the faith women have in democracy and its institutions and their strong belief in the power of voting. All these factors show a slow but a desirable shift in women's increased role in Indian democracy.

REFERENCES

Bhalotra, S., Irma, C.-F., & Lakshmi, I. (2013). *Path-breakers: How does women's political participation respond to electoral success?* Working Paper No. 14-035. Harvard Business School BGIE Unit.

Chari, A. (2011). *Gender, social norms and voting: Female turnout in Indian state elections.* RAND Working Paper Series, No. WR-900.

Chattopadhyay, R., & Duflo, E. (2004). Women as policy makers: Evidence from randomized policy experiment in India. *Econometrica, 72*(5), 1409–1443.

Deshpande, R. (2009). How did women vote in Lok Sabha elections 2009? *Economic and Political Weekly, 44*(39), 83–87.

Fornos, C., Power, T. J., & Garand, J. C. (2004). Explaining voter turnout in Latin America, 1980–2000. *Comparative Political Studies, 37*(8), 909–940. https://journals.sagepub.com/doi/10.1177/0010414004267981

Giné, X., & Mansuri, G. (2011, June). *Together we will: Evidence from a field experiment on female voter turnout in Pakistan.* World Bank Policy Research Working Papers 5692.

Kapoor, M., & Ravi, S. (2014). Women voters in Indian democracy: A silent revolution. *Economic and Political Weekly, 49*(12), 63–67.

Kumar, S. (2013, December 5). Over reading the turnout. *Indian Express.*

Mishra, V. (2010, November 24). The day before, paler, bitter Lalu. *Indian Express*.

Norris, P. (2002). *Women's power at the ballot box: Voter turnout since 1945*. Report by the International Institute for Democracy and Electoral Assistance.

Seppälä, S. (2004). *Women and the vote in Western Europe: Voter turnout in Western Europe since 1945*. Report by the International Institute for Democracy and Electoral Assistance.

Yadav, Y. (2003, June). The new Congress voter. *Seminar*. Retrieved April 8, 2019, from http://www.india-seminar.com/2003/526/526%20yogendra%20yadav.htm

CHAPTER 10

Achievements and Challenges for Gender Mainstreaming in the Employment Sector of the Maldives

Mohamed Faizal

INTRODUCTION

Gender mainstreaming focuses on the institutional barriers to equality for women (Daly, 2005). This chapter discusses the progress women have made in paid employment in the Maldives, and the remaining institutional constraints on progress. Women in the Maldives have traditionally been an integral part of the economy, especially due to their central role in the fisheries industry. The changing economic landscape, which involved a shift toward manufacturing and providing services in combination with migration to urban centers, inadvertently diminished women's participation in economic activities, confining a significant proportion of them to household duties. However, along with academic progress and economic development, the last decades have once again seen a steady increase in the number of women joining the workforce. In some professions they now outnumber men. Nevertheless, although policies for promoting gender

M. Faizal (⊠)
National Pay Commission, Malé, Maldives

I. Jamil et al. (eds.), *Gender Mainstreaming in Politics, Administration and Development in South Asia,*
https://doi.org/10.1007/978-3-030-36012-2_10

mainstreaming have had some success, women face an uphill battle for upward mobility, especially as regards gaining positions of leadership and narrowing the pay gap.

The relationship between economic development and women's participation in the workforce is complex, with participation considered an outcome of various economic and social factors (Verick, 2018). In this regard, the level of education has been found to have a positive impact on women's participation (Collet & Legros, 2016). However, the sectoral and occupational segregation of women in employment is a common phenomenon. According to Goldin (1990), women are often drawn into paid work due to the expansion of female-dominated jobs in the public sector as well as certain feminized professions such as teaching and nursing. It is also common for some professions to reflect a polarized view of women's employment. For instance, in some contexts, employment in the tourism industry has low status and is assumed to require a low level of skills, while in other contexts, it is perceived as glamorous (Riley, Ladkin, & Szivas, 2002). The unsociable working hours and at-times low pay in the tourism sector can be perceived by the local community as demeaning (Ruhanen & Cooper, 2009). Participation in the workforce can be further influenced by how gender practices relate to the extent of mobility to seek employment. More specifically, in the context of island nations, mobility can play an integral role in accessing livelihoods (Christensen & Gough, 2012) and has often been considered an adaptive strategy that is influenced by cultural, religious, economic, and social factors (Stojanov, Duží, Kelman, Němec, & Procházka, 2017). In the case of women, some argue that physical and occupational restrictions on mobility exist because women lack freedom to make choices and judgments for themselves (Lama, 2018). However, as far as breaking the proverbial glass ceiling to top management is concerned, Jauhar and Lau (2018) find that organizational culture, networking, and practices have a significant impact on women's career advancement, while family-related factors and personality traits have no significant impact. Complementarily, Budig, Misra, and Boeckmann (2012) examine country variation in the association between motherhood and earnings, in cultural attitudes surrounding women's employment, in childcare, and in parental leave policies. They conclude that culture and politics interact to create outcomes for women, particularly mothers, and argue that culture plays a role not only *through* policy, but in its interactions *with* policy. This chapter focuses on how factors such as those outlined above affect women's employment in the Maldives, and it identifies the achievements and challenges of gender mainstreaming in employment.

The chapter begins with a historical overview of women's employment in the Maldives. This is followed by a synopsis of the progress women have achieved in education, which is thought to be a primary reason for their increased employment. The chapter then explores the extent of women's participation in the workforce and how they are represented across professions, government sectors, and in the tourism industry. Additionally, it examines how women fare in politics and managerial positions. The next subject to be addressed is the pay gap between women and men across occupations, how the gap is affected depending on the level of education attained, and achievements in narrowing the gap in the civil service. The chapter then provides a brief description of government policies for gender mainstreaming that have had an impact on employment. Despite achievements in Maldivian women's employment, numerous cultural and institutional challenges remain. In this regard, it is contended that gender roles and responsibilities are defined within a particular cultural framework dictating that men tend to migrate more to seek employment and that men have the responsibility to protect women. In addition, it has been held that the archipelagic nature of the country relatively favors paid employment for men. In the chapter, it is argued that institutional policies developed for gender mainstreaming and additional work benefits for women have been inconsistent and inappropriately targeted, resulting in women's inability to break the glass ceiling and narrow the gender pay gap. The chapter concludes by arguing that a more focused, strategic, and holistic realignment of gender policies is needed, so that women can build on recent achievements, assume an even greater presence in positions of leadership, and continue to narrow the pay gap.

WOMEN'S EMPLOYMENT IN THE TRADITIONAL ECONOMY

For centuries, the majority of the Maldivian working population have been engaged in fishing and related activities (Phadnis & Luithui, 1985). Women came to play a central role in the fishing industry, specifically in processing fish for local consumption and export. As Maloney (1980) notes, some of the roles women played included boiling the fish fillets in salt water, smoking them for a few days, and drying them in the sun for a couple of weeks until the desired hardness was attained. Women also lent their muscles to beach the fishing boats for servicing.

The shift toward mechanizing fishing vessels and the emergence of fish processing centers, however, alienated women from participating in the industry (Shaljan, 2004). As men switched occupations, often commuting to other islands in search of better employment, women were consigned merely to household duties and childcare. This was particularly evident between 1977 and 1990 when women's overall workforce participation dropped from 63 to 20 percent (Shaljan, 2004). The progress women have since made in increasing their level of education has helped reverse this trend.

PROGRESS IN WOMEN'S EDUCATION

Maldivians have always placed great emphasis on education. History shows that no discrimination was evident against girls. On the contrary, girls used to continue their formal education longer than boys did, because boys terminated their studies at some stage to start apprenticeships with their fathers (Razee, 2000). Societal emphasis on education has ensured that the island nation continues to show remarkable literacy rates, with the 2014 Census showing a 98 percent female literacy rate and a 97.4 percent male literacy rate in the mother tongue (National Bureau of Statistics [NBS], 2015a). There is no difference in literacy rates between men and women in the atolls when compared with literacy rates in the capital city Malé, implying the nation-wide importance placed on education.

A shift from traditional educational institutions to formal education began in 1927 when the first boys' school was established. This was followed by the first girls' school in 1944. Over the years, schools were opened on all the inhabited islands and the government invested heavily in developing the education sector. The present generations have been the beneficiaries of these developments. Records dating from the turn of the twenty-first century show that net enrolment rates in primary education (grades 1–7) have remained mostly above 95 percent for both girls and boys (Ministry of Education, 2010, 2018). The same records show that for lower secondary (grades 8–10), those rates have shown remarkable increases during the last decade, with over 80 percent net enrolment for both girls and boys. This is further complemented by the phenomenal increase in the higher secondary rates (grades 11–12), where girls' net enrolment rose from 1.4 percent in 2001 to 50.4 percent in 2018, and

Table 10.1 Resident Maldivians attending higher education institutions, census 2014

Education level	Female	Male	% of female	% of male
Certificate	3318	1655	67	33
Diploma	2917	1708	63	37
First degree	3248	2084	61	39
Master's degree	428	446	49	51
PhD	14	17	45	55
Total	9925	5910	63	37

Source: NBS (2015a)

boys' net enrolment rose from 1.3 percent in 2001 to 38.9 percent in 2018. The growing and continued emphasis on education has been followed by significant increases in women's employment.

The achievements in secondary education have also filtered into higher education. According to data from Census 2014, the percentage of the resident female Maldivian population who attended higher educational institutions in 2014 was significantly higher than the male percentage: 63 percent female and 37 percent male (Table 10.1).

Apart from private funding for higher education, the government provides numerous scholarships. There is no gender disparity in the awarding of scholarships: from 2000 to 2017, a total of 1234 males and 1220 females received scholarships for diploma, first degree, master, or doctoral study programs (NBS, 2018a). However, the rate of female graduates is somewhat lower: recent data from local higher educational institutions show that the graduation rates for men were 55 and 57 percent for 2016 and 2017 respectively, compared with 45 and 43 percent for women (NBS, 2017, 2018a).

Women's achievements in higher education are now starting to be reflected in employment, at least to some extent. The Household Income and Expenditure Survey conducted in 2016 revealed that employed women are in fact relatively more educated than men. As shown in Table 10.2, women with a certificate, diploma, and/or degree are at 33 percent, while the level for men remains at 21 percent. This is primarily due to the dominance of women in education and health professions, as will be highlighted later in the chapter.

Table 10.2 Education level of the employed population (%)

	Female	Male
Not stated	1	2
Never attended	6	7
Higher secondary education	6	6
Degree and above	11	7
Certificate/Diploma	22	14
Primary education	23	27
Secondary education	31	37

Source: NBS (2018b)

Women in the Workforce

In most sectors of the Maldives' workforce, women's participation rates, although rising, are still lower than men's. After the decline in women's participation in the 1980s, gains were seen by the turn of the century. The 2006 census revealed that workforce participation rates for 15-year-olds and above were at 42 percent for women and at 70 percent for men (International Labour Organization, 2013). Since then, the rate for women has stayed at around 40 percent, although men's participation has incrementally increased to 77 percent in 2018 (NBS, 2018b; International Labour Organization—modelled estimates, November 2018).

Despite lacking progress in women's general workforce participation over the last decade, their increased level of education, when seen in combination with economic developments, shows significant improvement in their participation in some professions. For instance, the nursing profession is almost entirely composed of women, while teaching is also dominated by women. Such distribution is arguably related to the traditional norms that encourage women to assume the roles of nurturer and care-provider. Additionally, home-based work and some industries that offer less physically demanding jobs are dominated by women, for instance, factory-based fish processing. However, for most industries, as shown in Table 10.3, men continue to dominate by a substantial margin.

The proportion of women employed by the government has increased significantly over the years. According to the NBS's historical records, female representation in government employment (including appointed officials, elected officials, and security services) increased from 20 percent in 1980 to 41 percent in 2007. Two events—the introduction of a Civil

Table 10.3 Proportion of employed resident Maldivian population by industries (in percentage), census 2014

	Female	Male
Mining and quarrying	1	99
Construction	2	98
Accommodation and food service activities	10	90
Transportation and storage	11	89
Agriculture, forestry, and fishing	11	89
Electricity	12	88
Water supply	18	82
Other services	20	80
Arts, entertainment, and recreation	21	79
Professional, scientific, and technical activities	26	74
Real estate activities	28	72
Public administration and defense	29	71
Wholesale and retail trade	30	70
Information and communication	33	67
Administrative and support services	46	54
Extra-territorial organizations	48	52
Finance and insurance	49	51
Manufacturing	60	40
Human health and social work	65	35
Household as employers	65	35
Education	68	32

Source: NBS (2015b)

Service Act in 2008 and the subsequent formation of numerous statutory institutions that were established along with the new Constitution of 2008—were followed by a halt in collecting consolidated data on all government employees. Thus, since 2008, the NBS compiles employment statistics only for the civil service (comprised primarily of government ministries, departments, and local councils), which is roughly half the total estimated government workforce. This means that data on the gender composition of the entire government, which includes civil service, security services, overseeing bodies, elected officials, and the judiciary (altogether estimated to be around 42,000 persons), is unavailable. For the civil service alone, more women have been employed than men in almost every year since the formation of the civil service in 2008. By the end of 2017, total civil service employment stood at 13,175 women (59.7%) and 8907 men (40.3%).

A closer look at different professions within the government sector reveals further signs of achievements as well as areas that need greater attention. Recent data published by the NBS (2019a) show that 66 percent of all trained teachers, 39 percent of lawyers, 10 percent of police officers and 4 percent of judges are women. Additionally, 70 percent of medical staff at health facilities are women (Ministry of Health, 2014).

The inception of tourism in the early 1970s transformed the nation from being one of the least developed countries to a lower-middle income country. Currently, tourism is the single biggest contributor to government revenue, with an estimated 35.8 percent share in February 2019 (NBS, 2019b). However, the proportion of local women working in the tourism industry has continued to be low and shows a surprising decline: from 5.87 percent in 2007 to 2.75 percent in 2014 (Ministry of Tourism & Civil Aviation, 2008; NBS, 2018a). A survey conducted in 2013 also revealed that in the tourist resorts, while there were 291 male workers per establishment, there were only 8 female worker per establishment (NBS, 2013).

Women in Politics and the Glass Ceiling

In terms of access to education, the Maldives has achieved gender parity, yet better education has not contributed to more women entering politics, for there are persistent low levels of female representation.

Historically, the Maldives had women rulers, most noteworthy being Queen Rehendhi Khadeeja (1348–1363; 1364–1374; 1377–1380), Queen Raadhafathi (1380–1381) and Queen Dhaainkaba (1385–1388) (Maloney, 1980). Nevertheless, they were the exception because they belonged to noble families: most women were excluded from broad political participation (Razee, 2000). The first Republic 1953, however, was a turning point, when the Parliament had one-fifth female representation (Razee, 2000). These gains eroded shortly after the dissolution of the first Republic. The birth of the second Republic in 1968 and the subsequent years saw little increase in female representation in politics.

This is evident at both the national and the local level. As shown in Table 10.4, relatively few women hold political posts. With the exception of the 2005 parliament, which had 12 percent women members, all parliaments since 1989 have had around 5 percent women (El-Horr & Pande, 2016; Ritchie, Rogers, & Sauer, 2014). The parliamentary elections held in April 2019 also did not show any progress. Of 395 candidates who

Table 10.4 Extent of women's representation in political posts (2014)

Political post	Percentage of women's representation: total number of representatives
Cabinet	17.65%: 3 out of 17 cabinet positions
State ministers and deputy ministers	15.3%: 10 out of 63 deputy ministers, and 5 out of 35 state ministers
Parliament members	5.88%: 5 out of 85 seats
Parliament election candidates	7.6%: 23 out of 302 candidates
Island councilors	5.92%: 56 out of 946
Atoll councilors	2.27%: 3 out of 132
City councilors	11.76%: 2 out of 17
Local council election candidates (island, atoll, city)	11.1%: 273 candidates out of 2458 island, city and atoll councils

Source: Ritchie et al. (2014)

stood for the election, only 35 (8.86%) were women, and only 4 were elected, that is, around 5 percent of the 87 parliamentarians (Elections Commission, 2019).

The representation of women in politically appointed posts—for instance, minister, state minister, and deputy minister—is, however, slightly higher compared with elected posts. In this regard, a noteworthy improvement is seen in the politically appointed posts of the current government that came into power in November 2018. President Maumoon Abdul Gayoom's last cabinet had 22 percent female ministers, President Mohamed Nasheed's cabinet had 21 percent female ministers, President Mohamed Waheed Hassan Manik's cabinet had 19 percent female ministers, and President Abdulla Yameen Abdul Gayoom's cabinet had 17 percent female ministers (Asian Development Bank, 2014). In contrast, the current cabinet of President Ibrahim Mohamed Solih has 35 percent female ministers. Additionally, 21 percent of state ministers and 30 percent of deputy ministers of the current government are women.

Female representation in managerial posts does not fare any better than in the political sphere. In 1999, women occupied only 8 percent of government decision-making positions (Razee, 2000). The Household Income and Expenditure Survey 2016 showed that of all people employed in decision-making and management roles, only 19.5 percent were women (NBS, 2018b). Similarly, there have been relatively few women in managerial positions in the tourism industry. Although recent data is unavailable, a study conducted in 2007 revealed that female Maldivian representation in managerial positions in the tourism industry was merely 3.9 percent (Ministry of Tourism & Civil Aviation, 2008).

Gender Pay Gap

The presence of a gender pay gap, despite major changes in women's educational patterns and employment participation, is common in many countries (Rubery, Grimshaw, & Figueiredo, 2005). The Maldives is no exception. The Household Income and Expenditure Survey 2016 revealed that women, in their main job, earned on average MVR7510 (US $487) compared with MVR11,977 (US $776) for men (NBS, 2018b) during the given pay period. Thus, the gender pay gap for Maldivians at the national level is 26 percent, meaning that on average, Maldivian women earn MVR22.51 (US $1.46) per hour less than do men (NBS, 2018b).

This gap is further reflected when we look more closely at different professions. According to the Household Income and Expenditure Survey 2016, the pay gap was highest among managers (61%), followed by professionals (39%), craft and related trade workers (34%), and services and sales workers (22%) (NBS, 2018b). In monetary terms, this means that on average, women in managerial positions earn MVR146.7 (US $9.51) per hour less than do men, and for professional positions, women earn MVR48.95 (US $3.17) per hour less than do men.

The pay gap based on location is also of interest. In this regard, at the center of the government and economy, the pay gap in the capital city Malé is even greater compared with the situation in the atolls. In 2016, it stood at 37 percent (NBS, 2018b). Although previous comparative figures are unavailable, related data from 2010 reveal a similar picture, implying that the pay gap has not narrowed since then (see Table 10.5).

As stated, women have made noticeable achievements in higher education, and one might expect these to be reflected in a narrowing pay gap. This is hardly the case, however, for a significant pay gap in average monthly earnings remains. Data from 2016 indicate that women who have acquired a degree or higher qualification earn US $968.94 per month, while for men, the rate is 49 percent higher, at US $1448.18 (NBS, 2018b) (see Table 10.6).

Compared with the overall labor force, the Maldivian Civil Service has in fact shown rapid progress in closing the pay gap. Records show that when only the basic salary is taken into account, the proportion of female civil servants with a basic salary between MVR10,000 and MVR14,999

Table 10.5 Mean monthly earnings of women and men, by occupation in Malé, 2010

Occupation	Women's earnings (US$)	Men's earnings (US$)	Women's earnings as % of men's earnings (%)
Legislators, senior officials and managers	731.32	990.34	74
Professionals	476.13	638.65	75
Technicians and associate professionals	470.62	629.12	75
Clerks	375.75	407.85	92
Service workers, and shop and market sales workers	395.72	524.45	75
Skilled agriculture and fishery workers	324.25	806.29	40
Craft and related trades workers	297.08	487.03	61
Elementary positions	301.30	493.06	61

Source: Adopted from Asian Development Bank (2014)

Table 10.6 Average monthly earnings (US$)—main job by education attainment

	Female	Male
Never attended	280.48	466.28
Pre-school education	285.41	504.22
Primary education	309.60	593.90
Secondary education	419.78	791.44
Higher secondary education	515.43	741.25
Certificate/Diploma	573.48	961.67
Degree & above	968.94	1448.18

Source: Adopted from NBS (2018b)

increased from 33 to 36 to 47 percent in 2015, 2016, and 2017 respectively (NBS, 2016, 2017, 2018a). In these same NBS sources, similar developments were also observed for the basic salary in excess of MVR15,000, where the proportion of female civil servants increased from 37 to 38 to 45 percent in 2015, 2016, and 2017 respectively. Such progress means that with the right policies of employment in place, the pay gap can be reduced.

GOVERNMENT POLICIES AND GENDER MAINSTREAMING

Over the years, various governments have taken significant steps to promote equal rights for men and women. One early step was the formation of the Women Development Committees to empower women in the communities. When these started in 1979, the initiative was primarily focused on Malé. They were renamed National Women's Committees when they were rolled out to the islands in 1984 (Ministry of Gender & Family, 2018). By 2010 the committees gained legal status, as their functions were specified in the Decentralization Act of 2010. These committees are considered to be an integral part of local governance, but concerns have been raised due to their restricted autonomy and mandate in the affairs of rural women (United Nations Committee on the Elimination of Discrimination against Women [CEDAW], 2015).

Central government agencies for women's development have also been a feature for three decades. Firstly, in 1986, the Office for Women's Affairs was established and mandated to promote women's participation in socioeconomic development (Asian Development Bank, 2001). In 1993, the Office was elevated to a ministry, which has continued ever since, although with name changes.

Various laws have also been passed with a view toward gender mainstreaming and protecting the rights of women. These include the Family Act (2000), Employment Act (2008), Domestics Violence Prevention Act (2012), Sexual Offence Act (2014), Sexual Harassment Act (2014), and Gender Equality Act (2016). The Employment Act in particular mandates non-discrimination on the basis of gender in employment, including remuneration, recruitment, training, and type of employment. The Gender Equality Act aims to bridge the gender gap in political, economic, and family life by taking affirmative action in sectors where women perform below average.

The Maldives has, since 1993, also been a signatory of the International Convention on the Elimination of All Forms of Discrimination Against Women (CEDAW). The nation also joined the International Labour Organization in 2009. Over the years, the Maldives, in its efforts toward gender mainstreaming, has additionally benefited from various donor-funded projects by numerous international and multinational aid agencies.

A number of regulatory policies are also aimed at gender mainstreaming. One such policy was introduced in the civil service at the start of 2016. Under the policy, employees can have flexible working arrangements during pregnancy, for instance, to work from home. The types of work that are allowed from home include research-based analysis, legal drafting, computer software and web developing, architectural work, and press-related work.

Also of significance are recent changes to maternity leave policies. The Employment Act of 2008 guarantees 60 days of maternity leave for mothers and 3 days of paternity leave for fathers. In March 2019, the government announced six months of maternity leave for mothers and one month of paternity leave for fathers. All government institutions and state-owned enterprises subsequently amended their benefit policies in accordance with the government's decision. Additionally, the Employment Act provides two 30-minute breastfeeding breaks per day, and an optional one-year unpaid leave after the maternity leave period.

CHALLENGES FOR WOMEN'S EMPLOYMENT

Cultural Challenges

Despite the achievements that support gender mainstreaming in employment in the Maldives, numerous challenges continue to inhibit progress toward women's parity with men. In this regard, cultural challenges are critical. Unlike many neighboring countries, Maldivian women face little discrimination in basic aspects of life such as health, survival, and access to primary education (El-Horr & Pande, 2016). Nevertheless, balancing family responsibilities and work is found to be one of the most challenging obstacles for women aspiring to become leaders (Eagly & Carli, 2007). Shaljan (2004) further states that the restrictions on women, which inhibit their ability to develop on par with men, stem from the somewhat patriarchal nature of the society and from development processes that give men easier access to the modernizing sectors. Gender roles and responsibilities are defined within a traditional cultural framework in which men usually occupy the top echelons of the social hierarchy: men are perceived as protectors of women, and women are perceived to be consigned to childcare and household roles. These cultural parameters are prevalent in many professions and industries.

Maldivian island communities have traditionally been close-knit and cohesive. Men and women socialize freely without any segregation. However, one factor that has hindered women from entering some occupations, which consequently prevents them from reaching higher levels of employment, is the aforementioned protectiveness displayed by men (Razee, 2000). This societally entrenched protectiveness reduces women's mobility, especially to travel to other islands. From an early age, girls are encouraged to develop what are thought to be feminine characteristics such as shyness and subservience, while boys are encouraged to develop what are thought to be masculine characteristics such as to be out-going, forward, and self-confident (Razee, 2000).

Protectiveness is particularly expressed in the tourism industry. Until quite recently, when guesthouse tourism started to emerge on inhabited islands, tourist resorts were developed on uninhabited islands. Despite women making up half of the population, their direct employment in the tourism industry was minimal. The reasons include societal stigmas associated with young unmarried women staying on resort islands for significant periods of time, social expectations inconsistent with working away from family, perceived risks of women travelling alone, the high cost of transport, and limited childcare facilities for resort employees (El-Horr & Pande, 2016).

A second factor for low levels of women in some professions is related to reasons behind migration. Compared with women, men tend to be more willing to migrate to seek better employment. According to census-based data, while the percentage of men who migrated for the purpose of employment was 30.05 percent in 2006 and 26 percent in 2014, for women it was 4.28 percent in 2006 and 4 percent in 2014 (Ministry of Planning & National Development, 2006; NBS, 2015c). The fact that these figures have remained relatively unchanged implies that while men continue to migrate to where they can find better employment, women tend not to do so for that purpose.

A third factor contributing to the low level of women's representation in some sectors is considered to be the archipelagic nature of the Maldives itself—a nation with 1192 islands (188 inhabited islands) scattered over 90,000 square kilometers of ocean. Since the ocean covers 99 percent of the country, seafaring and dependence on the sea for daily livelihood are ingrained in history. The physical nature of spending the entire day out in a boat meant that many jobs were confined to men; women were expected to take charge of domestic affairs. The low level of representation in the tourism industry is also partly due to women being unable to spend long periods away from home on account of social expectations and their family responsibilities.

To some extent, the high degree of urbanization in the capital, where over 40 percent of the entire Maldivian population now reside (NBS, 2018a), has counteracted such challenges, since urbanization has led to greater female participation in the workforce. Nonetheless, the level of women participating in other islands, where the level of development is low relative to Malé, remains significantly low. Census data from 2006 and 2014 reveal that while men's workforce participation increased by 57 percent in the capital city, it increased by 32 percent in other islands during that period. Comparatively for females, there was a 75 percent increase in the capital, and a 36 percent increase on other islands during the same period (NBS, 2015b).

Guesthouse businesses established on inhabited islands have rapidly increased over the last decade. Over 450 such establishments are currently registered in 87 inhabited islands; and the number continues to increase rapidly (Ministry of Tourism, 2018). This expansion increases the opportunities for women to overcome the constraints of travelling and staying away from home, because they can now contribute to and be employed in tourism-related businesses while staying on their own islands. However, to get into tourism-related businesses, women need support in the form of training and financial assistance, and by countering societal stereotypes through community awareness programs. Through such targeted initiatives, women could regain the employment opportunities they lost through the modernization and mechanization of traditional sectors such as fishing.

Institutional Challenges

Institutional challenges that stem from employment-related policies also pose hurdles in achieving gender parity in the Maldives. This is because policies developed for gender mainstreaming and providing additional work benefits for women have not taken into consideration factors such as job and workplace characteristics that are directly or indirectly linked to breaking the glass ceiling and addressing the gender pay gap.

In relation to management, the concept of organizational culture as described by O'Connor (2011) refers to the myths, values, and practices that confine women to lower-level positions in an organization, and to see managerial positions as masculine. Acker (1990) states that masculinity pervades organizational processes and creates gender segregation by marginalizing women. These gender misconceptions lead to the belief that women cannot be good leaders because they lack 'masculine' leadership qualities. Such misconceptions may therefore lead to reducing women's opportunities for promotion to higher positions in organizations (Waheeda & Nishan, 2018).

An important factor for institutionalizing government policies for gender mainstreaming is the stability of the government framework mandated with that responsibility. In this regard, the continuous instability of Maldivian government structures that address gender concerns is arguably a challenge (El-Horr & Pande, 2016). Since the first gender committees in 1979, gender portfolios within the ministerial structure have shifted frequently, at times making it difficult to sustain programs, advocacy, and policies aimed at gender mainstreaming (Hope for Women, 2012). Similar to portfolios such as those for finance, education, and health, a common understanding—one required across the political spectrum—is that relative stability in supporting the gender portfolio is important. This understanding will send the right message, namely, that cross-party political commitment and accountability toward gender mainstreaming will continue to be on the government agenda.

One of the biggest hurdles to women's active participation in employment is the lack of childcare for working mothers. Presently, there are no government-funded childcare facilities, and private childcare facilities are expensive and not readily available (Ritchie et al., 2014). The government's role has so far been only to act as the regulator of day-care facilities (Ministry of Gender & Family, 2018). Successive governments have so far been reluctant to intervene and provide such facilities at affordable rates, although the issue has been raised during various assessments (Hope for Women, 2012). Childcare facilities are vital if women are to participate more in the workforce, because childcare is the mother's responsibility in the vast majority of households. Such facilities will help women find desirable and flexible working options. While in the islands, extended family members can provide childcare in most cases, this is quite different in Malé, where people are increasingly living in nuclear families. Government action and concrete policies are therefore needed for the provision of day-care facilities, which will subsequently contribute to further enhancing women's participation in employment, helping them gain higher positions, and narrowing the pay gap.

One further policy that needs reviewing in this regard is flexible working arrangements in the civil service for pregnant women. So far, the policy has not yielded notable benefits. The types of work specified as covered under the policy do not take into account the occupations with substantial participation by women. As a result, the professions dominated by women do not benefit from the policy. Occupations in public administration and professional scientific and technical work (see Table 10.3), which were the focus of the flexible work arrangements policy, had only a small female representation. Combined with the lack of a conducive working setup in most households, this has meant that only a handful of women have taken up the offer of flexible working arrangements.

The effects of the recent extension of maternity leave will need to be analyzed in due course. The challenges to studying the benefits of such policies in a proper way stem from a lack of empirical data and a lack of research on such issues. Although numerous studies have included statistics on gender issues, a focused institutional approach—one in which such issues are continuously and periodically studied through primary empirical data collection—is needed to observe the trends that in turn can be used to review and revise the policies related to gender mainstreaming in employment.

Challenges associated with access to higher education and professional training may also hinder women's attempts to reach higher echelons in their workplace. An analysis undertaken by the United Nations Development Programme (2011) revealed that the restrictions women face to reach executive and senior management positions stem from the lack of awareness regarding professional and employment opportunities, and the lack of training and tertiary education opportunities. At present, most of the higher educational and professional training institutions are concentrated in the capital, although the number of these institutions is gradually increasing in the atolls, and the use of alternative modes of training through information and communication technology is expanding. While these are steps in the right direction, a more targeted approach in which all possible hurdles are reduced through effective policies is required for any meaningful impact. That is because, for instance, as stated earlier, the percentage of female graduates from local higher educational institutions is lower. This phenomenon needs to be further explored; it is insufficient simply to state that the reason for women dropping out of the workforce is that they get married and become mothers.

One of the few Maldives-specific studies to explore possible reasons for the low representation of women in managerial posts finds that as far as the higher educational institutions of the Maldives are concerned, women face a number of specific challenges. These include the heavy workload of women who have to balance formal work with household responsibilities, the lack of opportunities for further career development, exclusion from decision-making, and the lack of proper support networks to manage their roles (Waheeda & Nishan, 2018). Such challenges have been highlighted in other studies as well. In a qualitative assessment conducted by the International Foundation for Electoral Systems (2015, p. 23), one woman summarized it succinctly:

> If a woman goes to work, her workload doubles. If a man goes to work, it is not compulsory for him to do any household work—that is what happens most often. There are exceptions. But if a woman goes to work, she has to go to work, do the cooking, take care of the children ... carry all the burden. Maybe that's why women do not come out to participate in public activities because their responsibilities are much more—not because they don't want to come out. .... the bigger responsibility of childcare falls on the woman. Even where the woman is earning more, her household work does not decrease.

For these institutional challenges to be properly addressed, barriers to women entering the political sphere need to be urgently targeted. The number of women who stand for and win elections is disproportionately and alarmingly low, especially considering their gains in education and gender rights. The political agenda is currently dominated by men. An assessment by Ritchie et al. (2014) concludes that possible reasons for women's low participation are the limited access to financial resources, reluctance to face gruesome campaign practices which often involve character assassination, unwillingness to travel away from home for long periods (often required in political posts), and reluctance to speak in public. Additionally, the Rights Side of Life Survey, conducted in 2012 by the Human Rights Commission of the Maldives, reveals that possible reasons for the low level of participation include the lack of women candidates, both in total and in terms of qualifications; limited support for women candidates from their families, other women, and society in general; the reluctance of men to vote for women candidates; and the reluctance of women to join public life (Human Rights Commission of the Maldives and UNDP, 2012). While there is no institutional discrimination against women running for parliament or local councils, the lack of a quota for women's representation has meant that these institutions continue to be male dominated (Ministry of Finance & Treasury and UNDP, 2014).

Providing affirmative action for women has been a subject of political debate, but without much serious consideration. Perhaps now is the appropriate time to bring the issue back into the public domain for a meaningful debate.

CONCLUSION

In the Maldives, women face little discrimination in basic aspects of life such as education and employment rights, and relative economic prosperity has contributed to decreasing basic gender inequalities. Despite these positive strides and in the absence of any legal hurdles in employment and participation in the labor force, deep-seated cultural beliefs coupled with inconsistent and inappropriate institutional policies continue to contribute to work and wage inequalities. All public-sector strategies and policies will have limitations, and no single approach is likely to achieve the desired goals of achieving gender mainstreaming in employment. Thus, multiple strategies and policies that are developed with the use of empirical data are needed for effective enforcement. Only through such a more focused, strategic, and holistic realignment of gender policies can the Maldives use the recent achievements to help women gain more positions of leadership and narrow the pay gap.

REFERENCES

Acker, J. (1990). Hierarchies, jobs, bodies: A theory of gendered organisations. *Gender and Society, 4*, 139–158.

Asian Development Bank. (2001). *Country briefing paper—Women in the Republic of Maldives*. Retrieved March 2019, from https://www.adb.org/sites/default/files/institutional-document/32556/women-maldives.pdf

Asian Development Bank. (2014). *Maldives gender equality diagnostic of selected sectors*. Retrieved March 2019, from https://www.adb.org/sites/default/files/institutional-document/149329/maldives-gender-equality.pdf

Budig, M. J., Misra, J., & Boeckmann, I. (2012). The motherhood penalty in cross-national perspective: The importance of work-family policies and cultural attitudes. *Social Politics, 19*(2), 163–193.

Christensen, A. E., & Gough, K. V. (2012). Island mobilities: Spatial and social mobility on Ontong Java, Solomon Islands. *Geografisk Tidsskrift-Danish Journal of Geography, 112*(1), 52–62.

Collet, R., & Legros, D. (2016). Dynamics of female labour force participation in France. *Applied Economics, 48*(30), 2807–2821.

Daly, M. (2005). Gender mainstreaming in theory and practice. *Social Politics: International Studies in Gender, State & Society, 12*(3), 433–450.

Eagly, A. H., & Carli, L. L. (2007). *Through the labyrinth: The truth about how women become leaders.* Boston, MA: Harvard Business School Press.

Elections Commission. (2019). *Parliamentary elections 2019 results.* Retrieved April 2019, from https://www.elections.gov.mv/

El-Horr, J., & Pande, R. P. (2016). *Understanding gender in Maldives: Toward inclusive development* (Directions in Development). Washington, DC: World Bank.

Goldin, C. (1990). *Understanding the gender gap: An economic history of American women.* New York: Oxford University Press.

Hope for Women. (2012). *Maldives NGO shadow report to the Committee on the Elimination of Discrimination against Women.* Retrieved March 2019, from https://www2.ohchr.org/english/bodies/cedaw/docs/ngos/HopeFor Women_MaldivesForPSWG.pdf

Human Rights Commission of the Maldives and UNDP. (2012). *The 'right' side of life: Second baseline human rights survey.* Malé: Human Rights Commission of the Maldives and United Nations Development Programme in the Maldives.

International Foundation for Electoral Systems. (2015). *Qualitative assessment: Perceptions about women's participation in public life in the Maldives.* International Foundation for Electoral Systems.

International Labour Organization. (2013). *Employment challenges in the Maldives.* International Labour Organization.

International Labour Organization. (2018, November). Modelled estimates. Retrieved March 2019, from https://www.ilo.org/ilostat/faces/oracle/ webcenter/portalapp/pagehierarchy/Page3.jspx?MBI_ID=7&_afrLoop= 760283628527267&_afrWindowMode=0&_afrWindowId=16do6tgm6m_1#! %40%40%3F_afrWindowId%3D16do6tgm6m_1%26_afrLoop% 3D760283628527267%26MBI_ID%3D7%26_afrWindowMode%3D0%26_ adf.ctrl-state%3D16do6tgm6m_57

Jauhar, J., & Lau, V. (2018). The 'glass ceiling' and women's career advancement to top management: The moderating effect of social support. *Global Business and Management Research: An International Journal, 10*(1), 163–178.

Lama, P. D. (2018). Gendered consequences of mobility for adaptation in small island developing states: Case studies from Maafushi and Kudafari in the Maldives. *Island Studies Journal, 13*(2), 111–128.

Maloney, C. (1980). *People of the Maldive islands.* Bombay: Orient Longman.

Ministry of Education. (2010). *School statistics 2010.* Malé: Republic of Maldives.

Ministry of Education. (2018). *School statistics 2018.* Malé: Republic of Maldives.

Ministry of Finance & Treasury and UNDP. (2014). *Maldives human development report 2014. Bridging the divide: Addressing vulnerability, reducing inequality.*

Malé: Ministry of Finance & Treasury and United Nations Development Programme in the Maldives.

Ministry of Gender & Family. (2018). *Promotion and protection of the rights of children, women, elderly and persons with disabilities 2013–2018*. Malé: Ministry of Gender & Family.

Ministry of Health. (2014). *Maldives health statistics 2014*. Retrieved March 2019, from http://www.health.gov.mv/Uploads/Downloads/Publications/Publication(23).pdf

Ministry of Planning & National Development. (2006). *Census analysis 2006*. Malé: Ministry of Planning & National Development.

Ministry of Tourism. (2018). *Tourism year book 2018*. Malé: Ministry of Tourism.

Ministry of Tourism & Civil Aviation. (2008). *Human resource situation in the tourism sector of Maldives*. Retrieved March 2019, from https://www.tourism.gov.mv/downloads/reports/survey_report_final_2008.pdf

National Bureau of Statistics. (2013). *Economic survey 2012–2013*. Retrieved March 2019, from http://statisticsmaldives.gov.mv/economic-survey-2013/

National Bureau of Statistics. (2015a). *Population & housing census 2014. Statistical release 3: Education*. Malé: National Bureau of Statistics, Ministry of Finance & Treasury.

National Bureau of Statistics. (2015b). *Population & housing census 2014. Statistical release 4: Employment*. Malé: National Bureau of Statistics, Ministry of Finance & Treasury.

National Bureau of Statistics. (2015c). *Population & housing census 2014. Statistical release 2: Migration*. Malé: National Bureau of Statistics, Ministry of Finance & Treasury.

National Bureau of Statistics. (2016). *Statistical year book of Maldives 2016*. Malé: National Bureau of Statistics, Ministry of Finance & Treasury.

National Bureau of Statistics. (2017). *Statistical year book of Maldives 2017*. Malé: National Bureau of Statistics, Ministry of Finance & Treasury.

National Bureau of Statistics. (2018a). *Statistical year book of Maldives 2018*. Malé: National Bureau of Statistics, Ministry of Finance & Treasury.

National Bureau of Statistics. (2018b). *Household income and expenditure survey (HIES) analytical report III: Employment*. Malé: National Bureau of Statistics, Ministry of Finance & Treasury.

National Bureau of Statistics. (2019a). *Women in Maldives*. Retrieved March 2019, from http://statisticsmaldives.gov.mv/nbs/wp-content/uploads/2019/03/Womens-Day-2019.pdf

National Bureau of Statistics. (2019b). *Maldives in figures—March 2019*. Retrieved March 2019, from http://statisticsmaldives.gov.mv/maldives-in-figures-march-2019/

O'Connor, P. (2011). Where do women fit in university senior management? An analytical topology of cross-national organizational cultures. In B. Bagilhole &

K. White (Eds.), *Gender, power and management: A cross-cultural analysis of higher education*. London: Palgrave Macmillan.

Phadnis, U., & Luithui, E. D. (1985). *Maldives: Winds of change in an atoll state*. New Delhi: South Asian Publishers.

Razee, H. (2000). *Gender and development in the Maldives. A review of twenty years 1979–1999*. UN Theme Group on Gender. Retrieved March 2019, from https://maldives.unfpa.org/sites/default/files/pub-pdf/Gender_and_Development_in_Maldives.pdf

Riley, M., Ladkin, A., & Szivas, E. (2002). *Tourism employment: Analysis and planning*. Buffalo: Channel View Publications.

Ritchie, M., Rogers, T. A., & Sauer, L. (2014). *Women's empowerment in political processes in the Maldives*. Washington, DC: International Foundation for Electoral Systems.

Rubery, J., Grimshaw, D., & Figueiredo, H. (2005). How to close the gender pay gap in Europe: Towards the gender mainstreaming of pay policy. *Industrial Relations Journal, 36*(3), 184–213.

Ruhanen, L., & Cooper, C. (2009). *The tourism labour market in the Asia Pacific region*. Madrid: UN World Tourism Organization.

Shaljan, A. M. (2004). Population, gender and development in Maldives. *Economic and Political Weekly, 39*(18), 1835–1840.

Stojanov, R., Duží, B., Kelman, I., Němec, D., & Procházka, D. (2017). Local perceptions of climate change impacts and migration patterns in Malé, Maldives. *The Geographical Journal, 183*(4), 370–385.

United Nations Committee on the Elimination of Discrimination against Women. (2015). *Concluding observations on the combined fourth and fifth periodic reports of Maldives*. CEDAW/C/MDV/CO/4-5, CEDAW, New York, NY.

United Nations Development Programme. (2011). *Women in public life in the Maldives—Situational analysis*. Retrieved March 2019, from https://www.undp.org/content/dam/maldives/docs/Democratic%20Governance/Women_in_Public_Life_Report.pdf.

Verick, S. (2018). *Female labor force participation and development*. IZA World of Labor, 87v2.

Waheeda, A., & Nishan, F. (2018). Challenges of women leaders in higher education institutions in the Republic of Maldives. *International Journal of Education, Psychology and Counseling, 3*(12), 8–22.

CHAPTER 11

Caught in the Cross-Fire of Religion, Culture, and Politics: Women's Sexual and Reproductive Health and Rights in Pakistan

Samreen Shahbaz

INTRODUCTION

Sexual and reproductive health and rights entered the international human rights framework through the Universal Declaration of Human Rights (UDHR), which calls for the right to life, the right to be free from torture and coercion, the right to the highest standard of physical and mental health, the right to privacy, the right to be free from discrimination, and the right to education. The International Covenant on Economic, Social, and Cultural Rights (ICESCR) (UN, 1966) and the Convention on the Elimination of All Forms of Discrimination Against Women (CEDAW) (UN, 1979) also clearly indicate that the right to health can be guaranteed through universal access to sexual and reproductive health and rights. This means states are obliged to take all necessary measures to fulfill, protect, and promote these rights.

S. Shahbaz (✉)
Asian-Pacific Resource & Research Centre for Women (ARROW),
Kuala Lumpur, Malaysia

© The Author(s) 2020   231
I. Jamil et al. (eds.), *Gender Mainstreaming in Politics,
Administration and Development in South Asia*,
https://doi.org/10.1007/978-3-030-36012-2_11

Pakistan is a signatory of several landmark international human rights instruments, including ICESCR and CEDAW, and has time and again, in international political contexts, reaffirmed its commitment to uphold women's human rights, including their sexual and reproductive health and rights (SRHR). These commitments include the adoption of the International Conference on Population and Development Programme of Action (ICPD PoA) (UN, 1994), the Beijing Declaration and Platform for Action (Beijing PfA) (UN, 1995), and the 2030 Agenda for Sustainable Development (UN, 2015). Nevertheless, the process of making good on these international commitments through laws and policies in the country itself has been stymied and still remains incomplete (ARROW & Shirkat Gah, 2014). To appease religio-political actors, state leaders deliberately allow the insertion of religion in the landscape of legislation and policy formation. They also promote a hegemonic national identity and culture, the boundaries of which are defined by the religious idiom and customary traditions and norms. Further, policy discourses on women's bodily rights and autonomy have been constrained in the name of protecting the national identity and culture, and often pro-rights laws and policies have been blocked before they can be formally presented for debate in legislative corridors.

Building on an existing body of literature, I dissect the limitations of the state's definition of sexual and reproductive health and rights through analyzing selected present and past laws and policies related to bodily rights and women's autonomy. By doing so, I try to understand the various factors that continue to shape law and policy-related discourses surrounding SRHR and which contribute to Pakistan's continuous inaction on its international commitments vis-à-vis SRHR, one example being the 2030 Agenda for Sustainable Development (UN, 2015).

I begin the chapter with a holistic, context-specific definition of SRHR by building on existing international definitions. I then look back in time, at the construct of Pakistan's national identity and how it intertwined with defining womanhood, particularly with respect to Pakistan as a post-colonial nation-state in the making. I then chronicle the making of selected laws and policies pertaining to SRHR, how this has interacted with political discourses on national culture and identity, and how rights have been restricted under the guise of protecting an imposed, hegemonic national culture and identity. Finally, I briefly shed light on emerging political scenarios and their potential impact on the legislative framework for women's rights.

DEFINING BODILY AUTONOMY AND SEXUAL AND REPRODUCTIVE HEALTH AND RIGHTS

Sexual and reproductive health and rights were formally articulated in the international human rights framework as part of article 12 of the International Covenant on Economic, Social and Cultural Rights (ICESCR) (UN, 1966). Here one reads that these individual rights entail that women make "free and responsible decisions and choices concerning their sexual and reproductive health and rights," without any discrimination or coercion (Locklear & Abeysekera, 2012, p. 12). The concept of nondiscrimination is further elaborated in the Convention on the Elimination of All Forms of Discrimination Against Women (CEDAW) (UN, 1979), which calls for substantive equality and nondiscrimination to ensure that women enjoy *de facto* equality "through law and other appropriate means," including addressing cultural and social determinants and influencers (Locklear & Abeysekera, 2012, p. 12).

The International Conference on Population and Development Programme of Action (ICPD PoA) (UN, 1994, p. 49) describes reproductive rights as "the basic right of all couples and individuals to decide freely and responsibly the number, spacing and timing of their children and to have the information and means to do so." This conference broke new ground by shifting the primary focus of family planning programs from reducing fertility and curbing population growth to ensuring women's autonomy and agency on reproductive matters. A year after ICPD, in 1995, member states reiterated and reaffirmed these agreements at the Fourth World Conference on Women in Beijing, China, as part of the Beijing Declaration and Platform for Action (Beijing PfA) (UN, 1995). The 2030 Agenda for Sustainable Development (UN, 2015), adopted by 193 member states including Pakistan in 2015, builds on the agreements outlined in the ICPD PoA (UN, 1994) and Beijing PfA (UN, 1995) and includes specific targets on gender equality and universal access to healthcare, including sexual and reproductive health.

Building on these frameworks, I (re)conceptualize bodily autonomy and SRHR with the following conditions and definitions:

1. Individuals must be enabled and empowered to choose their sexual partner with full and free consent, to decide whether to be sexually active, to engage in consensual sexual relationships, to enter into a marriage with a partner of their choice, to be able to assert individual

autonomy and agency within a marriage, and, finally, to pursue a safe and pleasurable sexual life.

2. Individuals must be enabled and empowered to make informed and consensual decisions about reproductive choices without any coercion, violence, and discrimination.

3. Individuals must have access to accurate information about, counseling for, and services for sexual and reproductive health matters, including access to comprehensive sexuality education; access to modern, safe, effective, affordable, and good-quality contraceptives of their choice; access to safe and legal abortion and post-abortion care; access to pregnancy and childbirth services; access to information and services for the prevention and treatment of sexually transmitted infections and HIV/AIDS, sexual dysfunctions, and reproductive cancers. Further, these services must respect individuals' right to privacy, confidentiality, and informed consent.

4. SRHR must ensure the prevention and remedy of all forms of gender-based violence and inequitable gender relations.

5. SRHR must ensure universal access to information and counseling, including psychosocial counseling related to sexuality, sexual identity, and sexual relationships.

6. SRHR must provide full protection from harmful cultural and customary practices such as female genital mutilation, honor killing, child marriages, and forced marriages.

METHODOLOGY

In this chapter, I follow a qualitative methodology, primarily by doing an intensive literature review of secondary sources. Building on existing publications, I try to gain an overview of the making of a hegemonic 'national identity' in Pakistan. Through analyzing laws and policies and by reviewing the literature, I seek to derive macro-level learning in order to understand how identity politics and the arguments relating to cultural authenticity continue to shape discourses on women's bodily rights and autonomy. The reviewed material includes academic literature, civil society organization (CSO) reports, and newspapers articles on SRHR and women's rights policies and laws in Pakistan.

What, then, are the challenges and barriers to Pakistan fulfilling its SRHR commitments, and how did the country arrive at the current situation?

CONSTRUCTION OF THE 'NATIONAL IDENTITY' AND PAKISTANI 'WOMANHOOD'

The history of men's opposition to women's emancipation is more interesting perhaps than the story of that emancipation itself.
  Virginia Woolf, *A Room of One's Own* (1929)

Benedict Anderson, in his book, *Imagined Communities*, describes a nation as a "political community," imagined by individuals who perceive themselves as part of that group, a "deep, horizontal comradeship" (Anderson, 1982, p. 7). Each nation is bound together as a single political unit by shared/common ideologies, which are often based on race, ethnicity, language, and religion. Nations hold onto these identities based on who they define as 'insiders' (people who belong to that particular nation and adhere to the common ideology) and 'outsiders' (those who do not belong to that particular nation by virtue of not relating to the common ideology) (Anderson, 1982).

Chatterjee (1989, p. 624) argues that the discourses around Indian nationalism in the nineteenth century can be framed by the dichotomy of 'the outer and the inner', the 'inner' being the spiritual Indian and Eastern identity, the 'outer' being the materialistic West. Therefore, in order to retain the significant difference between East and West, it was important to hold on to and strengthen the distinct Eastern values, which shaped the nationalist discourse in India.

Pakistan came into being in 1947 as the homeland for Muslim Indians. Rich in diverse ethnic and linguistic populations, the religious sentiment was relied on as the common ideological underpinning binding people together (Haqqani, 2005), and the idea of 'Muslim nationhood', counterposing the hostile 'Hindu India' and the larger world, was promoted. A dichotomy of 'insider' versus 'outsider' can be identified in the nationalist discourses promoted by the political elites and politico-religious organizations in Pakistan, with the 'outer' understood as the immoral West and the hostile and conspiring India, and the 'inner' understood as the pure, spiritual 'Pakistan', where Muslims live in accordance with the teachings and requirements of the Quran and Sunnah. Since these discourses are mostly politically motivated, diverse interpretations of Islam have been used during different political regimes to frame the yardstick of pure and spiritual Pakistan, all according to personal and political agendas (Shaheed, 2009).

The contours and parameters of womanhood and women's roles in the public and private spheres were inevitably framed within the inner versus outer dichotomies of the nationalist discourses of cultural authenticity and the 'true Pakistani', and a specific definition of womanhood in the Pakistani context was formulated and promoted, one which did not emulate Western values and codes (Shaheed, 2009; Jafar, 2005). Any deviation, actual or perceived, from these moral boundaries would result in backlash and condemnation (Jafar, 2005; Toor, 2007). This thinking is also embedded in the frameworks presented by Deniz Kandiyoti, who proposes that "post-independence trajectories of modern states and variations in the deployment of Islam in relation to different nationalisms, state ideologies and oppositional social movements are of central importance to an understanding of the condition of women" (Kandiyoti, 1991, p. 2).

Women were given the role of keepers of social traditions and upholders of moral values as outlined by the Quran and Sunnah, and as biological reproducers of the nation (Shaheed, 2009; Jafar, 2005). While women stepped out into the public sphere during the freedom movement, their political participation after independence was redirected toward relief and charity work for the masses of immigrants coming from India, as these roles were aligned with their traditional gendered roles of caretakers, nurturers, mothers, sisters, and wives. Women were also able to join the formal workforce as doctors and teachers. But any transgression of the traditional roles was not tolerated by the state institutions and the political elites (Mumtaz & Shaheed, 1987).

At the same time, it would be reductionistic to argue that Islam was the only ingredient in the process of painting the image of a true Pakistani woman. In fact, while it was the key ingredient, it constantly interacted with other local and feudal/tribal traditions and norms (Toor, 2007), which, as we will see later in the chapter, were also deployed in the process of defining women's roles and rights over the years.

Pakistani Women's Social and Cultural Lived Realities and Its Linkages with Their Bodily Autonomy

The social and cultural context in Pakistan is primarily patriarchal. While women do participate in formal and informal labor outside the four walls of their homes in both rural and urban areas, a very vivid demarcation between gender roles remains ingrained in the society. For example, women are expected to take care of the households, whereas men are inscribed with bread-earning and financial responsibilities of the family and other matters outside the house. The notion of *purdah*[1] and gender segregation is institutionalized at social level through this clear division of gendered roles and responsibilities, which ultimately also limits women's mobility and access to public spaces outside their homes (Rizvi, Khan, & Shaikh, 2014).

The social unit of family for a married woman is extended beyond the spouse and the offsprings, and includes her immediate family members, for example, her spouse's parents and siblings. There is a strong emphasis on the interconnectedness of the *khandaan*[2] and the *biradari*[3] and it reflects in the decision-making processes within the family regarding their day-to-day matters (Mumtaz & Salway, 2009). While this pattern is prevalent across the country, its nature and degree varies across class, caste, and regions (rural versus urban). Hence, decisions regarding a woman's reproductive choices are not made in a silo by the husband and wife, and in fact, it takes place in consultation with other extended family members, especially the elderly ones (Mumtaz & Salway, 2009).

Further, the honor of a *khandaan* and *biradari* is associated with their women's sexual behavior and practices of purdah. For unmarried women it often translates into strict scrutiny of their behavior in public spaces and

---

[1] *Purdah* is the practice of keeping women from being seen by unrelated or stranger men. Purdah is practiced through either keeping women in a certain part of the house which is not accessible to the public, or by covering women's faces and bodies with an additional piece of garment.

[2] *Khandaan (literally, "family")* comprises of immediate kinfolk including parents, siblings, uncles, aunts, first cousins and grandparents. Often members of the *khandaan* live in the same house and this kind of joint family living is very common in both rural and urban areas.

[3] *Biradari (literally "community")* is a network of extended family/blood relationships and close community members who belong to the same caste and often live in the same village.

interactions with *na-mahrem*[4] men which ultimately severely restricts their mobility outside their homes and their access to education, health services, and employment opportunities.

The rigid gender roles, notions of community and social codes around purdah culminate into lower literacy rates among women and girls, women's lack of participation in the formal and informal employment sectors, women's economic dependency on the males of their households, and women and girls' lack of autonomy over their decisions regarding their health and overall well-being (Rizvi et al., 2014). These systemic barriers are rarely challenged or addressed by the laws and policies on women's sexual and reproductive health and rights. In fact, in many instances, as illustrated in the latter sections, the legislative and policy frameworks propagated and/or legitimized the social and cultural status quo.

"No Laws Will Be Passed Which Are Repugnant to the Quran and Sunnah"—Inserting Islam in the Constitutional Framework of the Country

The Constitution of Pakistan serves as the supreme legal document of the country and defines the foundation of Pakistan's legal system.

Once the *raison d'être* of Pakistan was established by the political elites as part of their nationalist discourse, the first step toward 'Islamizing' the constitutional framework was to insert the Objective Resolution in the preamble of the 1949 draft of the Constitution. This stipulated that "Muslims shall be enabled to order their lives in the individual and collective spheres in accord with the teachings and requirements of Islam as set out in the Holy Quran and Sunnah" (Shaheed, 2009). The Objective Resolution was later embedded as Article 2A when the Constitution was formally adopted in 1956, and it essentially requires all laws to be consistent with Islamic injunctions (Shaheed, 2009). Further, through constitutional amendments, the Federal Shariat Court (FSC) and the Shariat Appellate Bench of the Supreme Court were established to review legislation for consistency with the 'Islamic injunctions.' An advisory body of *ulemas* (religious scholars), formally known as the Council of Islamic Ideology (CII), was also established to achieve the aforementioned objectives vis-à-vis state institutions and legislation (Shaheed, 2009).

---

[4] *Literally, "not related by blood".*

At the same time, the Constitution offers many of the human rights articulated in the Universal Declaration of Human Rights (UDHR), including equality, nondiscrimination on the basis of sex alone, equal protection for all citizens, and the right to life (Yefet, 2009).

Matters are further complicated by the presence and general acceptance of the *jirga* system,[5] which exists at the community level in some rural and tribal parts of the country. The attempt to provide legal protection for women's rights has been an arduous battle to bridge the vast gap between these contradictory norms within the constitutional and legislative framework.

THE HUDOOD ORDINANCES OF 1979 AND REGULATION OF WOMEN'S SEXUALITY AND SEXUAL AUTONOMY

The most explicit form of Islamization, which was under the guise of defining a hegemonic notion of 'national identity,' happened in the era of General Zia ul Haq, who took over the country after deposing the elected Prime Minister Zulfiqar Ali Bhutto in 1977. He took it upon himself to implement the *Nizam-i-Mustafa* ('social order of the Prophet') through aggressive legal and policy-based measures, specifically targeting women's already restricted rights. Through a series of martial law orders, women's mobility and visibility in public were curtailed (Toor, 2007). Women were allowed to appear on the government-controlled media only when absolutely necessary and then with a mandatory headscarf at all times. Through media policies and public statements by Zia himself, the regime sought to construct a more rigid Islamic 'national culture', free of obscenity and 'Hindu' and/or 'Western' elements (Toor, 2007). Any ideas or perceptions of culture and nationhood that contradicted this status quo were thus made crimes against Islam and the state (Toor, 1997).

In 1979, Zia introduced the Hudood Ordinances—a set of 'Islamic' laws defining 'legal' sexual activity. The ordinances covered adultery, fornication, and rape, making each a crime against the state. None of these recognized rape within marriage. One ordinance required the testimony of four adult Muslim male witnesses of 'good moral character' to prove

---

[5] *Jirga* is a traditional assembly of local community leaders, gathered to resolve community disputes through consensus-based decisions and in accordance with the local community's traditional customs and practices. Jirga is also known as *faislo* in many areas of the Sindh province, and as *panchayat* in rural Punjab.

the charge of rape by a woman. Failure to produce necessary witnesses would be considered confession to illicit sexual intercourse, and hence result in prosecution (Mir-Hosseini & Hamzić, 2010).

"Legislation sets limits for the social imagination through the construction/imposition of a normative ideal" (Toor, 2007, p. 257), and in this context, the effectiveness of Zia's legislative measures is evident from the fact that the ordinances normalized the regulation of individual bodies and their sexualities and embedded the definition of a normative social order in the country's legislation. Further, the ordinances legitimized the tribal and feudal norms (paradoxically, often considered 'un-Islamic') around kin and family ownership of women's bodies and sexualities and made the state complicit in that ownership (Khan, 2003).

IMPACT OF NATIONALIST AND RELIGIOUS FUNDAMENTALIST DISCOURSES ON POPULATION AND HEALTH POLICIES

The discussion on women's reproductive health entered the mainstream arena in the late 1950s when Begum Saeeda Waheed, a member of the All Pakistan Women's Association (APWA), started advocating for access to birth control. This was after her maid died from a failed abortion attempt. She founded the Family Planning Association of Pakistan (FPAP), which received financial support from the Ministry of Health through a Parliamentary vote (Khan, 1996). The first formal family planning program was launched in 1965 by General Ayub Khan,[6] in support of his administrative priority of controlling population growth and increasing economic growth per capita (Khan, 1996). External resource mobilization and donor-funded initiatives also provided motivation to launch a national family planning program in Pakistan (Khan, 1996). The program's scope, however, was limited to family planning and access to contraception for married couples only, as opposed to the recognition of women's reproductive rights and agency over their reproductive capacities and choices. At the same time, it was vehemently protested against by both left-leaning political parties and the religious organizations who termed birth control as a means to promote "free sex" (Riddel, 2016). In 1962, soon after the launch of the state-run Family Planning (FP) program, Mufti Mehmud, leader of Jamat-i-Islami (JI), carried out countrywide protests against the

---

[6] General Muhammad Ayub Khan was a military dictator and the second president of Pakistan. He assumed the presidency in 1958 and resigned in 1969.

program (Riddel, 2016). In the same year, Moulana Abul A'la Maududi, founder and leader of JI, authored the book *Birth Control: Its Social, Political, Economic, Moral and Religious Aspects*, which opposes the FP program on multiple grounds. Labeling birth control a modern phenomenon with historical roots in the West's "materialistic and sensate view of life," he claimed that FP did not have a place as a social policy in Islamic culture and society. A chapter of the book was distributed in the form of pamphlets in 1966, during protests by religio-political parties against the FP program.

When General Yahya removed Ayub and took over the presidential position in 1969,[7] the population control program continued receiving both governmental and international financial and administrative support. Then came Zulfiqar Ali Bhutto.[8] During his era, threats by religious and political factions to the continuation of the program became a real risk. After Bhutto became prime minister in 1973, the program was temporarily discontinued as a move to appease religious actors. Bhutto also wanted to discontinue the country's acceptance of Western aid. However, in a very short time, he realized he would not be able to deliver on his socialist promises without financial help from abroad (Khan, 1996). It was in this context that a committee was established to make recommendation vis-à-vis a population control program in Pakistan, and in response to the committee's report, the family planning program was re-approved with financial support from USAID and other funding agencies. It is noteworthy that other recommendations of the committee, including the legalization of abortion and increasing the legal age of marriage to 18, did not result in any policy or programmatic action (Khan, 1996).

The population control program was dealt a huge blow by the regime of General Zia.[9] While Ayub and Bhutto had to face religious interference during the policy-making processes, Zia made the right-wing religious argument his official political ideology and hence gave religious actors

---

[7] General Agha Muhammad Yahya Khan was a military dictator who took over the presidency after General Ayub in 1969 and continued in that capacity until 1971.

[8] Zulfiqar Ali Bhutto was president from 1971 to 1973. After the adoption of the 1973 Constitution, he handed over the presidency to Fazal Ilahi Chaudhry and assumed the position of prime minister, continuing in that role until 1977, when General Zia declared martial law.

[9] General Muhammad Zia-ul-Haq was a military dictator. He assumed the role of president after declaring martial law in 1977. He continued as the head of state until his death in 1988.

pronounced and explicit space in discourses on laws and policies (Khan, 1996; Shaheed, 2009).

In 1977, when Zia came to power, he froze the population program and international aid, which had focused heavily on the program. The aid money was rerouted to Zia's crude political agendas. It was during this time, due to political clashes and conflicts between Pakistan and the USA, that Pakistan stopped receiving external development aid from the USA (Khan, 1996). In 1980, amid increasing foreign pressure from the United Nations and bilateral agencies such as the World Bank to invest in education, health, and population control, Zia reinstated the program, though he never publicly supported it, nor did he allow any media campaign to raise awareness of it (Khan, 1996).

In 1984, the Council of Islamic Ideology (CII) issued a report declaring the FP program to be against the spirit of Islam; this resulted in a call for the government to cancel the program. The report was scheduled to be presented to Parliament for a vote, but Zia's government managed to stop the report in its tracks, and it never made an appearance in Parliament. Zia needed the program to run as part of the new aid deal with the US (Khan, 1996).

Under later regimes,[10] the religious threat to the family planning program has lessened in political corridors. The program has undergone several administrative changes, including the formation of a separate Population Welfare Ministry. Later, a cadre of community health mobilizers and 'Lady Health Workers' was also introduced by the Ministry of Health, to provide grassroots-level reproductive health services to rural women who, due to socio-cultural norms and other social determinants, faced mobility-related restrictions. While the program has received considerable support from the policymakers and relevant ministries, the Lady Health Workers continue to experience significant religious threats from the imams (priests) of local mosques (Tahira Naz, personal communication, September 2014). In some parts of the country, they are the target of violent attacks by religious fundamentalists and the Taliban (Din, Mumtaz, & Ataullahjan, 2012; ARROW & ARWC, 2014).

---

[10] Benazir Bhutto's elected government (1988–1990) and (1993–1996); Nawaz Sharif's elected government (1997–1999); General Pervez Musharraf's martial law (1999–2001) and presidency (2001–2008); Asif Ali Zardari's elected government (2008–2013); Nawaz Sharif's elected government (2013–2017).

The threat to the family planning program in political corridors has resurfaced recently, in the form of a new wave of non-government organizations (NGOs) regulations issued by the government. Fueled by state agencies' mistrust of NGOs—this came after the arrest of an NGO worker for affiliation with the CIA—the newly issued regulations have severely restricted foreign donors' contributions to the program and closed doors for NGOs that were providing reproductive health-related information and services (Shaheed & Zaman, 2018). Further, the CII proposed a 'model' bill for women's rights in Pakistan, which called for a ban on contraception and several other reproductive health-related services. A ban was also issued by the Pakistan Electronic Media Regulatory Authority (PEMRA) on airing advertisements on all TV and radio channels. Though the ban was removed after a few days, following a strong backlash against it by the civil society, PEMRA allowed the ads to air, but only after 11 pm.

After the 18th Constitutional Amendment in 2010, federal health and population welfare ministries were dissolved, and provinces were tasked to devise their own policies. So far, only Punjab, Sindh, and Khyber Pakhtunkhwa (KPK) provinces have passed a population policy, whereas Balochistan is in the process of drafting and approving its provincial-level population policy. Only the Punjab Provincial Policy (2017) recognizes reproductive health as a human right, but the mention of women's and girls' sexual and reproductive health (SRH) needs in other provincial policies remains minimal. The rights of youth and adolescents, including girls, are the subject of provincial youth policies, but these policies remain silent on many aspects of young people's sexual and reproductive health and rights. This is largely because the law, which criminalizes consensual sex outside marriage, also restricts acknowledgment of, or any discourse around, the sexual and reproductive needs of unmarried individuals.

While the FP programs and population policies have paved the way for greater access to contraception information and services, they have done little to challenge or address cultural norms and patriarchal power dynamics within households and how these affect women's reproductive choices. For instance, the Lady Health Program and the male mobilizers at Family Welfare Centers (the Population Welfare Department's counseling centers at the village level) tried to hold discussions and awareness-raising sessions with husbands, as a strategy recognizing that husbands play a huge role in decision-making at home. While a worthy initiative, it did little to challenge and address the power dynamics in families that often lie at the root of denying women reproductive autonomy. In addition, the stigma against providing unmarried girls with information on reproductive health or even menstrual hygiene management continues to remain unchallenged, and despite the information program's wide outreach, it has been unable to effectively bridge the massive information gaps among young girls.

Finally, while unsafe abortions remain a big contributing factor to Pakistan's incredibly high maternal mortality rates. The political environment around women's reproductive rights is so sensitive that rights advocates do not wish to open up any discussion on the country's abortion law, as they fear that it would lead to a more restrictive and regressive legal framework. Instead, they have opted for lobbying for post-abortion care services to mitigate the health risks (Sharma, Dhillon, Shabbir, & Lynam, 2019). Currently, the law only permits abortion in cases where the mother's health is in danger.

Implementation of a Sexuality Education Program

Policy discourses on sexuality education, although a critical component of sexual and reproductive health, have remained very limited and are always imbued with arguments relating to morality and cultural authenticity. Arguably, no other aspect of sexual and reproductive health and rights has received as much opposition in the policy discourses and during the implementation phase as the attempts to introduce sexuality education in the formal education system.

The HIV epidemic in Pakistan in the late 1990s and early 2000s paved the way for a conversation with policymakers on the integration of education and awareness-raising components themed on safe sex. The National Health Policy of 2001 was the first health policy which referred to mass awareness-raising campaigns as a strategy to reduce and prevent HIV, however, the focus was narrow and limited to HIV only. NGOs and international donor agencies used the opportunity as an entry point to start a broader discourse on the need to incorporate life skills-based education (LSBE) in the formal school curricula. References to LSBE were added to consequent policies on education and provincial youth policies. A model curriculum was also developed, which had components on puberty, menstrual hygiene, negotiation within a relationship, early marriage, and family planning (Chandra-Mouli, Plesons, Hadi, Baig, & Lang, 2018). Although it did not meet the international standards of a comprehensive sexuality education framework, it was nevertheless a groundbreaking initiative, as no previous policy or programmatic interventions had referred to SRH information for young people and adolescents. A Memorandum of Understanding (MoU) was signed by various NGOs and the provincial governments to launch the curriculum in provincial schools. However, the pilot program encountered huge resistance from local religious leaders, and soon after, amidst this backlash, provincial governments cancelled the MoU to implement the pilot program in public schools. Consequently, the program as such was also rolled back (Svanemyr, Baig, & Chandra-Mouli, 2015).

In subsequent years, through several dialogues and consultations with community leaders, parents, school teachers, and education department officials, the curricula were revised. Further consultations with religious scholars were held and their inputs were incorporated into the revised module. While NGOs have heralded this approach as a successful strategy (Svanemyr et al., 2015), and while it has been used to generate support and acceptance for other interventions including a vaccination program (Yusufzai, 2016), the practice of engaging religious scholars as arbitrators for matters related to fundamental rights has been criticized by women's rights advocates as a dangerous trend; such rights, they argue, should not be conditional to opinions of religious figures.

The current LSBE module contains information on sexual abuse and harassment, human rights, and early marriage. The curricula were formally piloted in selected public schools in the Sindh province (Svanemyr et al., 2015). Further, NGOs and rights advocates started to use child sexual abuse as a supportive argument to advocate for the integration of LSBE to increase awareness among young people to reduce their vulnerability. In 2017, when a case of child sexual abuse garnered huge local and international media attention, the Sindh government signed an MoU with the NGO 'Aahung' to integrate LSBE modules in the curricula. However, the move did not go unnoticed by the religious political parties who called it a 'Western' agenda. The political environment in other provinces, especially Khyber Pakhtunkhwa and Punjab, is still very hostile to LSBE programs, primarily due to the large number of conservative legislators sitting in the respective provincial assemblies. Furthermore, so as not to ruffle cultural sensitivities, the approved curricula is limited in scope, to the point of not talking about issues relating to menstruation and puberty (Shirkat Gah, 2018).

Customary Practices, Legal Impunity, and the Colonial Hangover

The interaction of formal legal institutions with informal justice mechanisms such as jirgas/faislo (tribal councils) and panchayats (village councils) adds another dimension to the state's judicial system. These informal justice mechanisms use the framework of consensus to resolve community disputes and conflicts related to *zan, zar,* and *zameen*.[11] In doing so, community harmony inevitably takes precedence over justice and the protection of fundamental human rights. Further, a deep-rooted concept in tribal settings is women's status as family property, just as are wealth and land. Women are therefore often used as a commodity that can be given to an adversary to resolve disputes. This practice is more commonly known as *vani* and *swara*.[12] In these cases, the exchanged women are often minors (Amnesty International, 1999; CRR, 2018).

Women are also considered custodians of the honor of the men they 'belong' to, and as such, must be chaste and protect their virginity, which should only be offered to the man chosen by their families. By engaging in an 'illicit' sexual relationship (actual or perceived), a woman is deemed to be defying the norms and defiling the honor of her family; she thus becomes *kari*.[13] Family members can only restore the honor by killing the kari woman and the man she was allegedly involved with—the *karo*.[14] If the karo manages to flee the village, a jirga or panchayat is called to settle the dispute between the families of the karo and kari. Since the ultimate aim of the jirga system is to restore the balance or compensate for the loss, in karo-kari cases, it is often done through cash compensation or through the exchange of women from the karo family. In some instances, women from the karo family are raped by men from the affected family.

Being an indigenous justice mechanism, the jirgas and panchayats hold great legitimacy among the local community, and their decisions are almost always considered binding. The dichotomy of 'outside' (in this case, state laws) and 'inside' (i.e., indigenous tribal/community traditions) (Chatterjee, 1989) has also been used to defend and legitimize the jirga and panchayat systems (NCSW, 2016). Furthermore, because the

[11] Literally means women, wealth, and land.

[12] *Vani* and *Swara* are cultural practices found in some parts of Pakistan whereby girls and women of a family are forcibly married to an adversary to settle disputes.

[13] Literally means 'black female', a metaphoric term for adulteress.

[14] Literally means 'black male', a metaphoric term for adulterer.

jirga system and panchayats have received legitimacy for almost a century from the state judicial system, as part of Frontier Crimes Regulation (1901) and Village Courts Act (1888) during the British era (Akins, 2017)—the British did not want to rock the boat in the tribal and rural belts back in the day—these mechanisms continue to override the national protective laws and policies that are in place today. As such, they have remained largely unquestioned by local authorities (NCSW, 2016). To make matters worse, in 2016, Parliament passed the Alternate Dispute Resolution (ADR) Act, in a move to reduce the burden on local courts. The law proposes constituting a panel of local men "of integrity and experience" to lead arbitration over matters ranging from commercial disputes to family law. Many have labeled it a move by the government to provide a constitutional cover for jirga systems (Khan, 2017).

Another glaring example of the state's deliberate acceptance of the jirga system is its continuation of the Frontier Crimes Regulation (FCR), even after Independence, as the law of the land for the Federally Administered and Provincially Administered Tribal Areas (FATA and PATA). The FCR effectively gives authority to tribal leaders in all community matters and hence isolates the tribal areas from the country's formal judicial system. It was only in 2018 that FATA and PATA were included in Khyber Pakhtunkhwa's provincial legal and policy framework through the FATA Reform Act, which was adopted as part of the 31st Constitution Amendment. To what extent it will be able to challenge the centuries-old systems, only time will tell.

Emerging Trends: Decentralization and Imran Khan's *Naya* (New) *Pakistan*[15]

Decentralization as a result of the 18th Constitutional Amendment has significantly changed the legal, policy-related, and programmatic landscape in the four provinces. While it aimed to increase provincial autonomy and provided the opportunity to make progressive and improved policies and laws at the provincial level, the process has been slow and

[15] Imran Khan became Pakistan's prime minister in 2018, after his party, Pakistan Tehreek-i-Insaf, won majority seats in the national assembly.

riddled with bureaucratic delays and challenges. As a result, key laws and policies have yet to be passed (e.g., the population policy received little attention in all four provinces in the country; only three provinces have adopted a youth policy; only one province has adopted a bill to protect women from violence). Furthermore, in Punjab and Khyber Pakhtunkhwa provinces, where conservative political parties have gained an increased number of seats in the provincial assemblies, advocates for progressive and rights-based law and policy-making processes are grappling with the additional challenges of arduous and lengthy debates with the conservative elements within the assemblies, simply to gain rights that are already ensured by the federal government and other provinces. For instance, when the Protection of Women Against Violence Bill (2015) was presented for debate and passage in the Punjab Provincial Assembly, members of the conservative and religio-political parties, including the Pakistan Tehreek-i-Insaf (PTI), walked out of the room (Jalil, 2016). The bill was successfully passed by Punjab due to a consistent push by women's rights activists. However, when a similar bill was tabled in the Khyber Pakhtunkhwa (KPK) Assembly, where the PTI led the provincial government and held the majority of seats in the legislature along with Mutahida Majlis-i-Amal (MMA) (a coalition of religio-political parties), the bill was deferred to the Council of Islamic Ideology (CII). In 2019, an amended version of the bill, which was drafted through consultation with the CII, was presented in the Assembly for approval, but members of the MMA and Jamat-i-Islami continued to resist it. While there have been some positive developments at the federal level regarding laws on women's SRHR (e.g., the Anti-Rape Act of 2016), trickling them down to all provinces will continue to remain a challenging task due to vocal religio-political actors in provincial legislative corridors.

In 2018, after the general elections, Imran Khan's PTI won majority seats and became the country's ruling party, with a promise to bring about a radical change and a *naya* (new) *Pakistan*. In his statements before and after the elections, Imran Khan has promised to uphold the rights of women and to empower women and girls through education. This was also claimed in the PTI's election manifesto. Only time will tell whether, and to what extent, the new government will be able to fulfill these ambitious promises. However, the PTI's past record does little to convince women's rights advocates, for it has traditionally made alliances with religio-political parties to gain political advantages. Imran Khan himself was a vocal opponent of General Musharraf's attempt to amend the

Hudood Ordinances in 2006. What is more, the fact that the PTI has only appointed three women to the National Parliament, only one woman to the Punjab Provincial Assembly, and no women to the Khyber Pakhtunkhwa Assembly gives little hope that women's voices will be meaningfully heard in legislative corridors.

Arrested Development of SRHR Laws and Policies and the Impact on Women's Lived Realities

Through a political use of religion and the concept of cultural authenticity during the making of the new-born nation-state, identity politics came to be part of Pakistan's legislative foundation. They have remained ingrained in legal and policy-related discourses on all matters since then. Identity politics have particularly affected the discourses concerning women's bodily rights, as women became the boundary markers of cultural authenticity. Women's fundamental bodily rights were contested and compromised under the guise of protecting and promoting a hegemonic national identity, a process in which the state remained complicit.

Pakistan continues to have the highest maternal mortality rate in the South Asia region (NIPS, 2018), and instances of unsafe abortions remain very high. The population and health-related policies have consistently focused on delivering family planning services and are mostly defined by an overarching goal of population control, as opposed to empowering women so they can make autonomous decisions about their reproductive health and capacities. The patriarchal design of power dynamics within households and at the societal level remains unaddressed and unquestioned by existing legislative and policy frameworks on population control and health, leading to women's limited agency over matters related to childbearing. Maternal health remains a serious concern till this date (NIPS, 2018) in both rural and urban areas, partly due to a shortfall in resources to cover maternal health needs at the grassroots level. The relevant policies and initiatives have therefore failed to reach out to a large percentage of the rural population. But a critical and very fundamental contributing factor is women's restrictive spatial mobility in rural areas, and hence their inability to access services for maternal healthcare (NIPS, 2018). Social and cultural norms that restrict women's spatial mobility have never been the focus of any policy or programmatic intervention for promoting women's rights, since challenging these norms would contradict the state's construct of Pakistani womanhood and national identity.

The number of child marriages and early marriages remains persistently high in the country (NIPS, 2013). This is also the case in Sindh province, where a law against child marriage has been passed. The law has failed to challenge the customary practices and informal justice systems such as *faislo*. Honor killings remain rampant in both urban and rural areas of Pakistan (HRW, 2018). The legislation meant to provide protection against harmful practices, such as child and forced marriage and honor killings, remains superficial, as there is little commitment to translate the laws into effective programmatic interventions. The passing of these laws faced heavy resistance at the community level and from religio-political leaders, and no effective measures are being taken to regulate traditional community-led justice systems and to reclaim the public sphere that has been co-opted by the religious right-wing in the country.

The sexual and reproductive health issues of unmarried young people, who constitute a large majority of the population, remain unrecognized and unacknowledged by the legislative and policy-related framework. Young girls face the double burden of these legal and policy gaps due to their age and gender. Gender-based violence, including domestic violence, is very common and often goes unreported in the name of protecting family honor. While two provinces have approved laws, little has been done to implement the laws and to provide effective protection and remedy to survivors of violence (Ali, Naylor, Croot, & O'Cathain, 2015).

In this context, achieving the targets of the 2030 Agenda (UN, 2015) and fulfilling Pakistan's international human rights commitments seem like a distant dream; a vast chasm will continue to exist between these commitments and the lived realities of women in Pakistan. In order to rectify the current situation, the state needs to start a bold discourse that challenges the concept of a single and hegemonic national identity. The state must also pay heed to the important lessons learned from past decades, about using religion for political gains, and it must establish a firm and clear stance on the prioritization of rights over identity politics through legislative and policy changes. Finally, it must invest in programs that challenge and address social and cultural norms and stigmas relating to women's SRHR, in order to ensure an enabling environment for implementing laws.

CONCLUSION

While Pakistan has signed numerous international human rights instruments related to sexual and reproductive health and rights, including the 2030 Agenda for Sustainable Development, this chapter demonstrates that the country has failed to translate its international commitments into local action. By promoting a hegemonic nationalist ideology, by using Islam as a political tool, and by arguing for a certain form of cultural authenticity, severe compromises have been made on women's fundamental rights vis-à-vis their bodily autonomy and agency. The gains achieved thus far in advancing women's sexual and reproductive health and rights are the result of a fierce and consistent push from civil society in past decades. But emerging issues, such as increased vocal religious opposition at the societal level and within the political corridors, pose an increased threat to women's already restricted rights. With the recently implemented stricter regulation of NGOs working with health-related issues, civil society's dissenting voices are under serious risk. If they are silenced, society's ability to hold the state accountable for its legislative and policy measures will be weakened. In order for Pakistan to truly fulfill its international human rights commitments, the state needs a fundamental shift in its perception of, and political commitment to women's SRHR. Swift action is required to address context-specific structural barriers by putting in place adequate, rights-based laws and policies across the country. Finally, the state also needs to tackle the persisting social and religious stigma and hostile political environment surrounding SRHR, thus to start a truly meaningful social discourse on women's empowerment through bodily autonomy and agency.

REFERENCES

Akins, H. (2017). *FATA and the Frontier crimes regulation in Pakistan: The enduring legacy of British colonialism* (Issue Brief). Retrieved May 21, 2019, from http://bakercenter.utk.edu/wp-content/uploads/2017/11/PolicyBrief5-2017.pdf

Ali, P. A., Naylor, P. B., Croot, E., & O'Cathain, A. (2015). Intimate partner violence in Pakistan: A systematic review. *Trauma, Violence, & Abuse, 16*(3), 299–315. https://doi.org/10.1177/1524838014526065

Amnesty International. (1999). *Honour killings of girls and women in Pakistan.* Retrieved May 21, 2019, from https://www.academia.edu/9872947/Honour_killings_of_girls_and_women

Anderson, B. R. (1982). *Imagined communities*. London: Verso.

ARROW & ARWC. (2014). *Our stories, one journey: Empowering rural women and sexual reproductive health and rights*. Kuala Lumpur: ARROW.

ARROW & Shirkat Gah. (2014). *Sexual and reproductive rights: Country profile of Pakistan*. Lahore: Shirkat Gah.

Centre for Reproductive Rights. (2018). *Ending impunity for child marriage in Pakistan*. Retrieved May 21, 2019, from https://www.reproductiverights. org/sites/crr.civicactions.net/files/documents/64785006_ending_impunity_for_child_marriage_pakistan_2018_print-edit-web.pdf

Chandra-Mouli, V., Plesons, M., Hadi, S., Baig, Q., & Lang, I. (2018). Building support for adolescent sexuality and reproductive health education and responding to resistance in conservative contexts: Cases from Pakistan. *Global Health: Science and Practice, 6*(1), 128–136. https://doi.org/10.9745/ghsp-d-17-00285

Chatterjee, P. (1989). Colonialism, nationalism, and colonized women: The contest in India. *American Ethnologist, 16*(4), 622–633. https://doi.org/10.1525/ae.1989.16.4.02a00020

Din, I. U., Mumtaz, Z., & Ataullahjan, A. (2012, March 21). How the Taliban undermined community healthcare in Swat, Pakistan. *Bmj, 344*, e2093. https://doi.org/10.1136/bmj.e2093

Haqqani, H. (2005). *Pakistan: Between mosque and military*. Lahore: Vanguard Books.

Human Rights Watch (HRW). (2018). *World Report 2018*. Retrieved May 25, 2019, from https://www.hrw.org/world-report/2018/country-chapters/pakistan

Jafar, A. (2005). Women, Islam, and the state in Pakistan. *Gender Issues, 22*(1), 35–55. Retrieved May 21, 2019, from https://link.springer.com/article/10.1007/s12147-005-0009-z

Jalil, X. (2016, February 26). Women protection law wins acclaim. *DAWN*. Retrieved May 25, 2019, from https://www.dawn.com/news/1242010/women-protection-law-wins-acclaim

Kandiyoti, D. (1991). Women, Islam and the state. *Middle East Report, 173*, 9–14. https://doi.org/10.2307/3012623

Khan, A. (1996). Policy-making in Pakistan's population programme. *Health Policy and Planning, 11*(1), 30–51. https://doi.org/10.1093/heapol/11.1.30

Khan, A. (2017, June 30). Pakistan's jirgas: Buying peace at the expense of women's rights? *Open Democracy*. Retrieved May 25, 2019, from https://www.opendemocracy.net/en/5050/pakistan-jirgas-womens-rights/

Khan, S. (2003). Zina and the moral regulation of Pakistani women. *Feminist Review, 75*(1), 75–100. https://doi.org/10.1057/palgrave.fr.9400111

Locklear, A. L., & Abeysekera, S. (2012). *Redefining and reclaiming rights: Guidance series: Analysing sexual and reproductive health and rights under the Convention on the Elimination of All Forms of Discrimination against Women*

(CEDAW) (Technical Report). Retrieved May 21, 2019, from https://arrow. org.my/wp-content/uploads/2015/04/Reclaiming-Redefining-Rights_ Monitoring-Report_CEDAW_2012.pdf

Mir-Hosseini, Z., & Hamzić, V. (2010). *Control and sexuality: The revival of zina laws in Muslim contexts.* London: Women Living Under Muslim Laws.

Mumtaz, K., & Shaheed, F. (1987). *Two steps forward, one step back? Women of Pakistan.* Lahore: Zed Books.

Mumtaz, Z., & Salway, S. (2009). Understanding gendered influences on womens reproductive health in Pakistan: Moving beyond the autonomy paradigm. *Social Science & Medicine, 68*(7), 1349–1356. https://doi.org/10.1016/j. socscimed.2009.01.025

National Commission on the Status of Women (NCSW). (2016). *Women, violence and jirgas.* Islamabad: NCSW. Retrieved May 25, 2019, from http://af.org. pk/gep/images/publications/Research%20Studies%20(Gender%20Based%20 Violence)/NB%20NCSW%20JIRGAS.pdf

National Institute of Population Studies (NIPS). (2013). *Pakistan demographic and health survey (PDHS) 2012–2013.* Islamabad: NIPS.

National Institute of Population Studies (NIPS). (2018). *Pakistan demographic and health survey (PDHS) 2017–2018.* Islamabad: NIPS.

Riddel, K. (2016). *Islam and the securitisation of population policies: Muslim states and sustainability.* London: Routledge.

Rizvi, N., Khan, K. S., & Shaikh, B. T. (2014). Gender: Shaping personality, lives and health of women in Pakistan. *BMC Womens Health, 14*(1), 53. https:// doi.org/10.1186/1472-6874-14-53

Shaheed, F. (2009). *Gender, religion and the quest for justice in Pakistan* (Report). Geneva: United Nations Research Institute for Social Development (UNRISD) and Heinrich-Böll-Stiftung.

Shaheed, F., & Zaman, S. (2018). *Health system governance strengthening for reproductive and sexual rights in Pakistan.* Karachi: Shirkat Gah.

Sharma, A. C., Dhillon, J., Shabbir, G., & Lynam, A. (2019). Notes from the field: Political norm change for abortion in Pakistan. *Sexual and Reproductive Health Matters, 27*(2), 1–7. https://doi.org/10.1080/26410397.2019. 1586819

Shirkat Gah. (2018). *Leaving the youth behind: The missing demographic in Pakistan's SRHR Policies and programmes.* Lahore: Shirkat Gah.

Svanemyr, J., Baig, Q., & Chandra-Mouli, V. (2015). Scaling up of life skills based education in Pakistan: A case study. *Sex Education, 15*(3), 249–262. https:// doi.org/10.1080/14681811.2014.1000454

Toor, S. (1997). The state, fundamentalism, and civil society. In N. Hussain, S. Mumtaz, & R. Saigol (Eds.), *Engendering the nation state* (Vol. 1). Lahore: Simorgh.

Toor, S. (2007). Moral regulation in a postcolonial nation-state. *Interventions, 9*(2), 255–275. https://doi.org/10.1080/13698010701409186

United Nations. (1966). *International covenant on economic, social and cultural rights (ICESCR)*. New York: United Nations.

United Nations. (1979). *Convention on the elimination of all forms of discrimination against women (CEDAW)*. New York: United Nations.

United Nations. (1994). *Programme of action adopted at the International Conference on Population and Development, Cairo, Sept 5–13, 1994*. New York: United Nations.

United Nations. (1995). *Beijing declaration and platform for action*. New York: United Nations.

United Nations. (2015). *Transforming our world: The 2030 agenda for sustainable development*. New York: United Nations.

Yefet, K. C. (2009). What's the constitution got to do with it? Regulating marriage in Pakistan. *Duke Journal of Gender Law & Policy, 16*(2), 347–378. Retrieved May 21, 2019, from https://scholarship.law.duke.edu/djglp/vol16/iss2/6/

Yusufzai, A. (2016, April 5). Pakistan and Afghanistan join forces to wipe out polio. *The Guardian*. Retrieved May 25, 2019, from https://www.theguardian.com/global-development/2016/apr/05/pakistan-afghanistan-join-forces-to-wipe-out-polio-taliban

Index[1]

A

Accessibility, 174, 207
Administration, vi, vii, 1–16, 41,
    87–106, 113n2, 124, 126, 129,
    132, 160, 164, 165, 167, 173,
    225
Affirmative policies, 9, 12, 38
Africa, 4
Agents of change, 5, 167
Agriculture, 3, 6, 163
American liberal, 3
Anti-poverty, 6, 12, 56

B

Beijing, xv, xvi, 2, 39, 140
Biological, 5, 173, 236
Bureaucracy in Bangladesh, 14

C

Capability, 7, 11, 63, 64, 145, 158,
    165, 166, 173

Caste, vi, 2, 4, 7, 12, 64, 95–96n6,
    131, 164, 165, 190, 192, 237,
    237n3
Characteristics, 9, 10, 42, 63, 82, 101,
    102, 115, 116, 128, 129, 222, 223
Choice, 7, 8, 23, 25, 33, 90, 94, 95,
    161, 166, 169–170, 210, 233,
    234, 237, 240, 243
Civil service, 9, 95, 96, 97n7, 97n8,
    105, 211, 215, 220, 224
Civil society, 5, 10, 15, 42, 46, 47, 57,
    138, 243, 251
Class, vi, 2, 4, 7, 9, 12, 63–68, 78–80,
    142, 147, 165, 192, 194, 195, 237
Code of ethics, 62
Commodity, 8, 246
Community, 6, 8, 11, 15, 39, 50, 57,
    63, 65, 78, 83, 96, 113, 114,
    116, 120–123, 126–129, 132,
    144, 146, 147, 157, 158, 163,
    167, 172, 173, 210, 220, 221,
    223, 237n3, 238, 239, 239n5,
    242, 245–247, 250

[1] Note: Page numbers followed by 'n' refer to notes.

Community engagements, 6
Conceptual clarity, 15, 151, 152
Controversies, 2
Creed, 63, 68
Cultural and religious values, 10
Culturally suitable judgment, 14, 121
Cultural norms, 83, 88, 112, 249, 250
Culture, 4, 11, 12, 26, 54, 58, 63–66,
    72, 84, 99, 102, 121, 127, 173,
    210, 223, 231–251

D
Decision-making, 2, 3, 6, 9, 11, 22,
    23, 55, 69, 71, 73, 82, 89, 93,
    98–100, 102, 105, 106, 112,
    139, 166, 176, 190, 217, 226,
    237, 243
Democracy, 27, 30, 42, 158, 181,
    182, 206, 207
Democratic process, 111, 205
Democratization, 7, 182, 206
Developing countries, v, 3, 6, 25, 27
Developing world, 2, 6, 12
Development, vi, xv, xvi, 1–16, 22–24,
    47, 54, 57, 72, 73, 96n6, 103,
    113, 114, 126, 127, 129,
    131n10, 132, 137, 138, 141,
    142, 145–147, 149, 150n2, 153,
    158, 159, 161–163, 166–169,
    171, 172, 174, 175, 193, 209,
    210, 212, 214, 219–221, 223,
    226, 242, 248
Disability, 7, 123, 126
Disparities, 1, 7, 144, 145, 152, 153,
    168, 170, 173, 177, 213
Doing gender, 63, 83
Double burden, 3, 250

E
Economic emancipation, 3, 130
Economic growth, 10, 137, 240

Economy, 1, 4, 6, 9, 10, 23, 27, 41,
    140, 145, 160, 165, 173–175,
    209, 211–212, 218
Efficiency, 6, 11, 12, 14, 24, 54, 141,
    145, 152, 164
Egalitarian, 4, 93
E-governance, 15, 157–177
Elections, 15, 20, 21, 25–28, 30,
    31, 33, 34, 45, 54, 56, 57, 92,
    112, 113, 113n1, 124, 127,
    131, 181–207, 216, 217, 226,
    248
Electoral participation, 15, 181–183,
    196, 205, 206
Electoral process, 15
Emancipation, 3, 15, 157, 159,
    173–177, 235
Employment, 6, 7, 22, 23, 38, 56, 87,
    89, 96, 96n6, 97, 97n8, 105,
    160, 161, 163, 164, 166, 167,
    170, 175, 209–227, 238
Empowering women, 145, 157–177,
    249
Empowerment, v, vi, 1, 2, 4–7, 9–12,
    14, 15, 22, 38, 52, 56, 57, 88,
    93, 94, 100, 106, 112, 114, 138,
    143–145, 157–159, 161, 162,
    166–169, 173–176, 251
Empowerment approach, 4, 7, 11, 56,
    93, 94, 145, 166
Equality, v, vi, 2, 5, 11, 12, 16, 22–24,
    28, 33, 38, 39, 43–46, 48, 49,
    51–53, 55, 56, 58, 67–69, 75,
    84, 93, 95n6, 97, 116, 117, 124,
    125, 127, 130, 137, 138, 140,
    141, 145, 146, 150–152, 171,
    173, 176, 209, 233, 239
Equal opportunities, 1, 2, 22, 64,
    95–96n6, 158
Equity, 5–7, 11, 12, 84, 94, 96,
    101–102, 105, 141, 143, 145,
    151
Equity approach, 7

Ethnicity, vi, 2, 7, 9, 64, 67, 235
Evaluation, 2, 13, 103, 105, 106, 150

F
Family, 1, 4–8, 26, 39, 43, 48, 49, 53,
    55, 65, 77–80, 82, 88, 94, 102,
    103, 106, 112, 122, 125, 162,
    171–173, 176, 189, 190, 216,
    220–222, 224, 226, 237, 237n2,
    237n3, 240, 243, 246, 246n12,
    247, 250
Female-male sex ratios, 8
Female students, 61, 68, 72, 74, 77,
    79, 82
Female vice chancellor, 61
Femininity, 63, 64, 79, 82
Feminism, 2, 4
Feminists, 2–4
Feminist theorists, 63
Formal economy, 6, 9, 10
Formulation, 1, 7, 9, 13, 37, 39–47,
    50, 52, 54, 57, 58, 138, 140
Free work, 6
Freedom, 5, 7, 82, 83, 96, 97n7, 116,
    170, 210, 236

G
Gap, 7, 8, 11, 15, 16, 20, 22, 141,
    143, 144, 153, 166, 177,
    181–190, 192, 193, 195, 197,
    199–201, 205, 206, 210, 211,
    218–220, 223, 224, 227, 239,
    244, 250
Garment sector, 10
Gender and development (GAD), vii,
    3–5, 11, 12
Gender and governance, 2, 137, 138
Gender as performance, 63, 83
Gender-based discrimination, 61, 62,
    64, 69

Gender-based harassments, 14
Gender-based violence, 14, 62, 65, 66,
    75–83, 234, 250
Gender budgets, 15, 139, 150–152
Gendered socialization, 14, 63, 64,
    72
Gendered subjectivities, 64, 83
Gender equality, v, vi, 2, 5, 11, 12, 16,
    22–24, 28, 33, 38, 39, 43, 44,
    48, 51–53, 55, 56, 58, 63, 67,
    75, 84, 97, 116, 117, 124, 125,
    127, 130, 137, 138, 140–142,
    144–146, 150–152, 173, 176,
    233
Gender identities, 14, 64, 66, 72, 82,
    83, 102, 141
Gender mainstreaming, v–vii, 1–16,
    141, 142, 147, 209–211,
    220–221, 223–225, 227
Gender parity, 29, 139, 145, 150n2,
    152, 173, 182, 188, 206, 216,
    223
Gender performance, 14, 63, 64, 83
Gender planning, 5–7
Gender policies, 11, 12, 14, 15, 143,
    150, 211, 227
Gender-sensitive individuals, 61
Glass cliff, 14, 87–106
Globalization, 7, 8, 10, 166, 174
Global village, 10
Governance, vi, vii, 6, 7, 10–13, 42,
    54, 58, 114, 126, 128, 131, 132,
    137–153, 158–160, 162, 163,
    165–168, 170, 174–176
Governments, v, vi, 1, 8, 9, 11, 14, 15,
    20, 21, 25, 38, 40–48, 50–58,
    88, 89, 95–97, 98n9, 106,
    111–132, 140–142, 146, 150,
    153, 158, 160–167, 172–177,
    188, 199, 211–218, 220–221,
    224, 242, 242n10, 243, 245,
    247, 248

Guidelines, 62, 146, 164
Guidelines for a Code on Sexual Harassment, 62

H
Harassment, v, 5, 8, 61–63, 65–67, 73, 75–77, 80–84, 102, 126, 169, 245
Higher educational institutions, 213, 225
Holistic approach, 4
Household duties, 15, 209, 212
Human Development Index (HDI), 188

I
Identities, 6, 16, 63, 64, 81, 83, 115, 165, 167, 192, 232, 234, 235, 249, 250
Implementation, 2, 7, 9, 11, 13, 14, 37–58, 123, 138, 141–143, 149, 150, 151n3, 153, 158, 165, 244–245
Inclusion, 1, 6, 7, 9, 21, 23, 58, 94, 119, 132, 138, 163, 168, 175
India, vi, 8, 13, 15, 25, 54, 111, 113, 128, 131, 142, 144, 158, 159, 163, 165–167, 173, 174, 176, 181, 182, 184, 188, 192, 196–198, 203, 205, 206, 235, 236
Indian democracy, 15, 181, 207
Indian electorate, 181
Industrialization, 3
Inequality/inequalities, 3, 4, 11, 14, 15, 33, 64, 66, 83, 97n7, 106, 126, 137, 139, 141, 145, 150, 152, 153, 157, 173, 227
Institutional accountability, 3

Institutional and behavioral challenges, 14
Institutionalizing, 2, 11, 224
Institutional policies, 3, 15, 211, 227
Institutions, vii, 3, 5, 8, 10, 12–14, 41, 96n6, 111, 117, 127, 130, 132, 170, 177, 207, 212, 213, 215, 221, 225, 226, 236, 238, 246
International actors, 11, 28
International system, 4

L
Lack of access to information, 10
Leadership, 6, 7, 10, 13, 14, 16, 22, 26, 31, 32, 42, 62, 74, 87n1, 88, 91–94, 98, 99, 101, 102, 105, 111–132, 210, 211, 224, 227
Legal framework, 14, 244
Legislation, 2, 24, 29, 45, 55, 111, 117, 138, 158, 232, 238, 240, 250
Local governance, 11, 126, 128, 132, 220
Local government, 9, 11, 14, 15, 20, 47, 111–132, 153

M
Male teachers, 61, 79, 81, 82
Manage economic activities, 10
Marginalization, 10, 68, 169
Marxist, 4
Masculinity, 63, 64, 81, 102, 223
Media, 8, 15, 183, 195–197, 239, 242, 245
Micro-credit, 12, 38, 122
Micro-finance, 10
Migration, 6, 15, 38, 209, 222
Minorities, 7, 8, 102, 159
Modernization, 3, 4, 223

N

National and international NGOs, 10
National Assembly, 203
National Family Policy, 62
National Health Policy, 62, 244
National plan of action, 62
National Policy on Youth, 62
Neo-Marxist, 4

O

Odisha, 15, 157–177, 185, 186, 190, 194

P

Pakistan, vi, xv, 11, 13, 16, 20, 25, 113, 144, 203, 231–251
Participation, 1, 3, 7, 9–12, 14, 15, 20, 22, 23, 28, 32, 38, 56, 68, 96–98, 111, 114, 115, 117–121, 128–129, 131, 139, 144, 158, 166, 173, 174, 181–186, 188, 189, 191, 193–199, 205–207, 210–212, 214, 216, 218, 220, 223–227, 236, 238
Participatory, 7, 162, 168
Patriarchal norms, 10, 112, 169, 193
Patriarchal structure, 14, 81, 83, 112, 158
The patriarchal structure of the institution, 14
Plan of Action Supporting the Prevention of Domestic Violence Act, 62
Policy frame, 2
Policy framework, 62, 141, 144–145, 152, 238, 247, 249
Policy process, 2, 3, 7
Policy-making, 14, 41, 42, 58, 88, 93, 99, 100, 106, 142, 241, 248
Political disempowerment, 15

Political leadership, 13, 92
Politics, vi, 1–16, 21, 22, 24, 25, 27, 28, 31–33, 100, 111, 116, 117, 127, 129, 130, 182, 189, 190, 196, 197, 207, 210, 211, 216–218, 231–251
Polling booth, 15, 181
Positive discrimination, 12
Post-colonial, 3, 232
Power differential, 10
Power structure, vii, 7, 12
Prevention of gender-based discrimination, harassment, and violence, 62
Private and public sphere, 1, 6, 9, 10, 12, 22, 62, 65, 68, 116, 173, 236, 250
Private-public dichotomy, 5
Private realm, 3
Processes, 3, 7, 9, 10, 12, 64, 72, 99, 111, 120, 140, 150, 152, 163, 170, 206, 221, 223, 237, 241, 248
Productive, 6, 9, 139, 162, 166, 171, 176
Professional competence and skills, 15, 138
Public financial incentives, 13
Public realm, 3

Q

Queer, 7

R

Race, 4, 38, 63, 64, 68, 95–96n6, 235
Radical social reform, 10
Redistributive policies, 10
Religion, vi, 4, 38, 39, 43, 48–50, 52, 63, 64, 95–96n6, 112, 231–251

Religious, 9, 10, 12, 14, 16, 39,
    42–44, 47, 49–58, 68, 74, 95,
    112, 121, 149, 192, 210, 232,
    235, 238, 240–245, 250, 251
Religious leaders, 5, 14, 47, 49, 245
Representation, 1, 7, 11–13, 15,
    20–25, 27, 68–75, 81, 89n2, 96,
    111, 114–117, 132, 169, 173,
    181–207, 214, 216–218, 222,
    225, 226
Reproductive, xvi, 6, 9, 126
Rights of women, 220, 248
Rights to own land and inheritance, 5
Roles, vii, 3–6, 8–10, 12, 14, 44, 63,
    82, 83, 88, 90–92, 102, 103,
    106, 111–132, 138, 211, 214,
    217, 221, 226, 236–238
Ruling regimes, 14

S
Self-reliance, 161
Senate of the University of Peradeniya,
    62
Sex, 5, 8, 38, 63–65, 68, 69,
    95–96n6, 234, 239, 243–245
Sex determination, 8
Sex-selective induced abortions, 8
Sexual and reproductive health and
    rights (SRHR), xvi, 16, 231–251
Sexual diversity, 2
Sexually harassed, 61
Small loans, 10
Social and development policies, 1
Social constructions, 4, 5, 12, 63
Social justice, 5, 15, 119–121, 132
Social mobilizations, 10, 130
Social organizations, 6, 41
Social transformation, 7, 10, 12, 87,
    112, 131
Social values and norms, vi, vii, 9, 10,
    145, 171, 182

Social welfare, 12, 123, 149, 159, 167
Society, vii, xv, 1, 2, 4–10, 14, 15, 23,
    31, 37, 39–42, 46, 47, 52,
    55–58, 62–65, 68, 79, 83, 90,
    91, 97n7, 99, 111, 112, 113n1,
    116, 119–124, 128, 129, 131,
    137–140, 145, 153, 157–159,
    161, 164, 166, 168–171, 173,
    174, 176, 195, 197, 207, 221,
    226, 237, 241, 243, 251
Socio-cultural norms, 16, 41, 242
Socio-economic development, 2,
    131n10, 162, 169, 193–196, 220
South Asia, v–vii, 1–16, 38, 39, 88,
    249
South Asian nations, 9–11, 152, 206
Sri Lanka, vi, vii, 13, 14, 144, 203
Sri Lankan universities, 63
State, 5, 6, 20, 38, 41, 62, 63, 65,
    67–69, 96n6, 122, 138,
    143–144, 158, 182, 185, 217,
    232
Subordination, 4, 5, 65, 142

T
Technological innovations, 4, 7
Third World, 4
Transformative politics, 15, 132
Transgender, 7

U
Unequally, 3
Unequal power relations, 14, 65,
    81–83
Unequal relations, 83
University Grants Commission
    (UGC), Sri Lanka, 62, 68
Urban, 13, 15, 38, 49, 130, 162, 168,
    175, 209, 237, 237n2, 249, 250
Urbanization, 3, 223

V

Values, vi, 9, 10, 12, 42, 52, 54, 58, 82, 83, 102, 112, 127, 141, 169, 201, 223, 235, 236
Values the characteristics, 10
Village court, 14, 120, 132
Violation, 3
Violence, v, 13, 14, 38, 52, 57, 119, 121, 122, 132, 137, 147, 160, 173, 220, 234, 248, 250
Voice, 12, 15, 43, 52, 55, 145, 181, 203, 249, 251
Voter turnout, 181, 194, 198, 199, 207
Vulnerable to disasters, 10

W

Welfare, 6, 11, 12, 15, 116, 123, 132, 159, 167, 174, 243
Window dressing, 12

Women and development (WAD), 3, 4, 12
Women in development (WID), 3–4, 12
Women's liberation, 15
Women's motivation, 13, 21, 31, 32, 191
Women's participation, 3, 7, 9–11, 15, 22, 23, 25, 28, 31–33, 38, 56, 82, 96–98, 114, 117, 118, 127–131, 139, 166, 173, 182–186, 188, 189, 193, 198, 199, 205, 206, 209–211, 214, 220, 223, 224, 226, 238
Women's representation, 117, 199–207, 217, 222, 226
Women's Reservation Bill, 199
Work and wage, 15, 227